THE WISDOM OF LOVE
IN
THE SONG OF SONGS

John B. Trinick, *Wisdom and the Lovers* (1964)

Stefan Gillow Reynolds

THE WISDOM OF LOVE
IN THE SONG OF SONGS

HIKARI
PRESS

First published in 2018
by Hikari Press, London

www.hikaripress.co.uk

Distributed in the UK by
Combined Book Services Limited
Paddock Wood Distribution Centre
Paddock Wood
Tonbridge
Kent TN12 6UU
www.combook.co.uk

ISBN: 978-0-9956478-2-4

Hikari Press gratefully acknowledges the financial support of
Arts Council England through Grants for the Arts.

British Library Cataloguing-in-Publication-Data.
A catalogue record of the book is available from the British Library.

Designed in Albertina by Libanus Press
and printed in the UK by Gomer Press

For my great uncle, John B. Trinick (1890–1972),
artist of the Song

———

For the Immaculate Heart of Mary,
Open Gate of Heaven, Fount of Wisdom,
Tower of David, Mystical Rose

For the monks of Mount Melleray Abbey,
where this book was written.

———

And for the Shulamite

'Blessed is the life of the man in whose heart is born
the pain of love for you.'
Mīr Sayyid Manjhan Shattārī Rājgīrī, *Madhumālatī*, 115

'You shall be a crown of beauty in the hand of the Lord.'
Isaiah 62:3

'Our sweetest songs are those that tell of saddest thought.'
Percy Bysshe Shelley, 'To a Skylark'

'Only the touch of the Spirit can inspire a song like this,
and only personal experience can unfold its meaning,
for it is the very music of the heart.'
St Bernard of Clairvaux, *On the Song of Songs* 1:11

Contents

Illustrations

Foreword

'The Song of Songs is a puzzle', St Augustine wrote (Augustine 1964: 289, sermon 46:35).[1] Can we say we have cracked the mystery of this enigmatic poem? We have advantages which Augustine and the other Church fathers and mothers didn't have: access to various ancient versions of the Song, a stronger sense of the historical aspect of scripture, and the human story behind it. We are much less orientated to symbolical meanings than those in the Classical era. We are, in other words, in a position to find the real human story in the Song – the ground on which any further meanings are built.

This poem, in the middle of the Bible among those known as 'the wisdom books', is popularly known as The Song of Solomon or The Song of Songs. Its actual title is The Song of Songs that is Solomon's. The attribution or association with Solomon expresses something of *what* or *who* inspired this poem; the superlative expresses the esteem in which it was held. The title doesn't mean Solomon wrote the poem but it does indicate that the *personality* of Solomon (not necessarily historical but as literary tradition shaped him) is our first and primary clue to its interpretation. Over the course of history people have read many meanings into the Song, a number of which may to the modern reader feel like castles built on air. To get into a house we need to start on the ground floor: to understand the Song we should begin with the literal meaning. Any other approach is not unlike an act of levitation (something to which the mystics were prone!) but modern readers may prefer to settle on the literal sense before climbing the stairs. There are other levels to the Song, but the human story is the foundation on which any spiritual reading can be discerned.

---

1 A comment from one who came close to piecing together the Trinity!

The importance of the literal sense was long ago underscored by St Thomas Aquinas: 'All the senses in Scripture are founded on one – the literal – from which alone can any argument be drawn, and not from those intended in allegory' (Aquinas 1981: I, 1:10, ad. 1). A word in Scripture, Aquinas writes, does not have a separate literal and a symbolic meaning, but rather 'the concrete things signified by the words can be themselves types of other things' (ibid.). The type, in other words, must fit its foundation in the literal sense. A square house can't be built on a round base: once the human story is clear only connected spiritual meanings are valid.

The Song is a love story. The secret of the story, however, is that it has both a human and a spiritual meaning. This ancient poem has inspired generations to read human love as somehow expressing divine love. Certainly, in the Song, human love is imbued with divine poetry, but until the eighteenth century it was presumed that the *eros*, the erotic relations portrayed in the Song, were really and only about longing for God. This interpretation corresponded with the period of the Song's greatest popularity: until the eighteenth century the Song was considered one of the most important books of the Hebrew Scriptures, a guide to mystical and experiential relationship to God. Since the eighteenth century, and still nowadays (despite parts being read at marriages) this beautiful text *as a whole* languishes largely unread. Many scholars of the Song see it as 'disconnected fragments' and it is only a few sections that are ever read in Church (unlike in the synagogue where the whole poem is read at Purim). Fragments do not make good reading: the aim of this book is to 'join the dots' so that the real story of the Song may be seen.

Despite its significance over the course of ecclesiastical history, the Song has remained for many 'a closed Garden, a fountain sealed' (to use one of its own images). And yet, the holiness of human love expressed in the Song could help illumine relationships today. Each generation must find for themselves the reasons why the lovers sing. With our contemporary interest in 'romantic love' there is no reason why the Song should not be *as popular* as it was in medieval times when the focus was on more spiritual themes. If there is no need to pin down the Song with religious meanings, we might ask why this outpouring of human love is found within the folds of the Bible? Or whether it actually reflects the often difficult reality of relationships? Many readers of the Song might feel like Thomas Hardy on hearing the 'darkling thrush':

> So little cause for carolings
>   Of such ecstatic sound
> Was written on terrestrial things
>   Afar or nigh around …
> (Hardy 1902)

If the divine is to be expressed in the human, the human side needs to be *fully human*, and convincingly so (as in the person of Jesus). The problem in the past is that the literal and symbolic meanings of the text have become split. Recent commentaries have not, on the whole, helped to bridge the gap. Those who take a literal approach read the Song simply as an expression of the desire for sexual union while the religious shore up its meaning as 'of the Spirit and not of the Flesh'. Such dualism impoverishes the poem on both fronts, for the Song expresses 'love'; both human and divine. It offers the embodiment of the spiritual and transfiguration of the sensual.

The poem does, however, need a key for its interpretation, and with today's sensibility it is time a convincing narrative reading came forward. This book unpacks the historical context in which the poem is set while bearing in mind its authorship was more than half a millennium later. Part One explains which keys can be helpful in unlocking what the original intention of the author may have been. Part Two uncovers the story aspect of the *Song*; why it was considered the greatest love song of all. Part Three shows how the story itself leads us on to a further level: the human relationship with wisdom. Reading the narrative as set within a particular historical era helps provide (1) convincing contexts, (2) real narrative plot and (3) consistent characterisation. All this may have been brought out when the Song was acted out or sung as a duet. The nature of the text as *poetic drama* needs, however, to be highlighted today. The Song also has parallels in later literature which help in its interpretation: Baile and Aillinn, Tristan and Isolde, Dante and Beatrice, Romeo and Juliet, Laili and Majnun. All star-crossed lovers – whose love cannot be realised in this world – are re-workings of the genius of this poem. Philosophy also has here a deeply personal expression of the love of wisdom (Sophia). Love and wisdom find fulfilment in contemplation: the Song has long been considered a guide to meditation.

The 'secret' of the Song of Songs is that romantic love, even in its most passionate and sensual forms, is not in contradiction to the pursuit of wisdom and peace. The love depicted in the Song is so strong that it points beyond what seems possible in this world, to an eternal love. It also unseals a longing for a peace that the conventions of this world can never give, and a desire for a wisdom that can only be a gift from heaven. The key to the Song is in the heart's longing. It points to a garden of paradise where human and divine love is one and the same and where man and woman are in harmony. The Song of Songs is indeed superlative because it expresses, and awakens in us, the 'non-duality of love'. This integrative power – that holds in balance the full spectrum of human experience – is wisdom.

Acknowledgements

This book is based on unfinished notes left to me by my great uncle John Trinick, poet, writer and artist in stained glass. In one manuscript, he proposed a new literal interpretation of the Song of Solomon that took account of the recent understanding of marriage as about mutual companionship and spiritual growth. I have endeavoured to draw many of his ideas into this book.

Special thanks to Isabel Brittain for supporting this project, for invaluable help with editing and all her work. Thanks to my parents Simon and Beata Reynolds for their continual kindness and for help with art and to Demetri Grey for challenging my argument until I got it right. Thanks to Peter Esmonde and Dr Tsehai Berhane-Selassie for friendship and for information on the Ethiopian tradition, to Fr Deacon Elutherius Price for helping with nuances of Greek, Laura Pooley for teaching me Latin, Sr Edmée Kingsmill SLG whose book *The Song of Songs and the Eros of God*: *A Study in Biblical Intertextuality* (2009) is undoubtedly the best recent book on the Song and gave me a great help with the nuances of Hebrew.

I am grateful to The World Community for Christian Meditation which, as a community of wise love, has nourished this book; especially Graeme Watson, whose *The Song of Songs: A Contemplative Guide* (2014) rekindled an old passion in me for the Song. Special thanks, however, to the Cistercians at Mount Melleray and Glencairn for their support: Sr Michele Slattery OCSO and Fr Denis-Luke O'Hanlon OCSO for being great friends to me; Fr Columban Heaney OCSO for his written and living teaching on Spiritual Friendship; and Sr Liz Deasy OCSO for help with the timeline. I have been shown again that, as in the Middle Ages, the Cistercians are the spiritual home of the Song of Songs.

Timeline of Pre-Modern Writers & Texts

Before Common Era below: Common Era opposite

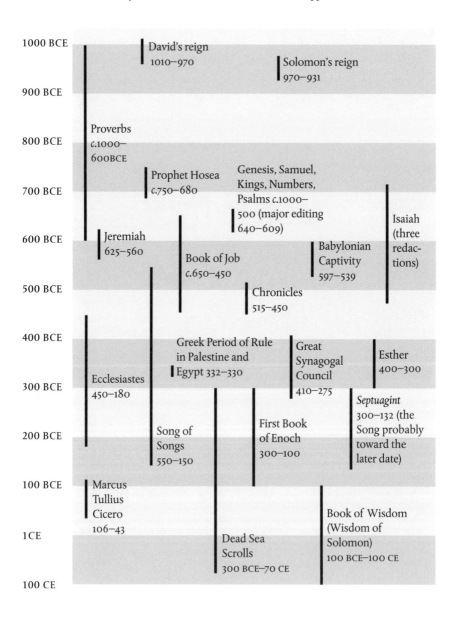

1000 BCE

David's reign
1010–970

Solomon's reign
970–931

900 BCE

Proverbs
*c.*1000–
600BCE

800 BCE

Prophet Hosea
*c.*750–680

Genesis, Samuel,
Kings, Numbers,
Psalms *c.*1000–
500 (major editing
640–609)

700 BCE

Isaiah
(three
redac-
tions)

Jeremiah
625–560

Book of Job
*c.*650–450

Babylonian
Captivity
597–539

600 BCE

500 BCE

Chronicles
515–450

400 BCE

Greek Period of Rule
in Palestine and
Egypt 332–330

Great
Synagogal
Council
410–275

Esther
400–300

Ecclesiastes
450–180

300 BCE

Septuagint
300–132 (the
Song probably
toward the
later date)

Song of
Songs
550–150

First Book
of Enoch
300–100

200 BCE

100 BCE

Marcus
Tullius
Cicero
106–43

Book of Wisdom
(Wisdom of
Solomon)
100 BCE–100 CE

1CE

Dead Sea
Scrolls
300 BCE–70 CE

100 CE

Christian Gospels 66–100 CE

Philo c.25 BCE– c.50 CE

Fragments of Song found in the *Dead Sea Scrolls* 30 BCE–70 CE   1 CE

Rabbi Akiva d.137   100 CE

Origen 185–254

Gospel of Philip 150–350

Mishna (the *Talmuds*) 100–300   200 CE

300 CE

Gregory of Nyssa c. 335–395

Vulgate Bible (translated by Jerome) 382–400   400 CE

500 CE

Gregory the Great c.540–604

Maximus the Confessor d.662

Qur'an 609–632   600 CE

700 CE

Masoretic Bible 700–900 (the Song probably around 800)   800 CE

900 CE

Kebra Nagest (*The Glory of Kings*) 750–1320   1000 CE

Bernard of Clairvaux 1090–1153

Aelred of Rievaulx 1110–1167

Sri Jayadeva d.1242   1100 CE

Jalaluddin Rumi 1207–1273

Thomas Aquinas 1225–1274   1200 CE

Highpoint of Zoharic Kabbalah

Dante Alighieri 1265–1321

Henry Suso 1295–1366   1300 CE

Margery Kempe 1373–1438   1400 CE

Nur ad-Din Jámi 1414–1492

1500 CE

John of the Cross 1542–1591

Teresa of Ávila 1515–1582

Mīr Sayyid Manjhan Shattārī Rājgīrī 1510–1572

The King James Bible 1603–1611   1600 CE

1700 CE

Note on the Text

Use of BCE (before the Common Era) and CE (Common Era) are used rather than BC (before Christ) and AD (*anno Domini*) as the Song is a shared text that crosses the Jewish and Christian traditions.

Biblical quotations are generally taken from the Authorised Version with some help in modernisation of language from the Jerusalem Bible, this being an ecumenical project.

The translation of the Song is based on the Douay-Rheims version – the earliest English translation of the Vulgate, completed in 1610 and recently reprinted (Douay-Rheims 2009: 691–695) – but with adjustments I have made in light of the Septuagint (as translated by Nicholas King in *The Old Testament: A Translation of the Septuagint*, vol. 3, 2008) and of the Masoretic text translated in the Authorised Version and also by Edmée Kingsmill. At any point of difference between ancient versions I have endeavoured to give weight to each authoritative text. In keeping with the Authorised Version and Douay-Rheims I have retained the old Englishisms (thee and thou, etc.) to give a sense of the ancient nature of the Song. I have also made reference to the Vulgate as the Douay-Rheims is not always accurate to Jerome.

The Song of Songs divided into episodes

FIRST EPISODE
Introductory verses – 'The meeting' (chapter 1, verses 1–5)

Shulamite: (Aside to her maiden companions) 1. *'Let him kiss me with the kiss of his mouth.'*

Solomon: (Echoing what the maiden companions have said previously about her) *'… because thy breasts are better than wine.*

2. *Fragrant with the best ointments: thy name is an oil poured out: therefore, have the maidens loved thee.*

3. *Draw me: we will run after thee to the odour of thy ointments.'*

Shulamite: *'The King hath brought me into his store rooms (inner chambers).'*

Solomon: (Expressing what the maidens had said) *'We will be glad and rejoice in thee, remembering thy breasts above wine: the upright love thee.'*

Shulamite: (Aside to her maiden companions) 4. *'I am dark but shapely, O ye daughters of Jerusalem, as the tents of Kedar, as the skin-shields of Solomon.*

5. *Look not closely upon me because I am brown, for the sun hath discoloured me: the sons of my mother contended against me, they set me as keeper over the vineyards: my own vineyard have I not defended.'*

SECOND EPISODE
Part 1 – 'The pastoral idyll' (chapter 1, verses 6–16)

Shulamite: 6. *'Show me, O thou whom my soul loveth, where thou feedest, where thou liest in the mid-day, lest I begin to wander after the flocks of thy companions.'*

Solomon: (In the guise of a shepherd) 7. *'If thou know not thyself, O thou fairest, among the women go forth, and follow after the traces of the flocks, and feed thy kids beside the tents of the shepherds.'*

(After an interval) 8. *To my mare among the chariots of Pharaoh have I likened thee, O my friend!*

9. *Thy cheeks are comely with circlets, thy neck with strings of beads.*

10. *We will make thee chains of gold, with studs of silver.'*

Shulamite: 11. *'While the king was reclining at table, my nard gave forth its perfume.*

12. *A bundle of myrrh is my beloved to me; he shall abide between my breasts.*

13. *A cluster of camphor my beloved is to me, in the vineyards of Engaddi.'*

Solomon: 14. *'Behold, thou art beautiful, O my friend! Behold, thou art beautiful … thine eyes of doves.'*

Shulamite: 15. *'Lo! thou (too) art fair, my beloved, pleasant indeed. Our bed is flowery.*

16. *Our house-beams are of cedar, our rafters of cypress.'*

Part 2 – 'Under the trees' (chapter 2, verses 1–7)

Shulamite: 1. *'I am a flower of the field, a lily of the valley.'*

Solomon: 2. *'As a lily among thorns, so is my friend among the daughters.'*

Shulamite: 3. *'As the apple tree among the wood of the forests, so is my beloved among the sons.*

I sat under his shadow, whom I desired, and his fruit was sweet to my taste.

4. *He brought me into the place of stored wine, he set in order the deep love within me.*

5. *Stay me with flowers, compass me about with apples: because I faint away with love.*

6. *His left hand is beneath my head, and his right hand shall encircle me.'*

Solomon: 7. *'I adjure you, O ye daughters of Jerusalem, by the roes and the harts of the fields, that you stir not up, nor make the beloved to awake until she herself please.'*

THIRD EPISODE
'Springtime' (chapter 2, verses 8–17)

Shulamite: (Soliloquy on awakening) 8. *'The voice of my beloved, behold he cometh leaping over the mountains, springing across the hills.*

9. *My beloved is like a roe and a young hart. Lo! He himself standeth behind our wall, looking through the windows, watching (me) through the lattices.*

10. *Lo! My beloved speaketh to me: Arise, hasten, my friend, my dove, my fair one, and come!*

11. *For winter has now passed over, the rain has subsided and gone away.*

12. *The flowers have appeared in our land; the time of singing is come: the voice of the turtledove is heard in our land.*

13. *The fig tree hath brought forth her green figs: the vines in blossom yield up their sweet odour.*

Arise, my friend, my beautiful one, and come!'

(After an interval) 14. *'My dove in the clefts of the rock, in the hollow places of the wall, show me thy face, let thy voice sound in my ears: for thy voice is sweet, and thy face is comely.*

15. *Catch for us the little foxes that destroy the vines, for our vineyard hath flowered.*

16. *My beloved to me, and I to him, who feedeth among the lilies.*

17. *Until the mid-day approach, and the shadows decline.*

Come back again! Be, O my beloved, like to the roe and to the young hart upon the mountain of Bether.'

FOURTH EPISODE

Part 1 – 'A tenacious maiden' (chapter 3, verses 1–5)

Shulamite: (Soliloquy as night falls) 1. *'In my bed by night I sought him whom my soul loveth: I sought him and I found him not.*

2. *I will rise, and will go about the city: by the quarters and the streets will I seek him whom my soul loveth.'*

(In the city): *'I sought him, and I found him not.'*

(After an interval) 3. *'The watchmen who keep the city found me: Have you seen him whom my soul loveth?*

4. *Even as I had a little passed by them, I found him whom my soul loveth: I held him.*

I will not let him go, till I shall bring him into my mother's house, and into the bed-place of her that brought me forth.'

Solomon: (On returning to the Garden) 5. *'I adjure you, O ye daughters of Jerusalem, by the roes and the harts of the fields, that you stir not up, nor awake the beloved till she herself please.'*

Part 2 – 'The bridal chamber' (chapter 3, verses 6–11)

Solomon: (Soliloquy at night) 6. 'Who is she that goeth up over the desert
as a slender rod of the smoke from aromatic (spices),
of myrrh, and incense, and all powders together of the
perfumer?'

(After a pause) 7. 'Lo! Threescore valiant, of the most valiant of
Israel, surround the bed of Solomon:

8. all possessing swords, and most experienced in war: every one
hath his sword upon his thigh because of fears in the night.

9. King Solomon made himself a litter of the woods of Lebanon:

10. He made its pillars of silver, its support of gold, the reclining
place of purple (cushions): the interior he filled with love,
on account of the daughters of Jerusalem.

11. Go forth, O ye daughters of Sion, and behold king Solomon in
the diadem wherewith his mother hath crowned him in the
day of his espousals, in the day of the joy of his heart.'

FIFTH EPISODE
Part 1 – 'The maiden described' (chapter 4, verses 1–7)

Solomon: 1. 'How beautiful thou art, oh my friend, how beautiful thou art!
Thy eyes as of doves were it not for that which lies hidden within
them.

Thy hair as a flock of goats, which come up from Mount Gilead.

2. Thy teeth as flocks (of ewes), which come up from the washing;
all bearing twins, and there is none barren among them.

3. Like a thread of scarlet are thy lips: and sweet thy speech.

As a piece of pomegranate, thus are thy cheeks, apart from that
which lies hidden within.

4. As the tower of David is thy neck, which is built with ramparts,
on which hang a thousand shields, all the armour of
valiant men.

5. Thy two breasts are like two young roes, twins of a gazelle, that
feed among the lilies.

6. Until the mid-day approach, and the shadows fall away, I will
go to the mountain of myrrh, and to the hill of incense.

7. Thou are wholly beautiful, my friend, and there is no blemish
in thee.'

Part 2 – 'The sister-bride' (chapter 4, verses 8–11)

Solomon: 8. *'Come from Lebanon, my bride, come from Lebanon, come; thou shalt be crowned from the top of Amana, from the summit of Senir and Hermon; from the dens of lions, from the mountains of the leopards.*

9. *Thou hast wounded my heart, my sister-bride, thou hast wounded my heart from one glance of thy eyes and one curl of thy neck.*

10. *How beautiful are thy breasts, my sister-bride! More beautiful are thy breasts than wine and the odour of your ointments above all aromatics.*

11. *A honeycomb distilling sweetness are thy lips, (my) bride: honey and milk abide beneath thy tongue, and the perfume of your garments as the incense of Lebanon.'*

Part 3 – 'The closed garden' (chapter 4, verses 12–16)

Solomon: 12. *'A garden closed up is my sister-bride, a closed garden, a fountain sealed.*

13. *Oh the perfumes sent forth from thee … a paradise of pomegranates … with the fruits of fruit trees … camphor with nard …*

14. *nard and saffron … sweet cane and cinnamon … with all the woods of Lebanon; myrrh and aloe … with all the most noble ointments.*

15. *O fountain of the gardens: O well of the living waters, which flow out with vigour from Lebanon.*

16. *Arise, O north wind, and come O south wind, blow over my garden and let flow the aromas thereof.'*

Part 4 – 'Eating the fruits' (chapter 5, verse 1)

Shulamite: 1. *'Let my beloved come into his garden, and eat the fruits of its fruit trees.'*

Solomon: *'I have come into my garden, O my sister-bride, I have gathered my myrrh with my aromatics: I have eaten the honeycomb with my honey.*

I have drunk my wine with my milk: eat, O friends, and drink, and be inebriated, dearest ones.'

SIXTH EPISODE

Part 1 – 'The importunate lover' (chapter 5, verses 2–3)

Shulamite: 2. *'I sleep, but my heart wakes …*
It is the voice of my beloved knocking (or 'who knocks'): Open to
me, my sister, my friend, my dove, my stainless one, for my
head is filled with dew, and my locks with the drops of the
night …
3. *I have put off my tunic, how shall I put it on? I have washed my*
feet, how shall I defile them?'

Part 2 – 'The desertion' (chapter 5, verses 4–6)

Shulamite: 4. *'… My beloved let pass his hand over the opening, and my*
inward parts/entrails trembled at his touch …
5. *I arose that I might open to my beloved: my hands distilled*
myrrh, and my fingers were abounding in quintessential
myrrh …
6. *I unclosed the bolt of my door to my beloved …*
But he had turned aside, and has passed by.
My soul melted while he spoke: I sought him, and I found him not; I
called, and he answered me not.'

SEVENTH EPISODE

Part 1 – 'Vulnerability' (chapter 5, verses 7–9)

Shulamite: 7. *'The Watchmen that go about the city found me: they struck me*
and they wounded me: those that keep the walls took away
from me my mantle.
8. *I adjure you, O daughters of Jerusalem, if you should find my*
beloved, that you make it known to him, that I faint with
love.'

Daughters of Jerusalem: 9. *'Of what manner is thy beloved from among the*
beloved, O thou most beautiful of women? After what
manner is thy beloved from among all the many beloved,
for that thou hast so adjured us?'

Part 2 – 'The lover described' (chapter 5, verses 10–17; chapter 6, verses 1–2)

Shulamite: 10. *'My beloved is white and ruddy, chosen out of thousands.*

11. *His head as the finest gold: his locks as crests of the Palm trees, black as the raven.*

12. *His eyes as doves over rivulets of waters, which are bathed in milk, and dwell hard by the most plentiful streams.*

13. *His cheeks like unto beds of aromatics planted by the perfumers. His lips as lilies distilling choice myrrh.*

14. *His hands as of lathe-turned gold, filled with hyacinths. The front of his body as of ivory adorned with sapphires.*

15. *His legs as columns of marble, which are set upon golden bases. His semblance as of Lebanus, excellent as the cedars.*

16. *His throat most sweet; and wholly worthy of desire is he … such is my beloved, and he – even he – is my friend, O ye daughters of Jerusalem.'*

Daughters of Jerusalem: 17. *'Whither has thy beloved gone, O thou most beautiful of women? Whither is thy beloved turned aside, and we will seek him with thee?'*

Shulamite: 1. *'My beloved is gone down into his garden, to the bed of aromatics, to feed in the gardens, and to gather lilies.*

2. *I to my beloved, and my beloved to me, who feedeth among the lilies.'*

EIGHTH EPISODE
Part 1 – 'The overwhelming reunion' (chapter 6, verses 3–9)

Solomon: 3. *Thou art beautiful, O my friend, sweet and comely as Jerusalem: yet terrible as the camps of an army ordained to battle …*

4. *Turn away thine eyes from me, for they have made me flee away …*
Thy hair is as a flock of goats, that appear from Gilead.

5. *Thy teeth as a flock of sheep that come up from the washing, all with twins, and there is none sterile among them …*

6. *As the rind of a pomegranate, so are thy cheeks, apart from thy hiddennesses …*

7. *Threescore are the queens, and fourscore the concubines, and numberless are the young maidens.*

8. *One is my dove, my perfect one, the only one of her mother,*
the elect of her that bare her. The daughters saw her and
declared her most blessed: the queens and concubines – and
they praised her …

9. *Who is she, that advances as the dawn arising, beautiful as the*
moon, all excelling as the sun, terrible as the camps of an
army ordained to battle?'

Part 2 – 'Being hurled over' (chapter 6, verses 10–12; chapter 7, verses 1–2a)

Solomon: 10. *'I went down into the garden of nuts, that I might see the fruits*
of the valleys, and that I might examine whether the
vineyard should have blossomed, and the pomegranates
should have budded.

11. *I knew not: my soul confounded me (hurled me over) on account*
of the chariots of Aminadab …

12. *Come back again, come back again, O Shulamite! Come back*
again, come back again, that we may look upon thee!'

Shulamite: 1. *'What would thou see in thy Shulamite, unless it be the*
multitudes of Mahanaim? (unless it be between the armies
drawn up for battle?)'

Solomon: 2a. *'How beautiful are thy steps in thy shoes, O thou prince's*
daughter!'

Part 3 – 'Looking upon the beloved' (chapter 7, verses 2b–7)

Solomon: 2b. *'The joinings of thy thighs are like neck chains wrought by the*
hands of a master craftsman.

3. *Thy navel is a finely tuned bowl, that never lacks mixed wine.*
The front of thy body as a heap of wheat set about with lilies.

4. *Thy two breasts like two young fawns that are twins of a gazelle.*

5. *Thy neck as a tower of ivory. Thy eyes like the fish-pools in*
Heshbon, which are in the gate of the daughter of a
multitude. Thy nose is like a tower of Lebanon that looks
over towards Damascus.

6. *Thy head like Carmel: and the hairs of thy head like kingly*
purple, gathered and bound in many channels.

7. *How beautiful thou art, and how seemly, my dearest, in thy*
charm!'

Part 4 – 'The garden of delights' (chapter 7, verses 8–11)

Solomon: 8. *'Thy stature is like a palm tree, and thy breasts to its clusters …*
9. *I said: I will go up to the palm tree and will take hold of the branches thereof: and thy breasts shall be as clusters of the vine … and the scent of thy mouth as of apples …*
10. *Thy throat like the best wine.'*

Shulamite: *'Worthy for my beloved to his drinking, and for the ruminating of his lips and his teeth.*
11. *I to my beloved, and his turning is (ever) towards me.'*

Part 5 – 'Up and away: nature and grace' (chapter 7, verses 12–14)

Shulamite: 12. *'Come my beloved let us go forth into the country, let us abide in the villages.*
13. *Let us go up early to the vineyards, let us see if the vineyards flourish, if the flowers be about to bring forth fruit, if the pomegranates blossom: there will I give thee my breasts.*
14. *The mandrakes yield up their odour.*
Within our gates are all fruits: the new and the old, my beloved, I have reserved for thee.'

NINTH EPISODE
Part 1 – 'The dilemma' (chapter 8, verses 1–4)

Shulamite: 1. *'Who shall give me to thee for my brother, sucking the breasts of my mother, that I may find thee outside and kiss, and kiss thee, and then may no one despise me? …*
2. *I would then take hold of thee, and lead thee into the house of my mother, and into the bedroom of her who taught me …*
and I will give thee a drink of perfumed wine, and new (or unfermented) wine of my pomegranates …
3. *His left hand under my head, and his right hand shall embrace me.'*

Solomon: 4. *'I adjure you, daughters of Jerusalem, neither arouse nor cause to awaken the beloved until she pleases.'*

Part 2 – 'Love is as strong as death' (chapter 8, verses 5–7)

Shulamite: 5. *'Who is this that cometh up from the desert abounding in delights, leaning upon her beloved?'*

Solomon: *'Under the apple tree I awakened thee: there was thy mother corrupted, there was violated she that bare thee.'*

Shulamite: 6. '*Set me as a seal over thy heart, as a token upon thy arm: because love is as strong as death, jealousy is hard (relentless) as the grave: the lights of love are lights of fire and of flames …*
7. *Many waters cannot quench (the fire of my) love, nor floods overwhelm it: if a man should give all the substance of his house for (my) love, people would despise him as nothing.'*

TENTH EPISODE
Part 1 – 'The little sister' (chapter 8, verses 8–10)

Shulamite: 8. '*Our sister is little and hath no breasts.*
What shall we do for our sister in the day when she shall be spoken to? …
9. *If she be a wall, let us build thereon defences of silver: if she be a door, let us make it fast with boards of cedar …*
10. *I am a wall: and my breasts as a tower, since I am become in the face of him (whom I love) as one finding peace.'*

Part 2 – 'The vineyard' (chapter 8, verses 11–12)

Shulamite: 11. '*There was a vineyard of Solomon ('the peaceable') in Baal-hamon (the populous place): he gave it over to keepers; a man will bring a thousand pieces of silver for its fruit …*
12. *My vineyard is in my own person.*
A thousand are for thee, Solomon ('the peace-giver'), and two hundred to those who keep its fruit.'

Part 3 – 'Last words' (chapter 8, verses 13–14)

Solomon: 13. '*O thou who abidest in the gardens, the children/angels/friendly ones hear and obey thee: make me also to hear thy voice!'*

Shulamite: 14. '*Escape (flee to the country) O my beloved, and make thyself even as a roe and a young hart (free) upon the mountains of spices.'*

PART ONE

The Literal Sense

Does literature have to be literal?

Generations have pored over these cantos: they have interpreted the lover's search, pondered the dark night, heard the beloved knocking, followed the lover down into the garden where the little foxes of the mind wreak havoc in the vineyards of the heart. The poetic symbolism ploughs deep, turning the furrows of the soul. The Song arouses and stirs up love. And yet it remains elusive, commentaries wander off in many directions. Fearing to misinterpret the Song, we must ask the one (and only) question the maiden asks of her lover, 'Show me, O thou whom my soul loveth, where thou feedest, where thou liest in the mid-day, lest I begin to wander after the flocks of thy companions' (1:7). We may, indeed, love the Song with its passionate, romantic and soulful images, but in order not to get swept away in personal interpretation we need to address what sources nourish it, by considering when the story was written and when it was set. We need to look at the Song in the 'clear light of day' to ask where the meaning lies. 'In the mid-day' – a time when no shadows are cast. 'Where is the summer, the unimaginable / Zero summer?', T. S. Eliot asked in 'Little Gidding' (Eliot 2015: 201). It is here the maiden wants to meet her lover. As interpreters of the Song we long to get ourselves out of the way and study the text objectively, but the shadows of millennia fall across their love. 'In the mid-day' – a time of rest for the Middle-eastern shepherd when, in the peace of contemplation among the monks and the mystics, the Song 'gives forth its perfume' (1:10).

'Until the mid-day approach and the shadows decline,' says Solomon (2:17, 4:6). To know the Song, we must suffer and pray with its passion, we must be *in the incense*. The meaning of the Song is personal to ourselves: 'If thou know not thyself, O thou fairest, among the women go forth, and follow after the traces of the flocks, and feed thy kids beside the tents of the shepherds' (1:8). There are many shepherds, over millennia, who have tried to guide the unruly flock of the words in this Song. Scholars have traced the meaning of many of the images. But when it comes to meaning many of them have pitched their tents in rather entrenched positions, seeing the Song as exclusively spiritual or exclusively secular, only mystical or only sensual. This book may graze by their tents, but only by searching our heart, knowing ourselves, will we find the secret of the Song. The Song provides a mirror for the longings of the human heart and, in the end, can only be read 'reflectively'.

Yet we do not have a blank canvas on which to paint our own projections. In the Song there is consistent characterisation, context and plot: not as clear as theatre, but within the idiom of poetry. The combined sense of words is expressive even when individual words or images seem opaque or baffling. Though the drama is a dialogue much of it is also soliloquy, though there is action much of it is within the inner-consciousness of the lovers. 'Only personal experience can unfold its meaning,' St Bernard says. In the Song we have a window into the *experience* of falling in love. Few people can doubt that at a literal level it is about human love. There is no obvious clue that one or other of the figures in the dialogue is actually God. Nor is there any explanation or key as to *how* it should be read as an allegory (as there is with the parables of Jesus) or that it carries a moral meaning (as with the Book of Job, contemporary to the Song).

The Song may be illustrating a real historical relationship between Solomon and a mysterious 'Shulamite' – but it may be just as well, or more likely, an imaginative work created by its author. Though written more than half a millennium after Solomon's reign, the Song's protagonist remains a potent and disputed figure within Jewish imagination and self-understanding. There is also an unprovable (though unlikely) possibility that the story was transmitted orally and handed down even from the time of Solomon.

The Song has never been placed either by Judaism or Christianity among the 'historical' books of the Bible. And yet its 'story' is set in a particular historical context, within the era of Solomon. A historical fiction, maybe, but also a commentary on the legendary historical figure it depicts. The Hebrew sense of the meaning in history – that God reveals God's self through the story of the Jewish people – means that even literary traditions were commentaries on the past. Solomon ruled c.970–931 BCE. The written text is much later, any time between 550 and 150 BCE. The Hebrew Masoretic text of the Song contains Aramaic forms and Hebrew words of Persian influence which show that this version, at least, could only have been written five centuries or more after Solomon's death; most likely around 350 BCE, but maybe as late as 100 BCE.

The literal sense is the form, nature and setting of the poem. The author would have known the book of Kings and, most likely, Chronicles, Proverbs (as an earlier 'Solomon text') and Ecclesiastes (which is probably slightly earlier than the Song). All of these fill in part of the *story* of Solomon that was handed down among the Jewish people. If the Song is of a later date, then the book of Sirach, composed around 200 BCE, would have been known. For poetic imagery and symbolism Sirach is the biblical book that has the closest parallels to the Song. The Book of Wisdom is, in all likelihood, later than the Song, written close to the beginning of the Common Era. With its much stronger personification of feminine Wisdom this late book may have been much influenced by the Song. There is a gradual transition from the more metaphysical presentation of Wisdom in Proverbs, at one end, to a more distinct characterisation in the Book of Wisdom.[1] If the Song is a wisdom text then it gives us by far the most human and incarnate portrayal of Wisdom (prior to the Gospels).

---

1 As shown by Gerhard von Rad (1972: 144–176). Von Rad, however, does not link the Song with this tradition.

The Song was written in a Jewish literary tradition that centred on two things: Wisdom and Solomon. The depiction of Solomon, and certainly the attribution of many of these books to him, is not necessarily historical. Solomon's reputation for wisdom could have come through his patronage of learning in the court that accompanied the temple he built. But there is enough 'story about Solomon' in these books and in other related texts to put together a clear *persona* for the male character in the Song.

If the Song as literature is set within this ambiance of Solomon, the question remains whether a 'literal' reading gives the whole and complete *meaning* of the text. Certainly, traditional exegesis has more often taken the male figure to be God. Solomon may have been a revered figure in the wisdom tradition of Judaism, but as a historical figure his ultimate sagacity is doubted by the influential deutero- nomic writers who composed (among others) the Book of Kings. Solomon can hardly be mistaken for God in Jewish exegesis; at best he is the one who received God's wisdom, and at worst the one who went on to lose it. Solomon is *too historical* to fit the allegories that were later placed on the Song. The figure of Wisdom, personified in the Jewish tradition as feminine, is *not historical enough* to really fit the very human figure of the maiden in the Song. So, one is left with a conundrum as to how the literal sense of the Song may be grounds for any symbolic meaning.

Recent exegesis proposes that the layers of symbolic meaning added to the Song are simply projections for which there is no basis within the poem (see, for example, Block and Block 2006). However, neither do they present a constant literal story: most modern exe- getes see it as a collection of 'fragments' or separate poems. The aim of this book is to show three things:

1   that there is a real story at the literal level;
2   that this does provide the basis for a symbolic reading; and
3   that these cannot in the end be separated.

The symbolic sense will be analysed in Part Three but it is necessary here to give some overview of how this has been read in the past so that we can assess how symbolic readings need not be wholly jettisoned but, when integrated with the literal and human, may remain in a specific form key to the enigma of the Song.

Introducing symbolism

Traditionally, in Christian as well as much Jewish exegesis, Scripture has been read at various levels: the historical, allegorical, anagogical and tropological. An example of this, from the Christian view-point, is given by St John Cassian (360–435 CE), analysing the word 'Jerusalem':

> The one and the same Jerusalem can be understood in a four-fold manner. According to history, it is the city of the Jews. According to allegory, it is the church of Christ. According to anagogy, it is the heavenly city of God, which is the mother of us all. According to tropology, it is the soul of the human being.
>
> Cassian 1985: 160)

Ancient commentators of the Song of Solomon give a variety of opinions as to the meaning of nearly all the phrases of the Song at nearly all the levels (nor do they stick to any systematic fourfold hermeneutic). St Bernard, commenting on 'Let him kiss me with the kisses of his mouth', says that *literally* it speaks of the Bride's desire for a kiss, *allegorically*, it speaks of the Incarnation; 'the mouth that kisses signifying the Logos, the Word of God who assumes human nature; the nature assumed receives the kiss; the kiss that takes its being from both the giver and receiver is a person formed by both [namely] Jesus Christ.' *Tropologically*, or morally, it speaks of the final stage of devotional union for 'one who is joined with Christ in a holy kiss becomes through his good pleasure, one spirit with him.' Finally, *anagogically* it speaks of the inner life of the Trinity for the 'kisses of the mouth are between the one who begets and the one who is begotten, between the Father and the Son, but the kiss itself – as the breath that passes between them is the Holy Spirit, in these words the Bride prays for the gift of the Spirit and is kissed by the kiss' (respectively, sermons 2:2, 3:3 and 8:1; Bernard of Clairvaux 1971: 10, 20, 45).

Jewish exegesis tends to read the Song as an analogy of the covenant of God with Israel and rarely as speaking of heavenly realms.[2] Only in the later Hassidic tradition was the Song read as an expression of an individual relation to God (tropologically) and only yet more recently as an expression of human relations between two lovers. Among the early fathers of Christianity different commentators had favoured modes of reading: Origen (185–254 CE) drew heavily from the Jewish Targum (the Aramaic commentaries on the Song that followed its acceptance as 'Jewish scripture' at the Council of Jamnia in 90 CE). For Origen the Bride is no longer Israel but the Church, and he gives a personal as well as a communal meaning to the Song. Origen was the pioneer in reading the tropological sense of the Song as a 'mystical eroticism' inviting an inner response or *tropos* (turn) of the soul's desire towards the divine Bridegroom. St Athanasius of Alexandria (296–373) gave a more theological analogy: the Song celebrated the Incarnation as a wedding of the Logos (or Word of God) with human nature – the embodiment of the Word in Christ is followed by the embodiment of Christ in the Church. St Gregory of Nyssa (335–394) followed Origen in stressing the personal exegesis. It is with the Latin commentators that the Song nearly always expresses the interior or moral development of the 'Bride' – the faithful soul – in response to God.

Neither Hebrew, Greek or Latin commentators focus on the

2   One exception is among mystically minded Jews in medieval Spain who read the Song as an expression of the 'Holy of Holies' in the temple, which embodied the presence of heaven on earth. See Elior (2007: 142, 147).

historical sense: if they did, like Origen (or Theodore of Mopsuestia), it was assumed that the Song was about the marriage of Solomon and the daughter of Pharaoh. The rest all believed the characters in the Song were figurative. Of all books in the Bible the Song alone had no historical or literal sense. Gregory the Great (d.604 CE), in the Latin west, writes:

> We must come to these sacred nuptials of the Bride and Bridegroom with the understanding proper to *interior* love, not mentally fixing on things that are outside of us … It is the same with the words and meanings of this sacred Scripture as it is with the colours and subjects of a painting; anyone who is so intent upon the colours in the painting that he ignores the real things it portrays is immeasurably silly.
>
> (Gregory the Great 1971: 144)

The 'real things' for Jewish and Christian commentators were the Song's hidden meanings. Yet, what seems 'immeasurably silly' to medieval minds – to look for the natural sense of the text – appears quite normal and sensible today. Even in art (since the Impressionists) beauty is to be found in the colours rather than the symbolism of pictures, so with the Song its attraction today is in the human love expressed in the words. If, in the Song, the sexual imagery is just the paint, the question remains: why paint in those colours?

What medieval commentators felt to be self-evident can seem tautological to modern ears: Gregory goes on to write of the Song that 'By way of words that express passion we are meant to make the transition to the virtues of dispassion and impassibility' (ibid.). For medieval writers, words that express physical things could carry symbolic meaning because of similarities of association: for example, 'the sun is luminous, Jesus Christ is luminous; hence the sun can signify Jesus Christ'. It is in this light that most of the imagery in the Song is read. To the modern reader the system of these associations seems arbitrary. Often it seems like a simple substitution of the heavenly or inner soul relationship for what, in actual words, express-es an earthly relationship between two flesh and blood lovers.

However, the richness of the Song is that it is a poem that can be intelligible on two registers. Only human love can speak of divine love. The aim of this book is to reconnect what seemed meaningful for medieval writers and what seems so to us today. It is necessary, however, to first restore (as well as we can) the natural, literal mean-ing of the text so that any further spiritual or hidden meaning may be rooted in a firmer foundation. Not all symbolism fits with the words. Despite what Gregory the Great says, no painting can be interpreted apart from the colours used in it.

Different senses of scripture carry their own distinct methods of interpretation, but for them to work in any consistent way they have to 'map onto' each other. This book aims for a holistic picture. For the sake of simplicity, we can conflate allegory, anagogy and tropol-ogy as *symbolic* modes, but these need to work in tandem with a literal reading of the story in the Song, or else we are building castles on air. The 'full picture', however, involves taking in not only distinct colours but overall form, not only the story but what it is trying to say. Poems or paintings can carry a meaning beyond what is actually expressed. The Song has parallels in symbolist art and poetry where the intention of the author is left open to an inspiration beyond their control and so there can be meaning which is unconscious to the author him/herself which is only discerned by later readers. The pio-neer of symbolism in modern poetry Charles Baudelaire (1821–1867) wrote that this mode 'seeks to find in outward and visible nature metaphors that allow the characterisation of pleasures and impres-sions of a spiritual order' (Baudelaire 1995: xvi). In his last writings, Baudelaire moved away from structured verse to '*poëmes en prose*', a form and ideal similar to the Song. In *Le Spleen de Paris* he speaks of 'the miracle of a poetic prose' as 'musical without fixed rhythm or rhyme, flexible and irregular enough to match the lyrical movements of the soul, the wave-motions of dream, the sudden starts of consciousness' (ibid.: xvi, xxxvi). Though speaking of the direction of his own work, Baudelaire could have been speaking of the Song.

Words are icons or images in sensible form, which express symbolic/spiritual likenesses. So too are human beings, who express the image and likeness of God (Genesis 1:27). At a purely anthropological level, therefore, the couple in the Song can be seen to represent God. 'Mercy has a human heart; / Pity, a human face: / And Love, the human form divine, / And Peace, the human dress', as a symbolist poet two generations before Baudelaire put it (William Blake, 'The Divine Image'; Blake 2008: 12). Every human virtue is the image of God and expresses what God is like. Yet the likeness is actually prior to the image for the latter can only be image so insofar as it is like something (we can only say something is like or unlike if we know what we are measuring it against). For Thomas Aquinas (1225–1274) in his *Summa Theologiae*, 'likeness is a kind of unity':

> As the good, the true and the wise, can be compared to each individual thing both as its preamble, and as subsequent to it, as signifying some perfection in it, so also in the same way there exists a kind of comparison between 'likeness' and 'image'. For the good, the true or the wise is a preamble to man or woman, in as much as man or woman is individually good, true and wise; and, again, the good, the true and the wise is subsequent to man or woman, in as much as we can say of a certain man or woman that they are good, truthful and wise, by reason of their perfect virtue. In like manner, 'likeness' may be considered in the light of a preamble to 'image', inasmuch as it is something more general than image: and, again it may be considered as subsequent to image, inasmuch as it signifies a certain perfection of image.
>
> (Aquinas 1981: vol. 1, p. 469)
> see also Aquinas 2015: ch. 19)

The Song, ultimately, is the realisation of the eternal image in the physical icon – peace in a peaceful person, wisdom in one who is wise, love in someone who loves – and the transfiguration of the icon into that which it symbolises, the human person becoming more and more what they exemplify. As the Gospel of Philip urges, 'Come, bind our angels to our icons' (Robinson 1977: analogues 14, 41). The spiritual is communicated directly through sensible form. *As above so below*, is the mystery of spiritual marriage: heaven and earth expressing each other. At the human level the Shulamite in the Song is in the process of self-discovery, of becoming more and more *who she is*. Yet as she approaches the likeness of her origin she becomes a sacred symbol, 'an outer sign that confers the grace that it signifies' (Definition of a Sacrament; Catholic Church 1994: 316). The earliest Jewish use of the symbol of the Star of David in the Kabbalah was as a protective amulet (*segulot*) known as the 'seal of Solomon': two triangles, one the inverse of the other ✡: as above so below. This may have links to what the Shulamite says at the end of the Song: 'Set me as a seal [*segulot*] over thy heart, as a token upon thy arm.'

The lover cries out in the Song, 'Come back again, come back again, O Shulamite! Come back again, come back again, that we may look upon thee!' (6:12). More than three-quarters of the way through the poem, this is the first mention of the name Shulamite, in Hebrew a feminine word, *Shulammith*. It is unlikely this is an actual name but expresses rather that she is the mirror image of her beloved: in Hebrew, Solomon is *Shelomoh* (masculine). Different in gender but united in peace – the root of both names being *shalom*. Some believe Shulamite is a reference to place, but there is no record of Shulam in Israel, the closest is Shunem (a village north of Jezreel and south of Mount Bilboa). There is a chance that this may identify her place of origin, but much more likely that it is a 'pet name' given to her in the relationship. This seems to please her as she refers to herself as '*thy* Shulamite' (7:1).

The name Shulamite (feminine form of Solomon) is also reminiscent of Abishag the Shunamite, the beautiful maiden from the village of Shunem, who kept David warm in his old age (1 Kings 2:13-25). The Book of Kings clearly states David's relation with the Shunamite was not sexual (in any usual sense). David's Shunamite was sacred in her virginity – a vestal virgin, who warmed the messianic figure grown cold. Similarly Solomon with 'his Shulamite' is a foretaste of 'the incarnation' – the kindling of David's line through the body of Mary. 'Concerning the Incarnation' is the subtitle of Rupert of Deutz's highly influential twelfth-century commentary on the Song. Deutz's commentary stands out in viewing the Song consistently as honouring the *vehicle* of the incarnation, the Virgin Mary.[3] Mary the God-bearer, a closed garden with respect to her virginity but the open gate of heaven with respect to her motherhood. Deutz's conviction that this motherhood is both physical and spiritual makes him rather unique among medieval commentators in his defence of the literal meaning of the Song: 'For indeed,' he writes, 'the mystical exposition will be more firm, nor will it be allowed to fluctuate with fantasy, if it is held to be built on the history of certain times and of rationally demonstrable facts' (Rupert of Deutz 1974: 7–8; my translation).

Grace builds on nature. In mystical interpretations of the Song ideas of 'grace' abound but the natural qualities of the maiden are rarely seen as the basis for the action of grace. Failing to discern any storyline in the Song, many recent commentators go so far as to say that the Song has no literal sense at all. Morris Jastrow (1921) sees it as a patchwork of forty-three relatively unconnected 'songs', Karl Budde (1894) sees seven separate poems within the whole, Ernst Würthwein (2011) connects twenty-four units referring to 'the wedding' with five independent poems woven in. None of these

---

3 Another example is the German poet Heinrich von Meissen (c. 1260–1318), known as 'Frauenlob' – meaning 'praise of ladies' – who rewrote the Song of Songs in his masterpiece the *Marienleich*.

commentators believe there is a consistent narrative. The tendency has been to dismember the poem into a series of disconnected, or, at best, loosely connected, episodes. Even when a thread is discerned it is in terms of the poem's liturgical *use* rather than in its *content*, so Würthwein reads it as a collection, in one form or another, of ceremonial marriage lyrics.

No wonder the ancient and medieval readings of allegory seem unconvincing. If the story itself is unclear, how do we effectively draw lessons from it? Good allegory has to be built on story; take, for example, Aesop's fables – they no doubt carry allegorical meaning (that was why they were written) but the allegory works through the stories. So the mystical sense of the poem, if there is one (which we conclude there is) has to work through the narrative sense. It is not something added on. To use Shakespeare again as an example: his ideas are conveyed through the *dramatis personae*. So it is with this poem. If metaphorical meanings to the Song are not castles built on air it is essential to find the human story, which then *may* act as a symbol for something more. The aim of this book is to pinpoint just such a literal meaning, and then hint at what symbolism may be built on this foundation. Aside from possible allegorical interpretations, it is possible to discern a coherent human narrative – i.e. not just a collection of disconnected lyrical effusions but a structured story, with a beginning, middle and end.

The aim of Part Two of this book is to show that the ultimate icon of the Song is the Shulamite: humanly she is wise; symbolically she *is* Wisdom. She represents the one Wisdom in two modes. These two modes could be seen as the literal and the symbolic senses of the Song, or the human and the spiritual, two approaches which have been juxtaposed in the history of the Song's interpretation. Up until the eighteenth century the latter dominated completely, but recently this whole level has been rejected as projection onto a collection of poems about human lovemaking. What is needed is an integral approach. In the Song itself, the Shulamite does respond to her lover's plea to 'come back' but by enigmatically asking whether she has to come back 'as it were between the armies drawn up for battle?' (7:1). This certainly symbolises how scholarship on the Song stands today: like armies drawn up for battle; the humanist on one side, and the religious allegorical on the other. The Shulamite maiden is, however, the symbol of peace, and her wisdom is key to the Song. There is, in the end, no separation between her and the divine wisdom she *receives* in discovering her likeness, and *gives* in her humanity.

The Song does what it says. It speaks of love and it transmits that love as wisdom and peace. Form and substance in a single operation: working on the one who receives (or in this case reads) that they may discover themselves in the words, and give themselves in the wisdom of love. Allegory need not mean dispassion, as that most emotional commentator on the Song St Bernard explains in his Sermon 79:

> In this marriage-song it is the affections behind the words that are to be pondered even more than the words themselves ... For love speaks in it everywhere; if anyone desires to grasp these writings, let him love! For he who does not love will hear and read the Song in vain; the cold heart cannot grasp its burning eloquence.
>
> (Bernard of Clairvaux 1980: 138)

That the original author of the Song intended to express love seems clear from the text. Within the text there are hints which, if followed, make the Song much clearer. In the end, however, the question remains, *what does it mean to us?* Like Jesus, the Song asks 'What about you? Who do you say that I am?' (Mark 8:29, Matthew 15:16). Wise love is relationship from a place of self-knowledge. In reading the Song we cannot in the end leave ourselves out of the picture.

The need for a new approach

The central line in the Song of Songs – with fifty-seven verses before and fifty-seven verses after – is that of a 'closed garden', of a 'fountain sealed'. The mysteriousness of much of the imagery of the Song, and the difficulty in finding its overall meaning, might make it seem as impenetrable as such a garden. A tenth-century Rabbinic commentator on the Song, faced with the plethora of interpretations even within the context of his own time, confessed, 'The Song is like a lock, the key of which has been lost' (quoted in Boyarin 1990: 115). Yet, throughout history, people have found in the beautiful, sensuous and mysterious lines of the Song hints of a magical half-hidden garden, and the promise of a source of living water for the thirsty soul. The Song is an untapped well of delight that just needs to be uncovered for it to flow again. It is a love story, related through dialogue but not spelt out – we are left with only snippets of a dream-like conversation. The poetry seems to speak of heavenly and earthly delights just beyond our reach, heartfelt musings that express our longing for human fulfilment *and* for the experience of God. It awakens and quenches that thirst through a realisation that heaven is here and now. Readers and scholars alike are left with the feeling that if we might yet obtain the key to the garden, if we might somehow find a way *into* the drama of the poem, the fountain might be unsealed and an eternal source of wisdom and love spring up again.

Despite its age the Song remains perennially fascinating, nourishing each generation. The search for the meaning of the Song is the quest for the Holy Grail. The poem's subtle enigma has enlisted the hearts and minds of many spiritual seekers. Many have seen in its elusive imagery a mosaic of meanings that often seem far-flung from the text. From the Jewish Hassidic and later Kabbalistic traditions, to the flowering of Christian monastic spirituality and the Sufi mysticism of Persia, spiritual devotees have loved to dwell on the lines, musing on its mystery. In the early Rabbinic period, *Mishnah Yadayim* 3:5 records Rabbi Akiva (*c*.50–135) professing, 'All the Scriptures are holy, but the Song of Songs is the holy of holies' (Neusner 1988: 1123). In the twelfth century, this poem became the most commentated-upon book of the Christian Bible. We know of thirty Christian commentaries in the twelfth century alone. In fact, in the whole Middle Ages, its popularity among commentators comes second only to the Gospel of John. Yet today, except for a few presaged passages which appear at weddings and a verse that is wrongly translated as mentioning God (8:6), the poem has become marginalised and lost in obscurity.

The fact is, the poem does not mention God at all; it is not overtly religious. And yet, the human love it depicts can seem quite idealised and lofty, to a level with which most, if not all, human relationships cannot relate. The imagery is distinctly Jewish (and speaks of an era long ago): outside the resonances of that tradition they can seem at times quite bizarre, even comic ('thy teeth are like flocks of goats …'). On the other hand, on a poem that speaks completely 'from the heart', scholastic commentaries can appear very dry (theological interpretations only adding to the oddity).

The poem's inclusion in the Old Testament implies that it was read spiritually from a very early age. Whether this was the author's intention remains a question. And yet the Jewish tradition has always affirmed *the human side* of the covenant with God. The Covenant must be expressed in the way we relate to each other (Leviticus 19:18). As a record of loving relations between two humans the Song is sacred. There is no need to add other dimensions.

Since this heart felt tract has influenced the faith of at least three faith traditions for the best part of 2,000 years, it would be a real loss if its capacity to inspire dried up. If it is approached as a religious text it has the great asset of bringing passion, sexual love, and the flow of libido back into faith. The diminished presence of the Song within contemporary culture is more illustrative of the breakdown (since eighteenth-century rationalism) of a long tradition of mystical *eros*. *Eros* is not the only way to love God and it is certainly not the only way to love our fellow human beings, but if we lose one of what C. S. Lewis called 'the four loves' – empathy, friendship, the erotic and the altruistic – we would lose part of our capacity to love, whether that be God or each other. In terms of poetic inspiration as well, to consign such a seminal text to the catacombs of history is a major impoverishment.

The multitude of allegorical interpretations that have evolved over time have, undoubtedly, led to the current cul-de-sac. Who is to say one is right over another? The impression is that each religion has merely projected its agenda onto an innocent poem. And yet the poem is not as innocent as it seems: it prompts, even provokes, mystical flights of fancy. A superlative poem speaking the language of sexuality: no wonder that it has been the seed ground for some unrestrained 'free-association', especially in the religious mind. The Christian allegorical reading, going back to Origen in the third century, was much influenced by Rabbinic readings. Both emphasised the mystical nature of the poem, reading romance as the soul's relation to God. For the Rabbis, God's covenant with his chosen people; for the Christians, Christ's love for the Church. Together they dominated interpretations up to the early modern era but fell out of fashion in the eighteenth century. With the rise of biblical hermeneutics in the nineteenth they were mostly considered simply as projections onto the Song.

Certainly, giving the Song *only* a spiritual meaning has drained it of much of its flesh and blood. Actual lovers have been sacrificed on the altars of ideals (however sincerely held). The Song is not about philosophy, which would be *love of wisdom*. The Song is about the *wisdom of love*. And yet, modern scholarship hasn't really helped to give back the real story of the lovers. Veering either towards a dry deconstruction of the poem into 'unconnected fragments' or dressing it up as a Bacchanite romp through the fields of sexual liberation, modern readings leave the lovers either emaciated or a little too hot-blooded than fits the text. Either way, this lyrical jewel has become trapped (like a vaquita in a net) between polarised branches of interpretation, none of them allowing the distinctive *characters* room to breathe within the poem: either a sense of consecutive story is denied, or the figures become generic male and female. But the Song is pre-eminently *personal*, and interpretation must be based on the real *personalities* of the lovers involved.

Modern analysis has primarily sought to strip back much of the symbolic 'overlay' that has been 'put onto' the Song, either to focus on the human relations between the two lovers or to deconstruct the poem into fragments denying any consistent narrative. The poem continues to be interpreted through a variety of proscriptive lenses: either as a secular love poem, an allegory not about mysticism but about sex, or as a ritual for Second Temple marriage ceremonies, or pagan fertility rites dressed up with Jewish symbolism.[4] Biblical hermeneutics has been somewhat at a loss to say what the poem is, or why it is in the Bible. What is needed is a new approach which brings together the human and the mystical aspects of the poem. The Song is based on a poignant and very human love at its core. It is a story about love: that most divine of human longings.

The hermeneutic I offer is a bridge between the traditional and modern perspectives, thereby bringing a deeper sense of cultural continuity to the interpretation of the poem. Jewish and Christian exegesis (in both patristic and medieval eras) may have veered into allegory which has only a tenuous link to the human dimension of the Song, but they still unpacked the symbolical *potential* of the Song in a way quite unmatched in modern scholarship. Modern readings have brought the man and the woman back to life, but the inclination to reduce the meaning simply to human relations tends to impoverish the depth of the poem (both vis-à-vis its journey

---

4 Respectively the positions taken by Block and Block (2006); Pope (1977); Davis (1989); Meek (1924: 48–79).

through history and as a resource for spiritual contemplation). The Song's cultural relevance today is no doubt different from the social context of earlier epochs, where everything was read through a lens of religious typology that went with literary culture. It is now possible to read the Song quite outside that. In many ways, this gives us a fresher view but it is no coincidence that the Song was a major part of literary and spiritual culture then whereas it is pretty much unknown even in consciously religious circles today.

The meaning of the Song, in the end, is in the telling. The approach I offer is to take it as a narrative whole, unfolding in distinct episodes, which correspond roughly to the section or chapter breaks that have come down to us in the early texts. By restoring, as best we can, the literal sense of the story we will be able to see what symbolic meaning corresponds with it, how the imagery in the Song expresses mystical or spiritual 'likenesses'. The actual story of the Song must be the guide to what is relevant to it within the broader Judeo-Christian tradition. Medieval exegetes tended too easily to 'follow the tracks of the companions' (Song 1:6), rather than stick with the authentic story of the text. The key to interpreting the meaning of the lovers of the Song is the mirror-like quality of their relationship: 'My beloved to me, and I to him' (2:16). They see each other through the same eyes: he says her eyes are 'as doves' (1:14 and 4:1), she says his eyes are 'as doves' (5:12). They look at each other with the same love that is winged (to the heights) and yet peaceful. 'I am become in the face/regard of him (whom I love) as one finding peace' (8:10). They know who they are through the mirror of each other: 'Show me where you are!' says the maiden, and her lover replies, 'If you but knew yourself!' (1:7-8).

The Song has many levels. The imagery at times asks for a simple natural reading, as for example when the maiden says, 'I am brown, for the sun hath discoloured me.' It is astonishing how many weird allegorical meanings have been attributed to the maiden's 'darkness' when the text itself explains it quite clearly. At other times the images serve to express a feeling or thought, as for example when the maiden says, 'Catch for us the little foxes that destroy the vines' – foxes do not destroy vines so we are prompted to look at this as an allegory for something else; in this case the clue is in her much earlier words: 'the sons of my mother contended against me … my own vineyard have I not defended' – she is remembering as if in a bad dream her brothers who tried to take her inheritance. Some images are explicable given topographical or etymological readings. At times the images are numinous with mystery, as in the lover's description of her as 'a closed garden, a fountain sealed.' Here, paralleling biblical texts, the insights of mystical theology or psychology can help.

Yet if the Song is properly and convincingly set within a narrative context it needs little more than the poetry of the text to explain it. The interpretative key *is* the story. At times things need to be 'brought from the outside' in order to 'get the story' – mostly these are from the historical era in which the Song is set (i.e. the time of Solomon). Writing in Hebrew for a Jewish audience which was highly conscious of its national history, the author would have assumed his readership to have a lot of this background knowledge. So the author doesn't fill it all in – we, however, need to be reminded. To appreciate the value of the concrete image as a carrier of meaning necessitates an appreciation of how any allegory is embedded historically. The more sacramental that allegory the more it must be approached as a real event in history, even if it be only 'story'. The Song is, in all likelihood, a piece of 'historical fiction'. However, it is accurately set within the time it represents. Whether or not the maiden actually existed … who knows. We are free to believe she did, and that the Song hands down some oral tradition that actually goes back to a real story in Solomon's life, but that cannot be proven. Nor do we need such a belief to make the poem real; literature (as in any great novel) brings people more than history to life.

In reading the Song imaginative perception is the presiding

hermeneutic, but as the Song is written a long time ago, and set at a time even further back, historical and linguistic analysis is needed. The aim in the end, however, is simply to 'get the story' for it is only on this that any further levels of meaning can be built. 'Become like little children,' Jesus said: for children imagination and reality interact and inform each other; they take stories as real and that is why they are so real for them. The Song is a very real story, and because of that it says much about life.

Translations/attribution of speakers

We have no 'original version' of the Song. The earliest surviving Hebrew texts of the Song are in the Dead Sea Scrolls: only fragments, and of a relatively late date, from 30 BCE–70 CE. Like most biblical texts found at Qumran they are close to the Rabbinic Masoretic text of the tenth century CE, the source of Protestant and Catholic Bibles today.[5] There are reasons, however, for not just sticking to the Masoretic text in a study of the Song. When looking at interpretations it is important to follow the history of the text, rather than referring to a Hebrew text which most commentators never knew. The Orthodox Church follows the third- to late-second-century BCE Greek Septuagint. This gives the earliest complete version of the Song. Early Greek commentators like Origen, Theodore of Mopsuestia, or Gregory of Nyssa, interact with the text they received (i.e. the Septuagint). In the Western Church, commentaries followed Old Latin texts and the fourth century CE Vulgate, which in its rendering of the Song is close to the Septuagint. Since the discovery of the Dead Sea Scrolls biblical scholarship is aware there was not 'one version' of Hebrew texts that came to make up the Bible. The concern

---

5   Such correspondences show that the Masoretic is an accurate transmission of *one* early text. The three main Masoretic texts, Leningrad, Aleppo and Cambridge, are collated and analysed by Piet Dirksen in 'Canticles' (Dirksen 2004: 8–10).

today is not to find one 'authentic' text – an impossible task – but to explain the common origin and early phases and revisions of Greek, Vulgate, Hebrew and Syriac versions. To study the Song properly we must use all that has come down to us. Each has a claim to be heard (though they be other to the original language of the poem). When deciding which to follow – normally that of Septuagint–Vulgate or the Masoretic – much depends on what question is being asked. Each version of the Song has its own history and geography of influence. It may not be possible to get back to a so-called 'original meaning of the text': we have versions in variant languages and later translations. The meaning of the text has evolved over time in different contexts. Shaped by distinct religious traditions, each lineage can be intolerant of others. The secular is even more intolerant, claiming a humanistic reading as the only interpretive key.

It would be humbler and more realistic to present a reading that draws on both the text as it has come down to us, *and* the interpretations that have been given. Attempts at 'original readings' often end up being readings from the perspective of today, so it is necessary to read texts in the context of their historical journey through time to provide a broader chronological objectivity.

This book (and its author) is shaped mostly by the 'western Christian tradition' and medieval commentaries so the translation I give is Vulgate-based, the Douay-Rheims being the first full English translation thereof. But at all variations with other ancient texts these parallel versions are considered. The Song was transmitted by the Synagogues in the early Common Era in Greek and early Hebrew texts. The Greek survives. Slight variations in the fragments of the Song at Qumran show how nuances evolved within the Latin, Syriac and later Rabbinic Hebrew versions. Taken together these versions provide a more rounded picture than using the later Hebrew Masoretic versions alone. The Vulgate is also helpful in approaching the literal sense of the Song for Jerome, translating from an early Hebrew source text, seems to have favoured more concrete meanings of words. When two possible alternative meanings of a Hebrew word or phrase are evident, the Rabbinic tradition chose valid but more abstract meanings. For example the Septuagint and Vulgate translate the second line of the first verse as 'For your breasts are better than wine'; whereas the Masoretic, through a different placing of vowels, reads it as 'For your love is better than wine.' This possible double meaning in the Hebrew is again read differently at 1:4, 4:10 and 7:13. It is likely the Rabbinic tradition chose the more metaphorical meaning to counteract claims that the Song was vulgar and licentious – there was a heated debate over the Song's canonicity during the formation of the Tanakh at the Council of Jamnia in 90 CE. However, the bodily sense of words proves helpful in studying the human context of the Song.

At most of the points where the Vulgate differs from the Masoretic text, it is supported by the Septuagint. Thus two of the most ancient full versions that have come down to us are in accord in their renderings of certain passages, which serve to highlight the narrative reading of the poem. At 1:6, for example, the Masoretic has the maiden 'working the vineyards' for her brothers; in the Septuagint–Vulgate these brothers 'set [her] to be a guard in the vineyards.' The sense of 'guarding' – φυλάκισσαν, *custodem* – throws light on the strange command to 'catch the little foxes' which, otherwise, seems to come from nowhere at 2:15.

In my commentary I have, however, made much use of the Masoretic text, especially where Hebrew meanings throw light on the meaning of metaphorical imagery used in the Song. The division of the poem into 'episodes' is also guided mostly by paragraph breaks within the Masoretic (as will be explained in Part Two). Unlike any of the ancient texts, I allocate the lines to speakers. The identification of speakers and their roles in any modern edition is drawn from the inner working of the text, but has also to be critically reviewed. The male/female/singular/plural distinctions are relatively clear in Hebrew. But the Masoretic text is late and may well reflect

Rabbinic interpretations, which were formulated with some intensity in response to Christian exegesis in the early centuries CE. In the Greek, Latin and Syriac versions things are not necessarily clearer, as gender is given to the subject but not the speaker of a sentence. Certain lines traditionally given to the man could also be seen as the maiden's rendering of his voice 'as it appears to her'. For example, at 2:8, 2:10, and 5:2 the maiden speaks of hearing 'the voice of the beloved.' Yet what follows 2:8 is the maiden's account of how she sees, or more likely *imagines*, her beloved arriving (the description is figurative, he doesn't literally 'leap over mountains'). 2:10 and 5:2 are, in the same verse, followed by speech. As there is no conjunction this is presented as direct speech, and yet this does not preclude that what is said is still within the narration of the maiden (especially as in poetic utterance, without grammar, conjunctions are often dropped). In fact, some lines after 2:10 the maiden expresses her longing for her absent lover and goes into the city to look for him: the implication is that at 2:10 Solomon is not actually there. 5:2 follows with the maiden's description of what Solomon does ('he put his hand …') so 5:2 could well be her account of what he says, or what she imagines him to say. The fact that at both 2:10 and 5:2 'the voice' begins in the same verse as the narrator hints that there is no change of speaker.

The Song is a hard text to pin down: any punctuation is a much later addition, and necessarily an interpretation. There is no capitalisation either in the early texts. The verse divisions may be the interpretation of the scribes, and yet ancient versions are in nearly complete agreement in demarking verses; cross-textual evidence that versification was in the texts they were working from. It does seem that, at times, a single verse could be split between speakers. 7:10 starts with Solomon adding another praise of the maiden (of her throat!) but is interrupted half way with the maiden inviting 'his lips' to delight in her. Verse 5:1 starts with the maiden inviting, 'Let my beloved come into his garden …' and then continues in the same verse, 'I have come into my garden, my sister-bride ...'[6] Similarly, the Masoretic and Septuagint verse 7:1 is counted as two verses in the Vulgate, and even a chapter break is made in the middle – a pointer that the collation into chapters is a scribal redaction (the Masoretic, as we will see, has different breaks). There can be time lapses within verses, for example 3:2 starts 'I will arise ... I will seek him' and ends 'I have sought him and I did not find.' Considering that the interval involves a walk into and through Jerusalem we can consider, even within one verse, a dramatic interval of some hours. The intervals within and between verses must be carefully gauged to keep the narrative sense.

It is noticeable that up to verse 7:11 the lines are roughly equally attributable to Solomon and the Shulamite. From this line on there are twenty verses attributable to the Shulamite and only three to Solomon. As the poem reaches its crescendo the maiden comes to the fore. 7:11, as we will see, is a key verse in reversing the relation between man and woman consequent to the Fall: 'I to my beloved, and his turning is (ever) towards me'. The fact that the turning of *his* desire is towards *her* contrasts with Genesis 3:16 where God says to the woman, 'your desire will be for your husband, yet he will rule over you.' In the mutuality of their love the maiden at this point is set free to take the leading role in the expression and direction of their love. After 7:11 only 8:4 is unambiguously spoken by the male figure ('I adjure you, daughters of Jerusalem, neither arouse nor cause to awaken the beloved until she pleases'). In 8:5b, which begins 'Under the apple tree I awakened thee ...', the one spoken *to* is given the masculine suffix implying that the maiden is the speaker, however, the much earlier Syriac versions have a feminine suffix to the one addressed (Pope 1977: 663). The Vulgate has a particular

---

6 I propose, in the following section, that this makes more sense of the opening verse: 1:1a as spoken by the maiden, 1:1b by Solomon. I propose this is not the case, however, at 2:10 and 5:2 for reasons given above. In text and here, a,b,c refers to the first, second and third lines of a verse.

verb *suscitavi* which means not so much awaken or arouse but 'lift up, raise, elevate' which links with the first line of 8:5, 'Who is this ascending (*ascendit*) from the desert …' Here the one ascending is clearly the maiden for she is 'leaning on *her* beloved.' So, following the Syriac and hints in the Vulgate, I take the maiden to be the one 'awakened' in 8:5b and Solomon the speaker of both parts of the verse. The penultimate verse 8:13 I believe to be spoken by Solomon (even though it concludes a long section in which only the Shulamite speaks) as it addresses 'you who live in the gardens': it is the maiden who came from the country, unlike the king who lives in Jerusalem. 8:13 ends, 'Make me to hear your voice!' The wisdom context implies that this verse is Solomon petitioning the maiden, who by the end of the poem has become synonymous with Wisdom, to teach him to rule well. As one of 'Solomon's Proverbs' was:

> Doth not wisdom cry out? and understanding put forth
>   her voice?
> She stands in the top of the high places, in the squares where
>   the roads meet,
> She cries at the gates, at the entry of the city, at the portals:
> 'Unto you, O men, I call; and my voice is to the sons of man.
> O ye simple, understand wisdom: and, ye fools, have prudent
>   hearts.
> Hear; I will speak of excellent things; open my lips for right
>   things …
> I am understanding; I have strength. By me kings reign.'
>
> (Proverbs 8:1-6, 15)

No ancient version, modern translation, or attribution of speakers among or within verses can be conclusive. But there are good textual reasons within the story context of the Song to make sensible allocations. A test case, that links translation with an attribution of speaker, comes right at the beginning of the poem, 1:1b and 1:3c. As noted, there is an important difference here between the Hebrew Bible (which most English versions today follow), and the Septuagint–Vulgate. The Hebrew of the Masoretic text at verse 1 is translated 'your *love* is better than wine', and verse 3: 'we will praise your love more than wine'. Both Greek and Latin use 'breasts'. The textual transmission is thoroughly analysed by Hebrew Scholar Edmée Kingsmill, who shows that it was Masoretic pointing around the eighth century which supplied the vowel *dôd* giving the meaning 'love' (Kingsmill 2009). The original Hebrew (from which the Septuagint scholars and St Jerome were working) would have simply the letters *dd*. As a double letter this is a plural in Hebrew and, in its context would normally take the simplest vowel form rendering *dd* as *dad* – breasts (pl.) (ibid.: 85–8). The evidence from the Dead Sea Scrolls similarly favours this reading. Among the remains of the four scrolls of the Song there are two fragments of the opening verses both without a vowel letter. The Qumran scribes typically added vowels when they sought to make clear a different meaning from the most obvious, but here they don't. On top of this, when the Masoretic scribes did reassign *dd* as *dôd*, the form is still maintained in its plural form, which makes very little sense of verses: 'your *loves* are better than wine', and 'we will praise your *loves* more than wine'.

So, it is not only the meaning of those lines in all English Bibles, which is inaccurately transmitted, but also the implication of who is speaking that is censored. This, Kingsmill points out, is the reason why the Rabbinic editors of the Hebrew Bible were so concerned that it was 'love' not 'breasts' in the opening lines. The Rabbinic tradition of scriptural interpretation was concerned to play down or take out anthropomorphic references to Yahweh especially when these could have a pagan cultic significance, or, indeed, significances that could play into Christian hands. Masoretic editors, in the eighth century CE, were aware that in earlier Jewish and Christian commentary these lines were presumed to have been spoken by the male figure – who represented God (or, for the Christian, Christ). The Masoretes sought to remove any notion of God as a fertility deity, as in Diana of the Ephesians, depicted with multiple breasts. They were also aware that Christian commentators (using the Septuagint or Vulgate) made the link in these lines with St John resting on the *breast* of Christ at the last supper, imbibing divine wisdom. In both cases, the Masoretes were concerned that God does not have breasts, so *dd* was pointed as *dôd*.

This whole problem is removed in a simple narrative reading of the text, if the person addressed in the lines is not taken to be God. The most natural philological meaning of *dd* can be restored. But also (and here I part company with Kingsmill) the natural subject of the lines can also be restored, namely that these lines were not addressed by the woman to the man as tradition has always assumed, but by the man to the woman, for whose gender 'breasts' is a much more appropriate.

Rabbinic and Christian commentary has, in all cases but one, attributed these lines to the male speaker but the one who places the voice in a different light is no less an authority than St Bernard (1090–1153) in his Sermon 9:4:

> Of whom are these words? The author does not tell us, leaving it to us to divine to whom they are most befitting. For myself, there lacks not motives for attributing these words either to the bride, or to the bridegroom, or even to the bridegroom's companions.
>
> (Bernard of Clairvaux 1971: 55–6)

Interestingly, his first choice seems to be the bride, then, maybe remembering tradition, the groom, but his strong sense of the exact wording of the text makes him think again, because the form is plural – 'breasts' – and, therefore, if attributable to male it must be to more than one. St John could lie on the breast of Jesus but hardly on his breasts (besides the New Testament word is *kalpō*, that is bosom/lap, not *mastos*). So Bernard adds a rather far-fetched allegory of the breasts as referring to the bridegroom's companions, that is, all the Apostles!

In any case, verses 1 and 3 of the Song make no mention of lying on but of being attracted to, nourished/inebriated by breasts. The natural subject of the image is the woman, the natural speaker a man. If there is still a doubt, the image occurs again later in the poem clearly as an address by the male to the woman: 'How fair are your breasts, my sister, my bride, how much better your breasts than wine' (4:10). As these initial verses of the Song orchestrate the reading of the poem, it is apposite to clarify who renders these lines. It could be argued that the nourishment to be received from these breasts is wine and not milk and, therefore, less tied to the physiology of woman; but wine, milk and for that matter honey (which appears often in the Song in a similar context) were much more closely *linked* in ancient understanding than today: all were considered to be the product of fermentation whereby something was transformed into something else. Grapes into an intoxicating liquor, nectar into sweetness, and, surprisingly maybe for us, blood into milk. As grapes made wine, in ancient and medieval understanding, milk was formed in the breasts through the fermentation of blood.

If the *prima materia* of the poem is a relationship between two human beings it is more natural for the breasts in question to be those of the woman and the desire for them to be that of the man. This is not to deny that this 'natural' reading cannot be transformed into a spiritual reading, but there is no wine without grapes, no milk without blood, no honey without nectar: any mystical reading of the Song must work *with* the human story.

Episodes of the Song/the great day

The Song of Songs, in the Septuagint and Vulgate, is divided into eight chapters. The Authorised Version kept the old chapter breaks (one assumes out of familiarity, as in other respects the translation follows the Hebrew). However, the Masoretic gives slightly different paragraph breaks, which form the basis of the ten major 'episodes', and the rationale for many of the 'parts' of episodes, here given.[7] For example, at 2:8, the Masoretic scribe intuits a break between the stillness we have been led into in verses 2:6-7 and the new action of 2:8 and puts a paragraph break after 5:1, suggesting a pause in the drama there, rather than at the opening of chapter 5.

Many modern commentators on the Song speak of the fragmentary style of the poem. Some see the 'episodes' marked in the Masoretic text as the beginnings of different 'phrase collections', which have been put together without any narrative connection, and 'gaps in the story' such that the Song is a series of 'independent poems' (Carr 2003: 115, 137). The 'ambiguity' and 'lack of closure' at the end is often noted; the last sections often seen as 'additions' (Block and Block 2006: 18–19). Some see in the Song 'no logical sequence', 'no story line … no narrative', that it is 'a dream transcribed, resistant of any simple decoding … a song that imitates the movement of a dream' (Davis 1989: 236–8). Certainly, the poetic idiom of the Song is strongly symbolic and imagistic rather than didactic (as is the majority of the Bible). Its dream like quality, however, should not blind us to the fact that it is telling a story.

The Song has more similarities to Greek drama than to biblical history: it does not try to say 'this actually happened', or give some message about the meaning of an event in time, but rather tells a story which reveals the depths of what it is to be human *at any time*. It uncovers the human soul. Theatre was not part of ancient Jewish culture, it was considered pagan. But there is one Greek word in the Masoretic text, *palanquin* at 3:9, which hints at an authorship

---

7 The Cambridge Masoretic text (Ms.Add.1753), for example, has *petuhah* paragraph breaks after 1:5, 2:7, 3:5, 4:7, 5:1, 6:9, 7:11, 8:4, 8:7 and 8:10 which correspond with the episodes I have given. Though the Cambridge Ms. doesn't have a break after 4:11, the Leningrad Masoretic text (EPB.IB.19a) does (Dirksen 2004: 8–9).

more familiar with stage performance.[8] The theatrical dialogue form of the Song – a form of literature not familiar to biblical scholars – does much to explain the changes in voice. If the Song is more like a drama then changes of scene within it between that of Jerusalem and the countryside are quite consistent with a unified plot and need not imply independent poems. It would, however, be better to use the term 'dramatic poetry' rather than 'drama', as the action of the poem is nearly all of a psychological nature.

Some of the episodes I give follow thematic or chronological breaks in the Song not given in the Masoretic. However, like those in the Masoretic versions, these clarify breaks or pauses in the narrative, often with readjustment of setting just as in a theatre. The Masoretic provides a paragraph break at 1:5, rightly illustrating that the dialogue has changed from between the Shulamite and Solomon to between her and the Daughters of Jerusalem. However, as the 'scene' remains that of the harem I have kept 1:5-6 as part of the first episode, introducing a new episode only with the introduction of the pastoral scene at 1:7. The Masoretic proposes a second paragraph break after 1:8 with the change back to regal imagery, however, as this does not mean a change of scene I retain 'episode two' until the end of the Septuagint/Vulgate chapter.

The episodes help orientate the story, presenting either distinct acts within the drama or a new subject of conversation (for example, at 8:8 when the maiden speaks for the first time of 'her sister') or changes of mood due to a lapse of time. Sometimes, in episodes, I have grouped dialogue according to speaker: with the exception of 4:16, all seventeen verses of chapter 4 and 5:1 are spoken by the male figure, so I have presented them as one episode.[9] A new episode starts with the Shulamite retaking the dialogue at 5:2.

---

8   The Song has not often been put to music, an exception being Forrest Reid (1875–1947) who created a libretto for an opera based on the Song.
9   The fact that 4:16 must be the Shulamite speaking can be discerned in that throughout the Song it is only she who uses the term 'beloved'.

I have further divided episodes into parts, which highlight transitions rather than breaks within the conversation. These are not dramatically distinct from the episodes (of which they are *part*). They imply no change of scene, lapse of time, or new encounter but are simply for the sake of textual exegesis.

What is discernible in the poem is that it frames *a great day*. The introductory verses 1:1-6 and the closing verses 8:8-14 are the frame, they occur before and after *the day*. The main body of the drama occurs between their meeting in the garden in the early evening (1:7 onward) to late in the night the following day. Within Semitic understanding a day starts in the evening before. The Song has two short 'nature ballads' within it: an aubade or *alba*-song that celebrates the dawn at 2:10-13, and a serenade or *sera*-song celebrating the evening at 7:12-14. These act as a morning and evening *raga*, or Matins and Vespers to *the day*. This day in many ways explicates the 'Yahwistic' account of man and woman in 'the garden' in Genesis 2-3. The movements within the Song of finding, losing and finding again, reflect the joy of Adam and Eve's discovery of each other, the pain and suffering of inevitable loss, and the rediscovery of each other 'outside of the garden' united in a new way even in tragedy. In the Song, however, the whole drama of human relations is lived in a day. It also offers a healing balm to the deep wound of humanity's mythic past. Where the couple of Genesis ate of the tree of knowledge of good and evil, at the centre of the garden those of the Song eat of the tree of life. There is very little concern for right and wrong between the couple in the Song, their only desire (anticipating John 10:10) is that 'they might have life, and might have it more abundantly.'

The movement of union and separation and finding again at a higher level is the *flow* of the Song. This movement was explored deeply in the Sufi tradition as well as among Jewish and Christian mystics. The Sufis followed the Song in using the motif of romantic love to express how God at times feels present, at times absent, and yet is always in union with the soul. Mīr Sayyid Manjhan, the great sixteenth-century Indian Sufi, depicts mystical union as cemented on the day man and woman were first created. For thus Monohar expresses his love for Madhumālatī *when they first meet*:

'Listen, dearest one!' the Prince then said,
'In a former life God created love between you and me … '

'I have heard that on the day the world was born,
the bird of love was released to fly.
It searched all the three worlds
but could not find a fit resting place.
So it turned and entered the inmost heart,
favoured it and never flew elsewhere … '

'You and I have always been together.
Always we have been a single body.
You and I both are one body,
two lumps of clay mixed in the same water.
The same water flows in two streams,
one lamp alone lights two homes.
One soul enters two bodies,
one fire burns in two hearths.
We were one but were born as two:
one temple with two doors.
>   We were one radiant light, one beautiful form, one soul
>   and one body:
>   how can there be any doubt in giving oneself to oneself?'

'You are the ocean, I am your wave.
You are the sun, I the ray that lights the world.
Do not think that you and I are separate:
I am the body, you are my dear life.
Who can part us, a single light in two forms?
I see everything through the eye of enlightenment.

Who knows how long we have known each other?
Today, O maiden, you do not recognize me.
Think back in your memory –
we knew each other on creation's first day.'

(Manjhan 2000: 48–50)

Certainly, there are many influences of Oriental mystical-erotic poetry in the imagery and allusions of the Song. In King Solomon's time, there was considerable cultural exchange between the Judaic kingdom and its Egyptian and Babylonian neighbours. Centuries later when the Song was written, the political influence of the Achaemenid Empire brought Persian dance and poetry to Israel. The motifs of the Song may, therefore, come from a Persian source common to later Sufi mystical poetry.

Egypt/Israel and the Song

Specific cultural use of terms like 'sister' for a bride may have derived from familial arrangement of marriage in the ancient world where the betrothed, even before marriage, was regarded as family. 'Sister' or 'brother' – implying one most loved and precious – is found in Mesopotamian sacred marriage poems predating 2000 BCE.[10] The style of the Song certainly has strong parallels with ancient Egyptian love poetry where, before the first millennium BCE, there was a turn from sacred-marriage poetry invoking fertility to the personal drama of love-longing. The Chester Beatty Papyrus illustrates the ancient Egyptian use of the sibling motif and other images that may have influenced the Song:

One alone is my sister, having no peer:
More gracious than all other women.
Behold her, like Sothis [a star] rising

---

10   On 'sibling love' see Carr (2003: 95–100).

At the beginning of a good year:
Shining, precious, white of skin,
Lovely, the look of her eyes,
Sweet, the speech of her lips,
She has not a word too much.
Long of neck, white of breast …
My brother torments my heart with his voice,
He makes sickness take hold of me;
He is neighbour to my mother's house,
And I cannot go to him!
Mother is right in charging me thus:
'Give up seeing him!'
It pains my heart to think of him,
For love of him has captured me …
Oh brother I am decreed for you
By the Golden One [Hathor].
Come to me that I may see your beauty!
May father and mother be glad!
May all people rejoice in you together,
Rejoice in you, my brother!

(Lichtheim 1976: 182–3)

The influence is not just on the content of the Song but also on its form as a *dialogue*. The Egyptian poem has two lovers speaking: the 'brother' expressing his admiration for the 'sister' which the 'sister' reciprocates in her yearning that he come to her side. Again, as with the early versions of the Song, the Chester Beatty Papyrus gives no gaps between speakers, so one has to discern (from content) who is speaking.

If the Song was composed in the post-exilic Jewish diaspora, and considering textual similarities to Egyptian love poems, the author was with some likelihood from the learned Jewish settlements in the Upper Nile. After the destruction of Solomon's Temple, a group of priests went to settle in Egypt.[11] Considering the one Greek word in the Song its composition could be after the Macedonian conquest of Egypt in 332 BCE.

There are three verses in the Song, which seem to show clearly that the author has a good knowledge of very ancient Egyptian history. Two concern the war between Tutmoses III and the siege of Kadesh in Syria of around the year 1450 BCE. Solomon compares the maiden 'to my mare among the chariots of Pharaoh' (1:8) – a strange expression since Pharaoh's chariots, like others, were drawn by stallions, not mares. However, there is a story about this ancient battle: the Prince of Kadesh contrived an ingenious and unexpected ruse; he released a mare before the line of Egyptian war chariots, each of which was drawn by a pair of stallions. The horses initially grew restive; the entire rank wavered and nearly broke up in confusion (Steindorff and Steele 1942: 59). As Ellen Davis says, '[Solomon's] compliment may therefore be 'translated': 'You drive strong males wild!' (David 2001: 70). Or, more metaphorically, that this women's beauty puts a spanner in the wheels of power. At 6:12, Solomon says, 'I knew not: my soul confounded me (hurled me over) on account of the chariots of [Heb.] *ammi-nādîb*.' If this is a Hebrew version of the name of the Egyptian hero Amenemhab, then the reference is to the same battle and the conclusion of the event, when Tutmoses' general Amenemhab rode his chariot up to the mare who was 'distracting' the stallions, leapt forth and with a stroke of the sword 'slashed open her belly, cut off her tail and tossed it before Pharaoh' (Virey 1890: verses 25–7). What Solomon is trying to say needs the more detailed exposition of Part Two, but he implies that he felt within him the unconscious instinct to 'open her belly with

---

11 Letters between them and the prophet Jeremiah show them defending their practice of devotion to a feminine Queen of Heaven alongside Yahweh (Jeremiah 44). Much later in the early centuries BCE this Jewish community in Egypt was the context for the Greek translation of the book of *Sirach-Ecclesiasticus* (which is the only version we have of the wisdom of Ben Sirach) and, further north in Alexandria, the *Book of Wisdom*, also written in Greek.

his sword.' It is likely a sexual metaphor. But, as an eruption of the unconscious, he says he was 'confounded, nearly over-turned', the Masoretic text says '[his] soul disturbed [him]'. Once more at 3:7-9 a third possible reference to ancient Egyptian history: Solomon speaks of having to have guards at his bed 'because of fears in the night' and goes on to speak of his royal travelling bed. There was a notorious assassination of Rameses III in 1155 BCE when a royal concubine Tiy in league with the harem supervisor Paibekkamen arranged for an attack while he was sleeping (with her) in his travelling palanquin. In these lines, Solomon is at his most distant, speaking of himself in the third person (as if that person was someone other than himself), remembering that the harem does not really express love.

Such oblique references do not prove that the Song was written in Egypt but, along with the similarities with native Egyptian and Jewish diaspora texts, there is strong evidence. Solomon himself had close dealings with Egypt, references to the pre-history of *his* reign fit with a Solomonic *setting* of the Song.

Yet the evident literary context of the Song is Israel. Edmée Kingsmill's book, *The Song of Songs and the Eros of God* (2009), draws on the sacred history of that people as the background to the metaphors of the Song. Kingsmill prefers the term 'metaphor' to 'allegory' as, for her, the former conveys an express 'intention of the original author' whereas the latter is something 'applied to the text by others' (ibid.: 42). So, to say that the two breasts of the woman referred to in the poem are the two tablets of the Law given to Israelites on Sinai for spiritual nourishment is *metaphor*, to say that the breasts are the Old and New Testaments is *allegory* for this is clearly an idea superimposed on a text written long before the New Testament era.[12] Kingsmill interprets the Song in terms of the sacred writings that would have been known to the author, and from which the author

---

12 The 'tablet' reading of the breasts comes from second-century CE Jewish Targum commentaries. The 'testament' reading of the breasts from the Targamists contempory, the western Christian apologist Hippolytus.

could have drawn the imagery consciously or unconsciously. Her thorough contextualisation of the Song within the Hebrew tradition means any extra-biblical influence (for example Egyptian) is played down. And by limiting herself to the texts the author might have known she gives little space to the prophetic nature of biblical texts, that the Song may be inspired to say things beyond what the author may be realising when he or she wrote it (cf. 1 Peter 1:20-21). Neither Rabbinic nor Christian interpretation has limited the meaning of scriptural texts to *only* what the human author intended or could have intended.

Moreover, Kingsmill gives little or no room to the literal narrative meaning of the Song. To equate the breasts of the woman to the stone tablets of the Law removes any sense that we are dealing with real people of flesh and blood and certainly deflates any romance. The relation of 'nature' and 'grace' proposed by Aquinas means that different senses, or levels, of Scriptural meaning should be able to co-exist: 'The literal sense of Scripture is not displaced by the spiritual typology it represents' (Aquinas 1956: verse 68297). The intrinsic relation between the human story of the Song and its spiritual meaning should be maintained. This does not mean that allegory (or metaphor, as Kingsmill prefers) need be completely dismissed as an unnatural imposition. 'It is of the very nature of thought and language,' C. S. Lewis writes, 'to represent what is immaterial in picturable terms' (Lewis 1936: 44). However, one has to look at the picture before one can discern the immaterial or hidden meaning. The Song conjures 'pictures' that are not only visual, but auditory, olfactic, sensate, and gustatory. We need to hear, smell, touch, taste as well as imagine the Song. Reading the Song should be an embodied experience. The fact that it is called a 'song' implies it was originally sung, maybe even enacted; perfumes may have been burnt with its recital, maybe even food served. The full sensual experience may be lost to us. Much of the imagery feels as from another culture, another world. But even today the Song is poetry before it is theology: it uses language to convey feelings rather than ideas, emotions rather than beliefs.

Parallels with Jewish wisdom books written in Egypt in the early centuries BCE (such as Sirach, or the Book of Wisdom) show that the Song may have come from the same milieu, that of Hellenised Jews prompted by the Greek philosophic search for wisdom. There are signs of Hellenic influence in the emphasis in the Song on the beauty of the human body. The Greek version of the Song from this era in the Septuagint is the earliest we have. There seems to be have been no dispute among these Jewish scholars in Egypt as to the canonical status of the Song (as there was later among the Rabbis prior to the Council of Jamnia). The Septuagint places the Song at the centre of the 'Wisdom Books' and it may well be that at this earlier stage, it was seen as an allegory for the relationship with 'Lady Wisdom' as depicted in Sirach and the Book of Wisdom. 'To Wisdom say, "My sister!" advises one of the Proverbs attributed to Solomon (7:4). Advice Solomon follows with the Shulamite in the Song.

Modern scriptural scholars, however, see no reason why the Song should be among the sapiential (Wisdom) books: 'A poem celebrating the joys of sex', as James Crenshaw puts it, could find no place among the 'historical' or the 'prophetic' books and was, there-fore, thrown in with those of 'wisdom' (Crenshaw 2010: 43). The Rabbinic collation of Tanakh (the whole 'Old Testament') placed the Song not among the wisdom books but among 'the writings' or Kethubim – a group that included the Psalms which are indeed closest in literary form to the Song. To read the Song as 'a wisdom text' involves an even stronger personification of Wisdom than that given in Proverbs, Sirach or the Book of Wisdom, and, as the Jewish tradition does not consider the latter two as canonical, it is unlikely they would have wanted to have the Song read in the light of these books, that is, as a parable of Solomon's search for wisdom. The strict monotheism of Rabbinic Judaism – particularly in response to Christianity in the early centuries CE – made any too strong personification of wisdom difficult, especially if it was expressed in such an 'incarnate' way as the Song. Christian association of Wisdom with the second person of the Trinity who became incarnate in Christ added to the Rabbinic dislike of too strong or too earthy a 'hypostatisation' of Wisdom. Could the much earlier Septuagint collators of the Bible, working recently after the Song's composition and (probably) in a geographically similar area to Egypt, not have had an understanding of the author's original intention?

Given the probable diaspora context for the authorship of the Song, it may even have been written by a woman. Certainly, the Song portrays well the woman's perspective within the love poem. Among both the 'Wisdom Books' of the Bible or the Kethubim of the Tanakh it counterbalances the rather 'male' perspective of Ecclesiastes, which is also attributed to Solomon and can be dated to a similar era to the Song. Egyptian 'wisdom texts' formed an integral part of scribal training in the Saite period of the sixth century BCE during which some Levitical Jews escaped to Egypt (while the rest were deported to Babylon by Nebuchadnezzar). If the Song was written within a Jewish community in Egypt, outside of the traditional religious environment of Jerusalem, then it is more likely that the experience of actual women could have been influential, even on a male writer (which would, admittedly, be the more usual for that time). An Egyptian scribe of this period called Ankhsheshonq complained about his difficulties in instructing women as being 'like pouring sand into a sack where the sides have been split open' (see Tyldesley 1994: 13, 118). From this one can assume, at least, that some women were educated (the only Egyptian woman depicted in hieroglyphics actually putting pen to paper was Seshat, the goddess of writing).

Alexander the Great conquered Palestine and then Egypt in 332 BCE, opening Jews in both places to the influences of an expansive empire. Certainly, of the spices mentioned in the Song, only henna and saffron are native to Palestine – frankincense, aloes and spikenard are from Arabia or India, cinnamon from China, and myrrh from Africa. If the poem is *set* in the time of Solomon then the cosmopolitan herbarium is not, however, anachronous for that time: 1 Kings records Solomon as having an empire from the Red Sea to the Euphrates and an expansive spice trade (4:29, 10:10). The Queen of Sheba is supposed to have brought exotic spices (1 Kings 10:2). Solomon used perfumes for both temple ceremony and for his private house, especially in the culture of his harem. The Prophet Jeremiah was later to complain about the uselessness of the elaborate perfumery of the Temple: 'To what purpose does Frankincense come from Sheba, or myrrh from a distant land?' (6:20). The conquest of Israel by the Babylonians in the sixth century BCE put an end to the Kingdom of Israel (which had already split after Solomon's reign), its role as a market with the destruction of Temple and palace, and route for the spice trade which was diverted along the Silk Road. Only Hellenised Jews of the post-exilic era would have known again the spices and perfumes of Solomon's reign as they are depicted in the Song.

The Song that belongs to Solomon

'The whole world is not worth the day on which this song was made.' So Rabbi Akiva stated his defence of the Song at the Council of Jamnia in 90 CE, and since then the Song was granted a very high status within the Jewish scriptures (*Mishna Yadadim* 3:5; Neusner 1988: 1123). What Akiva is saying, however, is that the Song was made on the seventh day, the Sabbath – the previous six days being the creation of 'the world'. The six days are not worth the day on which God and humanity rested, and the Song speaks of that 'great day'. Rabbi Akiva defended the Song as more than worthy of being in the Bible through insisting that its meaning was allegorical: it spoke of God's covenant with the Jewish people, a covenant which led to the restoration of paradise. Since then, until today, the Song is read in the Synagogues only on the Sabbath during Passover. The title of the Song itself says it is the greatest of songs: all other songs are 'about *this* world', the Song expresses the culmination of creation, when God rested. Rabbi Akiva compared it to the central point of the temple built by Solomon: beyond time and space, there the angels of God dwell.

The Song's title also shows it is *ăšer lišlōmō* – 'belonging to Solomon'. In saying this, the writer or later scribes situate the poem within the 'wisdom tradition', which had long been associated with Solomon, the third king of Israel. This title does not claim that the Song is 'written by' Solomon but that the subject matter is 'of Solomon'. The word *tirṣâ* in the Masoretic text (at 6:3) was the name of the main city of the northern part of Israel destroyed after Solomon's reign. The fact that this is used here in harmonic conjunction with Jerusalem implies that the poem is *set* in a time when Northern and Southern Israel were together, hence the time of Solomon (they split after his death and were never reunited).[13] The title may be hinting at an oral tradition whereby the Song has come down 'from Solomon'. To say the poem was *set* then doesn't mean to say it was *written* then. Solomon's association with gnomic wisdom may have been more as a 'patron of the arts' rather than a quality of his own character.[14] The title may be a later superscription.[15] Still, as a later scribal addition it still gives the literary and spiritual context in which the Song was to be read and gives the major clue as to its interpretation.

13   The notion that *tirṣâ* (Tirzah) is the city appears, however, only with the English 1611 Authorised Version of the Song, neither Septuagint nor Vulgate take the Hebrew as a place name but simply in its Hebrew meaning as 'beautiful'. This does lead to a slightly strange phrase at 6:3, 'you are as beautiful as beauty [itself]', in context this makes good sense though.

14   Von Rad sees a flourishing of wisdom schools and writings in Israel (mirroring those of neighbouring states of Egypt and Mesopotamia) at the time of Solomon as due to the cosmopolitan influences and through his patronage of the Temple (von Rad 1972: 15).

15   R. E. Murphy points out that *ăšer* is a different word for 'belongs' from that used in the Song at 1:6, 12 and 6:5 (Murphy 1990: 119).

Writings closer than the Song to the time of Solomon show that he had 'wisdom and understanding beyond measure, and largeness of mind like the sand on the seashore, so that Solomon's wisdom surpassed the wisdom of all the people of the east, and all the wisdom of Egypt', and that 'he composed some 3000 proverbs and wrote 1005 songs' (1 Kings 4:30, 32).[16] The idea of Solomon's wisdom may be legendary but was established, at the very latest, by the final editing of Book of Kings in the sixth century BCE and, two centuries later, in Chronicles. The dispute between these two records of Jewish history as to the ultimate 'wisdom' of Solomon may be reflected even in the Song. 1 Kings 11:4 says, 'His heart was not perfect with the Lord his God'; criticising his tolerance in having altars to other Gods erected in Israel for the sake of his 'pagan' wives, and his love of riches which led to tyrannous oppression and taxation of his own people.[17] Because of his commitment to 'things in the world' even in the Song Solomon seems only to half meet the challenge presented to him through this maiden. The Song shows that the prerogatives of kingship constrained his freedom to love.

The actual subject matter of Solomon's wisdom given in 1 Kings 4:33 is more agrarian than moral and spiritual:

He spoke of trees [in his proverbs and songs], from the cedar tree that is in Lebanon even to the hyssop that grows out of walls; he spoke also of beasts, and of fowl, and of creeping things, and of fishes.

An understanding of the natural world does not fit with what is attributed to him in the Book of Proverbs. It does, however, fit with

16   Specific Proverbs 10:1-22, 16, 25:1-29, 27, even post-biblical criticism, are considered potentially authored by Solomon.

17   'King Solomon forced 30,000 men from all over Israel to work for him', 1 Kings 5:13. It has been estimated this is the equivalent of 5 million Americans in the mid-1940s.

the imagery of the Song. Solomon is not just in the title of the Song but is mentioned many times within the poem. These are in the third person, suggesting he was never intended to be the narrator but a character within the poem. Some modern commentators argue that the figure of Solomon is merely added to a pastoral love poem to give it an aura, in a similar fashion to how many of the Psalms were attributed to King David.[18] Yet biblical criticism has actually shown that many Psalms do date back to the era of David and Solomon. The Song is much later than the Psalms, but an earlier oral or even written tradition could go back to the inspiration of Solomon himself. The Torah and most of the prophetic writings received a final redaction around 550 BCE. Therefore, most of the books of the Bible were not written down in the form we have (handed down by the Deuteronomic scribes) until the post-exilic era, that is, just prior to when the Song was written. Though the Pentateuch – the 'Books of Moses' – may not have been written by Moses, Moses still remains the key actor in Exodus, and textual transmission cannot rule out Moses's influence on what was written down more than five hundred years after his death. So too with the Song, written more than five hundred years after Solomon's death, yet the historical and legendary figure of Solomon still remains key to its interpretation. The author (or authors – though the coherence of the poem indicates one poetic voice) may have collected fragments from an earlier tradition or woven a poem out of what Solomon represents in the sacred story of Israel. If Solomon was seen as a 'friend of wisdom' then the author of the Song may have had the words of Isaiah in his mind (coming down to us from the period between Solomon and the time the Song was written):

---

18   Though there is stronger narrative construction in Shakespeare's plays than in the Song, it would be clearly nonsense to say that *King Lear* is not about King Lear because it was not written by King Lear. Yet this is often what is said about Solomon and the Song.

> Let me sing to my friend
> the song of his love for his vineyard.
> My friend had a vineyard …
>
> (Isaiah 5:1)

The maiden in the Song speaks of herself as a vineyard and of her lover as her 'friend'.

If the male character in the Song is Solomon we can fill in many of the gaps in the narrative. In the Bible Solomon represents humanity's search for wisdom; expressed in his prayer on becoming king. The other characteristic of Solomon is that, unlike his father, he was a man of peace (and thus was eligible to build the Temple). The root of his name is *shalom*.[19] Solomon also had a taste for women, and a slightly syncretist approach to religion – for both of which he is berated in Kings (such criticisms are not, however, in Chronicles). He built the first temple in Jerusalem – and many of the images in the Song come from temple construction and symbolism. There is also something of pageant associated with Solomon: unlike his father he didn't dance in his loincloth! The Bible records him as sumptuously attired, seated on high thrones and leading processions.

This can seem like a far cry from the 'pastoral' imagery of the Song, but one has to remember the jump from shepherd to king is not so extreme – Solomon's father made exactly that jump. That, at 1:6-7, the male and female figures in the Song briefly appear in the guise of a shepherd and shepherdess has been given disproportionate importance by some Victorian commentators. These read the lovers as a pastoral pair, and King Solomon as a third character who arrives with predatory intent on the shepherd's wife. The shepherdess remains loyal to her original husband (whom she finds again, grazing his sheep, at 2:16 and 6:1-2) and the Song becomes a Victorian

---

19   Though the Kingdom of Israel may have been at peace under him, his exploitation of his people is recorded to have caused the revolts that split Northern and Southern Israel after his death, 1 Kings 12:4.

morality tale about resisting seduction. There does seem to be a brief 'shepherd scene' at 1:6 but this can be explained as an attempt by the king to meet the maiden on her own ground, as a country girl without the trappings of court life. There is no need to read evidence of another character in the Song and create a love-triangle!

Solomon's play-acting as shepherd is well intended but forced, and dies out within a couple of lines. The further pastoral references are part of a spectrum of images drawn from nature. Solomon's ease with a landscape of fauna and flora need be no surprise if we remember the type of 'wisdom' he was remembered for in 1 Kings 4:33. Although the rural setting of the Song forms much of the backdrop of its poetic drama, the socio-political context of the royal palace is equally important in understanding the narrative of the poem.

The so-called 'shepherd theory' tries to make sense of the juxtaposition of royal and pastoral settings in the poem by positing a three-character love story – woman, shepherd-lover and king. Solomon, it is argued (the days of his father's original profession long over) could hardly be seen as pasturing a flock (as in 1:7). In the early nineteenth century Heinrich Ewald and Johann Jacobi popularised the view that the key to understanding the Song was to recognise three main characters in the book: Solomon, a rustic Shulamite maiden, and her husband, a shepherd. According to this dramatic plot a beautiful woman was in love with her shepherd companion, but King Solomon attempted to take her for himself (a little like Don Juan does with Anna, or Faust with Gretchen). The king had carried off the maiden by force to his harem, but when she resists his advances he permits her to return to the country. Jacobi suggest-ed that the purpose of the Song was to celebrate the fidelity of true love: the Shulamite maiden is the heroine of the book for remaining true to her humble shepherd husband despite being tempted by Solomon with all the luxuries and splendours of his court (still proposed today by Hill and Walton 2010: 300-01).

However, there is nothing definite in the text to indicate the change of male characters or to imply that Solomon is the villain of the story. We are left with an artificial parcelling-out of the verses between king and shepherd. Some of the passages assigned to 'the shepherd' contain references to spices that would not be familiar (let alone possessed) by one in that humble profession. It is much more likely that the shepherd guise is one taken by Solomon as part of his courting, meeting the maiden – as a country girl – on her own ground, by going back to the humble roots of his own family. Was not Solomon son of one 'who tended the sheep'? (1 Samuel 16:11, 17:20). And it was a guise he could easily take as one who 'possessed many flocks' (Ecclesiastes 2:7). If he intended to develop his relationship with this woman outside the intrigues and conventions of the royal harem then it is natural for them to arrange to meet outside the city in one of the royal park-gardens, and stay there. The rural context described is not the sheep-grazing uplands of Judea: there are lilies, blossoming flowers, fig trees, vines, pomegranates, terraces of spices – it is a royal garden.

A two-person narrative interpretation was presumed by the early Church fathers; some, like Origen and Theodore of Mopsuestia, saw the woman as the Egyptian princess, one of Solomon's wives; others even proposed the Queen of Sheba. Nineteenth-century commentators saw that the numerous associations of the maiden in the Song with the work of keeping a vineyard were hardly in keeping with such royal personages. However, it took a nineteenth-century Lutheran exegete to reinstate the poem as a two-person drama. Franz Delitzsch's commentary is still infinitely more perceptive than most modern commentaries. From the text, he saw that the woman is no Egyptian princess but, rather, 'a country maiden of humble rank, who, by her beauty and by the purity of her soul, filled Solomon with a love for her which drew him away from the wantonness of polygamy, and made for him the primitive idea of marriage – as it is described in Genesis 2:23 – a self-experienced reality' (Delitzsch 1975:

3). Delitzsch also sees the foil to her rustic purity in the sophisticated city girls, the 'Daughters of Jerusalem'. As Delitzsch writes:

> We cannot understand the Song of Songs unless we perceive that it presents before us not only Shulamite's external attractions, but also all the virtues which make her the idea of all that is gentlest and noblest in woman. Her words and her silence, her doing and suffering, her enjoyment and self-denial, her conduct … gives the impression of a beautiful soul in a body formed as it were of flowers.
>
> (Delitzsch 1975: 3)

Delitzsch and Jacobi are similar in representing a nineteenth-century concern to find in the Song a story with ethical implications for marriage. Both see the romance of the Song as 'more about character than about sex' (an insight that forms my approach in Part Two of this book). With the development of psychoanalysis in the twentieth century interpretations become less concerned with tracking a conscious narrative than observing hidden innuendo. However, there are flaws in the nineteenth-century approach. For Delitzsch the love story progresses through a rather respectable form of meeting, betrothal, and married life. Solomon raises this woman (of humble origins but exalted virtues) to be his queen, and he renounces his polygamous life, and in fact, according to Delitzsch, his whole royal station, in order to live a simple rustic life with her. This is a rather romantic view probably derived from the pervading Romantic poetic ethos of the time. In any event, it is true neither to the poem's historical context, nor to the drama as it is depicted. Delitzsch wants a happy ending but the poem doesn't have one (except in pointing to some fulfilment beyond this world). The marriage is one of souls rather than lives: the yearning in the poem is for something tasted but unrealisable under the conditions of the time.

If Rabbinic and Church Patristic expositions of the Song seem like projections of the concerns of the author so can some modern readings. Delitzsch is not unaware that the Song could have multiple levels of meaning but he reads the 'divine truth' in the Song in a conventional way: Solomon is a personification of Yahweh in relation to the maiden who is the congregation of Israel or, for Christians, the Church. Delitzsch plays down the anagogical possibilities of the poem – God's relation to the soul in the hereafter – which made it such a rich text for the mystics who proffered no abiding city in this life.

The open-mindedness of Delitzsch's acceptance of *both* narrative and allegorical meaning, however, remains, a hermeneutic key for the Song. In seeking a literal meaning one need not claim that is the *only* meaning, or deny or discredit the validity of allegorical and mystical interpretations (a reductionism many post-Freudian commentators fall into). Inspiration, especially if one accepts the divinely inspired nature of this poem, has many levels. However, any allegorical or mystical interpretation – being as it were a fruit of grace – works much better if it is founded on nature.[20] If a longing for union lies at the heart of the Song, then we cannot shirk from the fact that it is the sexual aspect of man and woman that is the *prima materia*, the narrative and literal sense, on which mystical meanings are based.

Wisdom in the harem

Now we come to what seems to be a clear historical context of the poem but which has been ignored because of the attempt to give a respectable 'religious' interpretation to the narrative. Such a context is even more scandalous if we posit, as we do, that the woman is the leading figure of the poem, and that this woman is one of Solomon's harem (from which she stands out and yet is still part of):

---

20 'Grace does not destroy nature but perfects it', according to Thomas Aquinas in his *Summa Theologica* (Aquinas 1981: 1:1, question 8, part 2).

> There are sixty queens
> and eighty concubines,
> numberless are the young maidens.
> One is my dove, my perfect one …
>
> (Song 6:8-9)

It is clear we are dealing with a description of a royal harem here. This is a conservative estimate: 1 Kings 11:3 says that Solomon 'had seven hundred wives as queens and three hundred concubines'. We will deal with each category, before we look how his 'perfect one' fitted in.

Queens were chosen for political and dynastic alliances. Solomon's marriage to the daughter of Pharaoh, according to 1 Kings 3:1, was early in his reign, before he started building the temple. In fact, alongside the Temple, Solomon built a royal palace, which would have housed the harem, and a palace for the daughter of Pharaoh. This may have been as she carried with her a substantial dowry, and had to be treated well, but 2 Chronicles 8:11 gives cultic reasons why no foreign wife could dwell in the royal palace on Zion (where the Ark of the Covenant had dwelt). In any case Pharaoh's daughter doesn't seem to have had children with Solomon, as the mother of the three official children, including his heir Rhoebham, was Naamah, this time an Amorite princess. Solomon went on to marry many women from neighbouring tribes, making space for them to worship their own gods. Naamah means 'pleasant'. Despite being of foreign descent she is described by some Talmudic commentaries as being 'righteous', which may mean she adopted the Israelite religion. She is the only one of all the queen mothers of Israel or Judah who was a foreigner.[21] As mother of a (future) king she would on his succession have been known as *Gebira*, meaning 'Great Lady' or 'Queen Mother'. A king had many wives but only one

---

21 On Naamah see 1 Kings 14:21, 2 Chronicles 12:13, *Babylonian Talmud: Baba Kamma* 38b (e.g. Goldin 1918: 34) and Berlyn (1996: 28).

mother, and this maternal co-ruler in Israel stood higher than any of the wives (1 Kings 2:13-21). Solomon's mother was Bathsheba (David had 17 sons through various wives and yet the intercession of Bathsheba proved decisive in his choice of Solomon as heir, 1 Kings 1:11-31). In the Song 3:11 Solomon asks 'ye daughters' to 'come forth and behold [himself] in the diadem wherewith his mother hath crowned him in the day of his espousals.' Any such official cultic ceremony of espousals, under the patronage of Bathsheba, would have been with a high-ranking princess, probably Pharaoh's daughter.

We have more information about the royal harems of Egypt, which would have been the nearest model for the neighbouring and much newer Kingdom of Israel. Those the Pharaohs actually married – the royal queens – were a select few. Too many legitimate heirs were not wanted. We may assume Solomon followed a similar practice to the Pharaohs who married many women but had only one royal consort or queen. In Egyptian practice this had to be one of as high a royal birth as Pharaoh himself – so much so that, at least in the Eighteenth Dynasty (some four to five hundred years before Solomon), only a full or a half-sister could be a queen of Egypt (Tyldesley 1994: 190–91). Despite the biblical record of Solomon's seven hundred wives only one official son is mentioned, Rehoboam, and two daughters, Taphath and Basemath (1 Kings 4:11, 15). The Ethiopian royal dynasty traces descent from Solomon from Malenik I (in Arabic Ibn Al-Hakim, 'Son of the Wise') who was supposed to be the royal child of Solomon and the Queen of Sheba. In all likelihood, therefore, the 'wives' mentioned in 1 Kings were not ceremonially married. Psalm 44, which, unlike the Song, and dating to the time of Solomon, is a real Hebrew royal marriage song, makes a distinction between 'the daughters of kings' who are 'among the ladies of honour' (in the harem) and the queen who is 'dressed in gold of Ophir' and stands at the king's right at solemn occasions (verse 9). It seems in this Psalm that the queen is, in fact, the royal mother, for she is introduced, standing on the king's right, before the 'bride to be' is 'led to the king with her maiden companions'. 1 Kings 2:19 reports how, after the death of David, Bathsheba went to King Solomon: 'the king got up to meet her and bowed before her; he then sat down on his throne; a seat was brought for the king's mother, and she sat down on his right'. The 'bride to be' in Psalm 44, however, is urged to 'pay homage to the king' as she approaches him. As a highborn bride she is dressed 'with splendour, her robes embroidered with pearls set in gold thread'. But the Psalm makes clear at the end that it is expected she will have 'sons who will become princes' and that *she* 'will make them rulers' – the high-bride will, to the next generation, become the royal mother who 'crowns' (Song 4:11).

The internal evidence in the Song (we will see) shows that the maiden Shulamite is not from such a background. In the harem she would, at best, have ranked among the secondary wives from local neighbouring tribes, but this is not likely. If the woman in the Song was selected for her beauty – as is clear from the text – then most likely she belongs to the category of the concubines. Beauty was the only criteria for the concubines whose role was to be attractive and alluring, and could come from humble backgrounds. The particular woman in the Song seems to have been chosen for her outstanding beauty, which is recognised by all on her arrival:

The daughters saw her and declared her most blessed:
the queens and concubines, and they praised her.

(Song 6:9)

It is necessary to make the historical leap of imagination to see these royal harems not as seedy extravagance: the harem for the Jewish kings (as for other monarchs of the time) was expected as a royal prerogative. Far from scandalous it was the respectable place for royal wives to live among serving women who also served the king in his bed representing their royal mistresses. The king was not expected to particularly love his wives, as these were politically arranged marriages. They retired to comfortable lives in the splendid harem. The concubines were seen as adjuncts to the wives, and some of them were expected to take their place in the marriage bed. High mortality in childbirth meant bearing too many children was dangerous; something avoided by those in higher stations in the harem. The highest 'queen' would be expected to have sons, but not too many (because of rivalry after the king's death). The relationship of a king with the women who stood in – or rather lay in – for the queen or nobly born wives never had any official standing. This was a duty which was professionally impersonal, the concubines standing in for the queen they served, and trained to do a better job, as wives were not chosen on the grounds of attractiveness but usually for political reasons.

The 'daughters' and 'young maidens' mentioned in the Song are a third category of servants to the harem – attending the needs of the wives and the cosmetic culture of the concubines and acting as nurses for the children.[22] Some of them may literally be 'daughters' of either the queens or the concubines (though the record of Solomon's two official daughters were that they married courtiers, 1 Kings 4:11, 14). The harem also served as a nursery, boys leaving at the age of maturity to be trained in the army, girls remaining to serve in the harem until they reached marriageable age. There was very little idea of a 'nuclear Royal Family' in ancient times. The role of 'the women's department' of royal courts was purely functional: as the kitchener provided meats and wines for the royal table, the harem provided sufficient female flesh and enticement for the royal bed. Any birth of children was a subsidiary effect, the children themselves the by-product of the institution, cared for generally by the harem (see Vaux 1997: 114–17).[23]

---

22 The Book of Esther 2:9 mentions these handmaids in this capacity.

23 In the Egyptian Harem this large group was known officially as 'the house of nurses' as, alongside being ornamental, they looked after the numerous children who were raised in the harem (Vaux 1997: 184).

If we take seriously the historical context in which the poem is set – that of the early Davidic monarchy – and the humble origin of the maiden depicted in the Song, then Solomon could hardly have 'married' her, certainly not in any monogamous sense. There is also no internal evidence within the poem that the lovers are married, nor does the poem end with marriage (in fact it ends on a somewhat tragic note with their separation). Queens (who cemented alliances) could go *into* the harem (where they were looked after by the harem maidens) but queens could not be made *from* the ranks of other woman in the harem. There was a clear pecking order between royal queens and the concubines who became royal mistresses of the harem – the latter could not rise to the rank of the former. The Davidic court knew the intrigues that would be caused if this rule was not kept: only by this were queens able to keep their status vis-à-vis the other women in the harem. In the story of Esther, set in a period later than that of Solomon, during the Jewish exile in Babylon, there is an example of an exception: a queen (and it seems at this time a unique role) is chosen from among women selected solely on the grounds of their beauty. However, the Book of Esther 1:13 makes clear that this was a very unusual precedent (brought on by the need to depose a previous queen), which needed to be ratified by the lawyers and sages of the kingdom.

The poem opens with the presentation of a new girl of exceptional beauty to the young king. The custom is clearly illustrated in the Book of Esther, which dates to about the same time as the Song.[24] Although the narrative setting of Esther is fifth-century BCE Persia the conventions of royal harems were long established and common to major kingdoms of the Middle East. It is worth quoting in length because it gives a setting which fits exactly with the opening episode of the Song. The author of the Song would *certainly* have read Esther. Despite having no mention of God in the story, it was accepted as

---

24 The Hebrew version of Esther dates to the fourth century BCE, the Septuagint version to late second century BCE so it is, probably, just a little earlier than the Song.

part of the Hebrew scriptural canon by the Great Synagogal Council, which lasted from 410 BCE to 275 BCE, and was read (twice aloud) during the yearly Jewish festival of Purim. This is a key text for understanding the Song author's perception of the conventions of a royal harem. It even gives a parallel to the beginning of the storyline of the Song:

> The king [Ahasuerus]'s servants who attended him said, 'Let beautiful young virgins be sought out for the king. And let the king appoint commissioners in all the provinces of his kingdom to gather all the beautiful young virgins to the harem in the citadel of Susa under the custody of Hegai, the king's eunuch, who is in charge of the women; let their cosmetic treatments be given them … So when the king's orders were proclaimed, and when many young women were gathered in the citadel of Susa in the custody of Hegai, Esther also was taken into the king's palace. The girl pleased the king and won his favour, and he quickly provided her with her cosmetic treatments and her portion of food, and with seven chosen maids from the king's palace, and advanced her and her maids to the best place in the harem … The turn came for each girl to go in to King Ahasuerus, after being twelve months under the regulations for the maidens, since this was the regular period of their cosmetic treatment, six months with the oil of myrrh, and for another six they used certain perfumes and aromatics. When the girl went in to the king she was allowed to wear whatever she asked for from the harem [wardrobe]. In the evening, she went in to the king's palace; then in the morning she came back to the second [level] of the harem in the custody of Shaashgaz, the king's eunuch, who was in charge of the concubines; she did not go in again unless the king delighted in her and she was summoned by name. When the turn came for Esther to go into the king, she asked to wear

nothing but what Hegai, the king's eunuch, who had charge of the maidens, advised. Now, Esther was admired by all who saw her. When Esther was taken to King Ahasuerus he loved Esther more than all the other women; of all the virgins, she won his favour and devotion.

(Esther 2:2-3, 8-9, 12-17)

In contrast to the maiden of the Song, Esther did in fact rise to be queen but the historical setting of the story (fictional or historical) presumes monogamist royal marriages (only one queen). Even here Esther's rising from the rank of concubine to Queen is shown as an unprecedented situation (maybe an intentional slight to the previous queen who Ahasuerus felt had dishonoured him). This was not the case for Solomon some four hundred years earlier. A monogamist marriage outcome of the romance depicted in the Song would not have been possible by the time of Solomon's reign. However, it is the Song rather than Esther that celebrates romantic love and herein reveals an evolution in social consciousness. Though Esther rises to be queen it does not seem a particularly close and certainly not equal relationship. When she is asked by her fellow Jewish people to go to the king to supplicate for them she points out, 'I have not been called to come to the king for thirty days' (4:11) – it was against the law and punishable by death for her to do so on her own initiative (16), and when she does approach him she relies on her outward charms rather than a heart-centred connection with him: 'Then majestically adorned … she was radiant with perfect beauty, and she looked happy, as if beloved, but her heart was frozen in fear' (15:5). Her charms do in fact calm the initial 'fierce anger' of Ahasuerus and he speaks to her tenderly 'as a husband' – but this was all against expectations, such were the precedents of court life vis-à-vis the harem.

Yet in the Song, which was written about the same time as the Book of Esther, we see extrapolated true personalised sentiment and most of all equality and complete freedom from fear in relationship.

The marriage of Esther to the king is providential for the Jewish people in the Persian Empire and saves them from persecution but it is the unknown maiden of the Song – for whom we have no name – who is the champion of real relationship. Esther works within the system for the sake of her people, the maiden of the Song challenges the whole system of organised and commodified sexual love for the sake of the real love she feels.

Though the king's mistresses were chosen because of their 'charms' (which were further augmented in the cosmetic culture of the harem) one gets the feeling that 'institutionally' the harem was a rather loveless place. If the maiden had stayed she would have taken her place among the concubines there selected for their beauty for the sexual gratification of the king. It is clear from the Song that Solomon responds to the maiden's desire for a *personal relationship*. However, given the historical context of the Song the difficulty of this should not be underestimated, even for a king. It would be problematic, in the long run, to flout social conventions within the harem; this explains why the setting chosen for their relationship is rural, where they could be free. It also explains the difficulty of their relationship continuing: the difficulty for the maiden to re-enter the official structure of the harem, which in all likelihood she would not have wanted anyway, and the challenge to the king to continue what in effect becomes an all-encompassing relationship while the structure of the harem is still in place.

It is in this paradoxical matrix – spiritual wisdom appearing in the context of sexuality, both positive and negative – that the Song is set. This is why the poem has been so baffling to interpreters, the spiritually minded finding carnal desire quite unthinkable, and those who read the poem as a celebration of human love faced with a context where the personal quality of human love as a choice of one for another is not expected. Yet herein lies the drama of the poem, of some of its most famous lines which demand an individuated love – 'Let him kiss me with the kisses of *his* mouth', and celebrate it – 'My love is mine and I am his.' But herein also is the tragedy of the narrative – that the love arrived at is impossible in the context. The story is evidently *not* a marriage song, nor is it a celebration of purely natural sexual relations – the emphasis is on the personal quality of love; a love that, both by the social standards of the time and the politics of the harem, would be considered taboo. It would kick up a storm in the harem if the king devoted all his love to one of his mistresses, to the exclusion of the queens and other concubines.

This explains why at the end of the poem there is a parting of the lovers that seems to imply that their love is not possible in the context of the king's royal estate. It is impossible to imagine this woman again in the harem at the end, when the entire action of the poem puts her in sharp opposition to that royal institution and all it stands for. Nor is it possible to conceive of her as the sole regnant queen beside her lover without a radical revolution in the arrangement of royal marriages for which the time was not ripe. As the narrative unfolds it implies that the man has to abandon his entire kingly destiny, his power and wealth, in order to stay with her in a new hidden identity, or to say farewell to her and separate from her forever. At a human level the romance is a matter of all or nothing, and the story ends in the recognition that this is a relationship that cannot be humanly fulfilled.

The very pathos of the human story may be the reason why religious commentators throughout the centuries have seen the Song as pointing to a spiritual fulfilment. It need not, however, be the unattainability of the human love depicted as much as the completeness of that love which means it can only be tasted briefly in the conditions of this world. The figure of the woman in this poem, therefore, has great similarities to that of Beatrice in Dante's life: a real human love and sexual attraction that is so all-encompassing that its meaning is much more than can be realised within this world, finding its full meaning only in heaven.

Rabbi Akiva said, 'The one lifting up his voice in a drinking house with the Song of Songs, and who treats it like a kind of secular song, will have no place in the world to come' (*Targum Sanhedrin* XII:10; Epstein undated). To say that the poem starts with Solomon's encounter with a woman in his harem does not mean it is a celebration of sexuality in such an impersonal context, quite the opposite. As Kingsmill (2009: 45) writes, 'It is not sexual desire which the song intends to arouse but *love.*' More recent understandings of marriage as 'being caught up into divine love' would point to this being more realisable in this life, but such was not the norm in the historical context set for this poem (Flannery 1992: 951). Despite the efforts of some recent Evangelical and Catholic commentators to enlist the Song as a manual for marriage, the literal sense of the Song points to no such conclusion (see Hocking and Hocking 1986 and, on the Catholic side, Mitch and Hahn 2013; see also Hahn 2009: 868). Maybe tragically so, it is more like *Romeo and Juliet*: a spousal love that cannot be realised. But unlike Shakespeare's play the Song is not swept along by instinctual sexual passion, but depicts an intensely personal love. The longing and desire in the Song is for personal relationship, rather than simply physical fulfilment. The first line of the Song sets the tone: 'Let him kiss me with the kisses of his mouth' – indicating that what the maiden wants in the kiss is *him*.

Solomon

At what age is Solomon depicted in the Song? The maiden says, at 2:9, 'My beloved is like a roe and a young hart.' An early Jewish commentary on the Song, the Midrash Rabbah, attests that 'Solomon wrote the Song of Songs first, then Proverbs, finally Ecclesiastes,' giving as evidence the natural course of life, for 'When a man is young, he composes songs; when he grows up, he speaks in proverbs; when he gets old, he speaks of vanities' (Neusner 1989: 54). In the Song Solomon seems to have some portion of his royal harem already in place: 'sixty queens and eighty concubines' (6:8). However, 1 Kings 11:3, recounting the latter days of Solomon's long reign of 40 years, says, 'he had seven hundred wives as queens and three hundred concubines.' So the numbers in the Song show an early stage. Also, on accessing the throne Solomon would have inherited the harem of his father, so the 'sixty and eighty' may be what was handed down, many of them old wives of David. 1 Kings 2:17 shows that Abishag, David's last and most beautiful companion, on his death was under Solomon's patronage.

Solomon seems to have expanded the harem exponentially in terms of wives over his reign, and proportionally less vis-à-vis his father's quota of concubines. The increase of this latter group for Solomon may have been mainly as handmaids to the numerous wives. The wives were, according to 1 Kings 11, political alliances to daughters of neighbouring tribes. Unlike his father, Solomon attempted and succeeded in ruling without warfare by uniting the Israelite kingship with the families of would-be aggressors. This policy is criticised in 1 Kings where it was said that 'when Solomon was old, his wives turned away his heart after other Gods, and his heart was not true to the Lord his God, as was the heart of his father David.' This criticism, however, is not in the Book of Chronicles, which covers the same events of Solomon's reign.

According to 1 Kings the troubles were simmering before Solomon's death. Something certainly went wrong in the Kingdom after Solomon's death: a major revolt against the Davidic line meant ten of the twelve tribes set up their own Kingdom. In all accounts, Solomon is both a most highly blessed and a tragic figure: given so much, building so much more, and yet knowing that it is all vanity and a chasing after the wind. The bitterness of a life of success and worldly wisdom comes through in Ecclesiastes (written about the same time as the Song, c.450 BCE–c.180 BCE). He is given wisdom without necessarily having compassion: after his death, the heads of the tribes requested his heir to 'lighten the hard service imposed by your father, and his heavy yoke that he placed on us' (1 Kings 12:5).

Twice in the Song the maiden expresses somehow the loss of youth in Solomon as someone trapped in the pomp of the royal court, the intrigues of palace and harem, the massive building projects that may still be witnessed in the archaeological sites in Israel. 'Better is a poor but wise youth than an old but foolish king,' says the Teacher in Ecclesiastes. And the maiden cries in the Song 2:17, 'Come back again! Be, O my beloved, like to the roe and to the young hart,' as if she was noticing, or foreseeing, that he would lose his youthful spirit. And, at the last line, she implores him, 'Escape (flee to the country) O my beloved, and make thyself free even as a roe and a young hart.' Solomon, according to Ecclesiastes, stays wise into his old age, but with the wisdom of knowing his folly:

> The words of the Teacher, the son of David, king in Jerusalem: Vanity of vanities! All is vanity! … I said to myself, 'Come now, I will make a test of pleasure; enjoy yourself.' But again, this also was vanity. I said of laughter, 'It is mad', and of pleasure, 'What use is it?' I searched with my mind how to cheer my body with wine – my mind still guiding me with wisdom – and how to lay hold on folly, until I might see what was good for mortals to do under heaven during the few days of their life. I made great works; I built houses and planted vineyards for myself; I made myself gardens and parks, and planted in them all kinds of fruit trees. I made myself pools with which to water the forest of growing trees. I bought male and female slaves, and had slaves who were born in my house; I also had great possessions of herds and flocks, more than any who had been before me in Jerusalem. I also gathered for myself silver and gold and the treasure of neighbouring kings and the provinces; I got singers, both men and women, and delights of the flesh, and many concubines. So I became great and surpassed all who were before me in Jerusalem; also my

wisdom remained with me ... Then I considered all that my
hands had done and the toil I had spent in doing it, and again,
all was vanity and a chasing after wind, and there was nothing
to be gained under the sun.

(Ecclesiastes 1:1, 17-18; 2.)[25]

Psalm 48 (written close to the time of Solomon himself) is in
many ways a template for Ecclesiastes; a wisdom psalm that shows
the futility of worldly success, the two parts ending with the refrain,
'In his riches man lacks wisdom, he is like the beasts of the field
which are destroyed.' And yet Ecclesiastes is at pains to show that
this king never lost wisdom (despite losing nearly all belief in its
value). A disillusioned wise man, bitter in his wisdom: Solomon as
an old man.

Solomon's wisdom is indeed ambiguous. The Bible recounts that
Solomon's gift of wisdom came after his prayers 'in the high places
of Gibeon' (1 Kings 3:3-12; 2 Chronicles 1:3-12). Kings, which emphasises a unique cultic role for Jerusalem, criticises the burning incense
and spices in 'the high places' of neighbouring mountains like
Gibeon – a criticism which the maiden in the Song (who by the end
comes to symbolise wisdom) may well be contradicting when, in
her last words, she says, 'Escape (flee to the country) O my beloved,
and make thyself even as a roe and a young hart (free) upon the
mountains of spices.' Even when ceremonial prayer was centred in
the new temple he built, she urges him to return to his youthful
prayer for wisdom. Later Jewish tradition (which also comes down
to us in the Qu'ran 27:16) says that, when he awoke from his sleep
after praying at Gibeon, the first sign of Solomon's gift of wisdom
was that he could understand the language of plants and animals.
This fits with the kind of wisdom attributed to him in 1 Kings 4:33.

---

25 Ecclesiastes is attributed to Solomon but, like the Song, is written centuries after
his reign. However, the subject matter, like the Song, speaks of the time of the reign
of Solomon, and the idiosyncratic nature of that king.

And yet, some of the Jewish writings turn this into a critique of Solomon: that in giving way to his love of wealth and pleasure he became too natural, that he was 'as the beasts'.[26] In fact some legends say that the beasts were wiser than him:

> Solomon once heard one ant say to the others, 'Quick enter your houses; otherwise Solomon's legions will destroy you.' The king asked why she spoke thus as he had no ill intent to them, and she answered that she was afraid rather that if the ants looked at Solomon's legions and their magnificence they might be turned from their duty of praising God alone, which would be disastrous to them. She added that, being the queen of the ants, she had in that capacity given them the order to retire. Solomon, perceiving her wisdom, desired to ask her a question; but she told him that it was not becoming for the interrogator to be above and the interrogated below, and moreover it was not fitting that he should sit on a throne while she remained on the ground. Solomon now placed her upon his hand, and his question was, 'Is there anyone in the world greater than me?' The ant replied that she was much greater; otherwise God would not have sent him there to place her upon his hand. The king, greatly angered, threw her down, saying, 'Dost thou know who I am? I am Solomon, the son of David!' She answered: 'I know thou art created of dust of the earth like all men; therefore thou oughtest not to be proud.' Solomon was filled with shame, and fell on his face.
>
> (*Sefer Hekalot*, 5: 22-29; Singer 1906: 82)

---

26 The *Mishnah*, a Rabbinic commentary on the Hebrew Scriptures, recorded in the first two centuries of the Common Era, is inclined to speak only of Solomon's weaknesses of character (the one exception among this group Rabbi Jose Halaafta who praised Solomon). Later Rabbinic commentators dropped the *Mishnah*'s critique of Solomon.

This story is in some ways an inverse parallel to Solomon's encounter with the Queen of Sheba. The Bible says only that the Queen of Sheba came to Jerusalem to test Solomon's wisdom 'with hard questions and riddles', which Solomon answered to her complete satisfaction (1 Kings 10; 2 Chronicles 9). They exchanged gifts (both accounts emphasise the 'abundance of spices' brought by the queen) after which she returned to her land. Jewish, Arabic and Ethiopic literature develop the story, however. These offer, as one might expect, slightly variant versions. The most complete is in the Kebra Nagast, the Ethiopian book of the 'Glory of the Kings', which reached its final redaction around 1320 but draws from earlier versions going back to the eighth century CE.[27] The Queen of Sheba is given a name, Makeda (in Arabic versions she is called Bilqīs).[28] In the Kebra Nagast, through a somewhat wily seduction Solomon turns Makeda's search for wisdom into a night of passion.[29] While sleeping together Solomon dreams that the sun is setting in Jerusalem and he awakes with a great sense of loss. He tries to persuade the queen to stay but she says she must return to her country; he gives her a signet ring as a seal and token of their love. Solomon, with the loss of Makeda – one queen he could not hold within his harem – realises

27 Translated into English by Wallis Budge as *The Queen of Sheba and Her Only Son Menyelek* (first published 1922, 2nd edition 2000). Whether what is recorded is story or history is debated but there is no doubt that the identity of the Ethiopian nation and monarchy is tightly bound up with it.

28 The story of the Queen's visit to Solomon is already slightly expanded in the Qur'an 27:15-44 in comparison to its Biblical counterpart. Her name comes later in Islamic commentaries and elaborations systematised by Al-Kisa'I and by Ath-Tha'labi in the eleventh century CE. In these accounts, unlike the Jewish and the Ethiopic, Solomon and Bilqīs do marry and there is no emphasis on seduction or an illicit relation as in the Jewish (who say Sheba seduced Solomon) or the Ethiopic (who reverse the transgression). See Pritchard (1974: 99).

29 Makeda resists Solomon's advances but on the last, or first, night of her stay (versions vary on this) Solomon makes an agreement with her that they will remain chaste on the condition that she takes nothing at all from his palace. She agrees but Solomon seasons their supper with an uncommon amount of salt and in the night she gets up with a great thirst and finds water only in a jug by Solomon's bedside. She drinks from it, and so he claims his side of the bargain and has his way.

that love is 'a chasing after the wind'. After Makeda returns to Sheba (Ethiopia), unbeknown to Solomon she gives birth to a son, Menelek. When Menelek has grown into a young man he sets off on the journey to meet his famed father carrying the ring back. When he arrives, Solomon, on seeing the ring, knows this is his son. Menelek lives with Solomon and then travels back to Ethiopia in the entourage of the eldest sons of the twelve tribes. They take with them the Ark of the Covenant and, spiritually, the sun sets in Jerusalem.

This is a late historic legend vis-à-vis the texts we have been looking at but it contains a particular slant that reflects the distinct Ethiopian Christian reading of the Song: in this tradition, the male figure is indeed Solomon (who is also assumed to have written the Song) but the maiden is read as symbolising the Ark of the Covenant which dwelt in Zion and for which Solomon built a temple, but which he loses. Ethiopic commentaries elaborate the end of the Song as expressing the separation of Solomon and the Ark which he loves, the focus of adoration in the Temple. The commentaries do not associate the Queen of Sheba as the maiden and the Kabra Nagast does not mention the Song. However, it does emphasise that, after his encounter with Makeda, Solomon's wisdom wanes and hers grows. In Chapter 89, she says of herself: 'I made of wisdom a shield for myself, and I saved myself by confidence therein, and not myself only but all those who travel in the footprints of wisdom' (Budge 2000: 132). She is praised by Azariah, another of Solomon's sons: 'Thy wisdom, O queen, so far exceedeth that of Solomon that thou hast been able to draw with thee the fruits of the tribes of Israel and the Tabernacle of the Law of God with the rope of thy understanding' (ibid.: 137).[30]

Though Ethiopic commentators on the Song, taking an allegoric approach to the maiden, do not associate the Shulamite with their

---

30 Compare (and contrast) with Matthew 12:42: 'The queen of the south will rise up at the judgment with this generation and condemn it, he came from the uttermost parts of the world to hear the wisdom of Solomon and, behold, a greater than Solomon is here.'

founding queen, such an association was made in the west (a tradition reviewed by Maccoby 1980: 98). The Shulamite at Song 1:4 says, 'I am dark but shapely', depicting, some say, that she was dark skinned, from Ethiopia or southern Arabia (the two places where Sheba has been identified). The Latin *nigra*, or Hebrew *šēhôr*, do both mean black, but Jerome tempers this in the next line (1:5) where he uses *fusca sim* – 'I am browned', and the Hebrew has a qualified adjectival form *šēhrim*, meaning 'like as if I am black.' The reason for the pigmentation seems clear from the text: 'for the sun hath discoloured me.' And it is to the clues given about her in the Song that we must turn if we might know more about this mysterious Shulamite, and where she comes from.

The Shulamite

What do we know of the maiden's background? Unlike Solomon she is not a historically known figure, nor one around whom a symbolic persona developed. We have only the words in the *Song* about her, and no name is given. So, we have to take careful note of what is given: 1:5, in particular, provides a very condensed narrative. When she is presented to the king she is brown 'for the sun hath discoloured me.' We can deduce from this that she is a country girl and has not been long in the royal palace or harem (where pale skin was considered beautiful). Solomon recognises her rural background and prepares for their relationship to unfold outside of the city, in a garden, probably one of his nearby hunting estates from where he can easily return to the city. Right at the end of the Song he remembers her as 'thou who abidest in the gardens' (8:13). In fact, despite this rustic but still somewhat royal setting she seems to long to be with him in her own world. 'Come my beloved', she says towards the end, 'let us go forth into the country (Latin and Greek versions have 'in the field'), let us abide in the villages' (7:12). *That* was where she was brought up, in the world of farmers and villagers. And more specifically she wants to be with him in the very world of her family's kind of work and the work she had done: 'Let us go up early to the vineyards, let us see if the vineyards flourish, if the flowers be about to bring forth fruit' (8:12).

An idyll, but not a royal background, no daughter of a local chieftain. Twice in the Song, when Solomon has left her for the night in the 'garden' she gets up and makes the short distance to the city herself, but she seems as one lost there, unable to find the palace where, obviously, her royal lover would be. The first time Solomon foresees her sortie and prepares for her to be guided to him. The second time he does not foresee it; she is not a 'known princess' so when 'the watchmen that go about the city found me,' she says, 'they struck me and they wounded me' (5:7). Hardly what one does to a royal queen! She is an unknown country girl.

Secondly, it seems that her family background had become very difficult. The Hebrew word used to describe her as 'black' – *šěhôr* –hints at her having gone through an ordeal. The word is used elsewhere in the Hebrew Scriptures not to describe a colouring of the skin but to express a state of great suffering, both physical and mental (Job 30:30; Lamentations 4:8). The maiden gives some information which may throw light on this, 'the sons of my mother contended against me.' The attitude of these 'sons of her mother' is strong, the Hebrew word used means 'incensed' or 'furious', the Greek and Latin means they 'fought against' her. She cannot bring herself to call them brothers – they are 'sons of her mother.' To be a brother is not ultimately a blood relation but a way of relating to another: these do not deserve the name in the way they treat her.[31] What did 'the sons of her mother'

---

31 Solomon does treat her 'as a brother', often calling her 'my sister', that is, as an equal. He is solicitous toward her, respecting her wishes, making sure she is not disturbed or troubled – 'Do not arouse or cause to awaken the beloved until she pleases' (8:4). This is the opposite of 'the sons of [her] mother.' At the end of the Song she knows that, 'I am become in the face of him (whom I love) as one finding peace' (8:10).

do to her? We are told: 'they set me as keeper over the vineyards'. One would think not such a terrible thing. But the Greek and Latin have a difference, which probably explains better what is going on: 'they made me to be a guard in the vineyard'. And this is confirmed in what follows; she is trying to 'defend' the vineyard. Whose vineyard? 'My own vineyard.' And she admits she has not succeeded (Song 1:5).

Who is she defending it from? The answer comes later in the Song when, as if remembering a nightmare scenario, she asks Solomon: 'Catch for us the foxes, the little foxes who destroy the vineyard, for our vineyard is flowering' (3:15). Who are these foxes? Real foxes do not destroy vineyards (just chickens). The key reference is to an early story in Jewish history, earlier than the Davidic line, going to the heart of rural Israel which tells of a family drama of perceived rejection and actual rejection, revenge and counter revenge and a spiral of violence that ends with Samson (the chief protagonist) hiding 'in the cleft of the rock' (Judges 15:1-8). In the line before the Shulamite speaks of the foxes she speaks of 'my dove in the cleft of the rock' (3:14). She is comparing Solomon to Samson (there are big differences between the cultured ruler and the titan of earlier history but they both had a liking for beautiful women who, at least in some accounts, proved to be their downfall).

Samson feels rejected when his wife is taken from him by her father, for she is married to another because Samson had been away too long.[32] Samson, rather typically, takes revenge on the neighbouring Philistines by burning up their vineyards. But the peculiar method of burning the vineyards was that Samson 'went and caught three hundred foxes, and took some torches; and he turned the foxes tail to tail, and tied a torch between each of the tails, and let the foxes go into the standing grain of the Philistines, and burned up the shocks and the standing grain, and vineyards' (Judges 15:4-5).

---

32 The key to the tragedy of Samson's marriage is his father-in-law who interprets Samson's absence as rejection of her and gives her away to Samson's best friend. He doesn't realise that Samson did love her.

In the Song, the maiden feels herself to be on the receiving end of this havoc and Solomon is asked to wind back the whole scenario. The foxes are (in all versions) in the present tense 'ruining the vineyards' and they need to be caught for her vineyard is now '*our* vineyard' which is 'in flower'. The meaning of this text continues into their relationship, in a new mode, as the foxes, 'the little foxes,' also represent the petty backbiting and gossip of the royal court, which yet has the power to wreak havoc on their love.

The details of the domestic drama in the Shulamite's family can only be guessed at; but close guesses are possible. The father of the maiden's household is not mentioned. We are given some information about her mother (who is also the mother of sons). At Song 6:8 Solomon describes the maiden as 'the only one of her mother, the elect of her that bare her.' How does this fit with her mother having 'sons'? It could be, symbolically, that the mother is Wisdom and she alone, among the siblings, is in relation to *her*. However, assuming that the Song has a literal as well as symbolic meaning, it implies the mother much preferred – elected – her daughter over her sons. There seems to have been a close relationship between this maiden and her mother. When she thinks of somewhere safe to which she can take her lover she says to herself 'I shall bring him into my mother's house, and into the bed-place of her that brought me forth' (3:4). And nearly the same again at 8:2: 'I would … lead thee into the house of my mother, and into the bedroom of her who taught me'. This may again be a reference to one taught by Wisdom but at a literal level her mother's bedroom had become hers. From which it also becomes clear that her mother has died: she imagines bringing her beloved to a house she loves, but an empty house, to a bed where her mother lay, but now an empty bed – for not once does she say 'I shall bring him to my mother'. One can hardly imagine anyway the three of them sharing the same bed.

Concerning the 'sons', if the maiden was her mother's favourite there may be jealousy, but there is something much more to make them 'incensed' or 'furious' and to 'fight' her ... There is no mention of a father: the maiden always speaks of her 'mother's house', 'her mother's bedroom', not 'her parents'; or, as one would have supposed in a patriarchal culture, her 'father's house' or, moreover, of her 'father's sons'. The fact that she had received an inheritance, 'my own vineyard', and that her brothers are making the decisions, implies strongly that her father had died. One could interpret the last line of 1:5 one way: in keeping 'the vineyards' of 'her mother's sons' she is made to neglect her own – 'my vineyards'. But it seems the situation is worse than this: it is hardly consistent with the maiden's character that she raises the subject just to complain that she was made to do more work, and put out in the sun more than was beneficial for her pale complexion!

One can imagine her father had died when she was young and her mother had remarried (as she speaks of her brothers only as 'sons of my mother'). And it seems her 'mother's house' is different from that of her half-brothers' for in the Song she imagines leading her beloved to the place where she felt most at home and secure (not a place where the inhabitants were 'incensed' and fighting against her). This 'mother's house' may have had its own vineyard, which became 'my own' when her mother remarried and moved to a larger farm designated separately as 'the vineyards.' But her brothers' fighting against her can be none other than their attempt to *get* her inheritance as well (probably on the decease of their common mother who protected her). Yet, even more than that, the foxes story implies that they tried to destroy her vineyard so she had no independent income. She had to go out in the midday sun 'to guard' when they tried to set alight the vines in the hottest part of the day. And they succeeded: 'My own vineyard I have not defended.'

'Foxes, little foxes', they are mentioned twice in all versions (except the Dead Sea Scrolls – whether this is an addition, or subtraction in the Qumran version is hard to know). 'The foxes' may be the brothers, 'the little foxes' the men they sent. One is reminded of a line from the Prophet Jeremiah:

> For even thy brethren, and the house of thy father, even they have fought against thee, and have cried after thee with full voice: believe not when they speak good things to thee. I have forsaken my house, I have left my inheritance, I have given my dear soul into the place of her enemies … Many shepherds have laid my vineyard waste, have trampled down my inheritance, reducing my pleasant inheritance to a deserted wilderness.
>
> (12:6-7, 10)

The expression implies also that the foxes are small and yet destructive, not openly aggressive or frightening, but cunning (as foxes), hard to stop and inflammatory; like gossip or slander. The Christian Letter of St James may provide the best commentary: 'The tongue is a small part of the body [but] a huge forest can be set on fire by a little flame.' In the context of Solomon's relationship with her, the foxes, as we will see, will be the slander of the court and the harem. Despite Solomon treating her 'like a sister' – that is, an equal – she in fact is not: in the eyes of the court and harem their family backgrounds are *vastly* different. That is why at the end her cry of despair is: 'Who shall give me to thee for my brother, sucking the breasts of my mother, that I may find thee outside and kiss, and kiss thee, and then may no one despise me?' (8:1).

The imagery in the Song has multiple meanings, even at a narrative level, because human beings know that what is, what was and what shall be all follow similar patterns. Returning to the original context, however, why would the non-brothers wish to deprive her of her independent income? Because she was very beautiful and they could make more money out of selling her – all this is expressed at the end of the Song (when she has to return to them). Her own vineyard, in the end, is not only a field, it is her: 'my vineyard is my own person' (8:12). It is now 'given over to keepers' ('the sons of my mother'); 'a man will bring a thousand pieces of silver for its fruit.' She is to be married for money. Maybe to an old man who has the means: 'If a man should give all the substance of his house for (my) love, he would still be despised as nothing' (Song 8:7). The maiden's arrival at the harem is because those 'keepers of her' 'contended against' her, by trying to marry her off – no doubt, considering her beauty, to a rich man, who'd take her to his estate and they'd have her house and vineyard anyway. Her constant refusal 'incensed' them, and their further venial rejection of her involved pushing her for selection for the harem.[33] *They* are pleased.

Is she pleased? She has lost her independence; she is a chattel in an institution where she will always be remembered as being of no important family; she has lost, forever, the house she loved, the vineyard she cared for and (as we later learn as the last bit of information about her life) the 'young sister' she is solicitous about. Her vineyard, her house, her independence, all must be found within her own self now: that 'room of her own' must be who she is. She has escaped from an arranged marriage, but now, in the harem, she has no possibility for marriage. She serves the queens, she is noticed as of particular beauty, a beauty honed maybe by suffering, and she is put through the cosmetic culture to await her summoning to the king. Whatever the details, it is clear that hers has not been an easy family background: there has already been major grief and loss in her life. Her wisdom has already been tested in the crucible of suffering. 'Where there is much wisdom there is much grief,' Solomon was later to reflect (Ecclesiastes 1:18).

At the opening of the Song she is faced with the only man she

---

33 In Esther it was only in the exceptional circumstances of King Ahasuerus' quest for a new High Queen that the king's attendants organised an active seeking for beautiful young virgins for the harem. In usual circumstances possible royal concubines were promoted locally. The family of the chosen maiden would have received payment.

can form any relationship with, the king. The expectations of that relationship, given her unroyal background, are not high but she has heard of this king, maybe seen him from afar, and she has learnt already to love him deeply. And she demands the kind of relationship that would not be expected, that of personal love. She is bold enough to ask for *his* kisses – concubines don't ask, they do. Very early in the Song, soon after their first brief meeting, she already speaks of him as 'thou whom my soul loveth' (1:7). She has lost everything but she has found love.

A maiden among the daughters

There are two verses in the Song that are attributed to speakers other than a man or a woman. Modern translations have called these 'the chorus' (Brugg 1995), or 'daughters of Jerusalem' (Murphy 1990), or even 'wedding guests' (Hess 2003).[34] These consist of two questions addressed to the maiden as to the identity and whereabouts of her lover: 5:9: 'Of what manner is thy beloved from among the beloved?' and 5:17: 'Whither has thy beloved gone?' It is, as we will see, as if they do not know, or need evidence, as to *who* he is.

This group are addressed, in second-person plural, as 'Ye Daughters of Jerusalem' – by the male as an adjuration (2:7, 3:5, 8:4), by the female as an address (1:4, 5:16) – but also as a request in the same words as her lover (5:8). When she adjures them they seem to be taken aback, and ask, in effect, 'from whence do you get the authority to make such formal requests to us!' (5:9). The maiden is no 'royal queen' who would have authority in herself to give orders. At one point the male speaks of the 'daughters of Jerusalem' in the third person plural, as them (3:10), immediately followed by a less formal request (3:11). In this last case, it is clear the 'daughters of

---

34 St Bernard, as we have seen, spoke of them as 'the bridegroom's companions'.

Jerusalem' is a respectful term generally for the women attendants of the harem. In the others, they are specifically for the handmaids allotted to the Shulamite.

In the poetic drama, however, they also act as a foil to the composed figure of the Shulamite. They might be conceived to represent a contrasting excitable and emotional component of female character. Literary echoes of this technique appear in the way Jane Austen emphasises some of the more nervous or even hysterical behaviour of women in her novels to highlight the sagacity, or at least calm-mindedness, of her heroines; or, to take a biblical reference, as Jesus addresses the 'daughters of Jerusalem' on the way of the Cross commending them to take care of themselves rather than get over-emotional about others (Luke 13:27-29). At three crucial points in the Song the male figure is concerned that these women 'do not stir up or awaken the beloved until she please' (2:7, 3:5, 8:4). The atmosphere of the lovers' meetings is to be calm: the maiden is not to be influenced by the expectations, gossip, ambitions, desires and conventions of others, she is to be given the space to respond to her lover in her own way. In other words, she is not to be pressured to conform to the standards of the harem, or be like any other 'daughters' in it. She is no concubine there simply to please the king. Nor is she portrayed in the Song as one prompted by her own unconscious instincts – the 'crowd' of her inner drives – to please herself. There is a deliberate 'enclosing' of the lovers (expressed in the repeated command of the king) so that the sexual energies awakened in them may be channelled towards love and not towards ungoverned emotionalism, desire or even hysteria. John of the Cross, in his Spiritual Canticle, has these outer or inner 'attendants' kept at a certain distance:

> You girls of Judea,
> While among flowers and roses
> The amber spreads its perfume,

Stay away, there on the outskirts:
Do not so much as seek to touch our thresholds.

(John of the Cross 1987: 224)

The link between femininity and hysteria, of course, has a long history, which Sigmund Freud attempted to challenge. The Greek root of the word *hysteria* comes from 'womb', which in pre-modern medicine was considered both deficient and insatiable and, therefore, always in a state of desire and disquiet. Freud came to the conclusion that symptoms of hysteria had no physiological origin but were linked to traumatic events in patients' emotional lives. For Freud hysteria always had its origin in a sexual event experienced during infancy or childhood, which is triggered much later when sexuality becomes conscious (see 'General Theory of the Neurosis' in Freud 1991). Certainly, in 5:2-8 of the Song, the maiden is driven to a state of panic through the disappearance of her lover at the very time when she is surrendering to him and offering to him the possibility of a fully sexual relation. In Freudian terms, this would be just such a trigger, which would release hidden traumas caused by sexual stimulation that, in an infant state, could not be brought to consciousness or fulfilment, and was experienced as abandonment.

It may well be that the deep wound of the maiden's early 'abandonment' by her father and mother – which as we will see fits the story of her 'family life' – wells up in her, causing the very disquiet that her lover had urged the 'daughters of Jerusalem' not to awake in her. In the end, it is not against 'feminine nature' that he must be wary but his own inner instability. His 'adjurations' become something of a self-fulfilling prophecy, as it is his own disquiet that becomes the cause and catalyst for a breakdown in her composure. She recovers when she reconnects with the image of her lover, as he is present in her memory and imagination *now*. She may have experienced abandonment and loss as a child, especially if her father died (as we can presume), but her lover is not dead or departed but is experienced as *still present to her awareness*. In Freudian terms, this moment of separation from her lover has led to a 'transference' of unconscious material and the realisation that now, as an adult, she is able to deal with the situation and there is no longer any need to ban the demands of the libido as a danger (see Freud 1991: 489–90, 497–8 on 'transference'). She has recognised the gap between her original 'feeling of rejection' and the present circumstance. In Jungian terms, psychological integration, at this point, comes with the assimilation of the *animus* – the masculine aspect of her own nature, which has been brought about *through* her relationship with Solomon. By first seeing him, in the sequence from 5:10-16, as *present within her* she is able, at 6:1-2, to see where he actually and physically *is*, and act to find him.

Similarly, the gift of nurture – rooted maybe most evidently in the maternal feminine instincts of compassion and empathy – are key to understanding the male figure in the Song. If the lover in the poem plays any directive role vis-à-vis the woman (as religious commentaries have normally, without much ground, interpreted into the relationship between them) then it is in a maieutic role. He provides through his own person an object for her desire; and through a tranquil context, an opportunity for the personal assimilation of newly awakened feelings. Her latent sexuality is brought into clear consciousness by being integrated with a new awareness of spiritual wisdom. This is why, as the poem progresses, she becomes the guiding force of the relationship. That Solomon understood the maternal feminine instincts of compassion and empathy is shown already in 1 Kings 3:16-28, in his judgment of who was the real mother of the child in the dispute between two harlots. It is no surprise that the demonstration of Solomon's appropriation of feminine wisdom is shown through his insight into the nature of motherhood. The Song also illustrates that Solomon was a man of *shalom* through the peace he created for his consort, supporting her, so that, at the end of the Song, she speaks of herself as '*leaning upon* her beloved' and as one who has 'become in the face of him (whom I love) as one finding peace' (8:5,10).

St Bernard says that that, 'Love is the good fruit, which is placed in the middle of Solomon's plate … There peace is added and all the other fruits of wisdom' (Bernard 1987: 104). Dante places Solomon at the heights of heaven for 'he doth breath by such a love that all the world here below is avid to know the news thereof' (*Paradiso* 10:109–11 in Dante 1986). As Dante was led to love by Beatrice; so, in the Song, is Solomon led by his Shulamite. The conversation between Solomon and his Shulamite, however, is not transparent: layers of symbolism are already built into it, and (as commentators through the centuries have shown) the associations of these symbols evoke further symbolism. All this gives the Song a depth of meaning, but one must still remember that this is based on a conversation between two human beings. To evaluate what allegory really fits with the story it is necessary to begin with an appreciation of the literal human relations. From this foundation, it will be possible to show how the symbolism of the Song does not detract from but brings deeper meaning to human relations.

Most people reading the poem have difficulty in picturing the conversation in any setting or context, as the author gives only arcane clues within the dialogue itself as to where the dialogues are taking place. Once the historical ambiance of King Solomon is accepted, the poem provides enough setting to make sense of the dialogue. In expanding on these I have not just provided 'imaginative filling-in of the gaps' but rather linked the hints given in the poem to the history of the era and person of King Solomon through the many centuries prior to and after the writing of the Song. The episodes are read as sequential and yet information given in later parts can illumine what is going on earlier. The Song does not start – 'Once upon a time …' but in mid-act, jumping immediately into the drama. Only as it commences does some of the background become clear. Clarifying the setting of this first conversation requires information gathered from later in the poem.

This presumes, however, that the poem can be taken as an interrelated whole. If, as some scholars have argued, the poem that comes down to us is fragmentary, then the 'abrupt' opening could be because an earlier introductory section is missing. The fact, however, that no ancient version (coming down to us through various lines of redaction), nor the fragments of the Song found at Qumran, give anything other than the lines we have makes the notion of an 'incomplete text' very unlikely. It may well be, however, that the Song was originally meant to be sung or even acted and a setting and even introduction may have been given visually or orally as a pre-amble. As a poem, however, the opening line is of such strength and originality that (like the opening lines of Wordsworth's poems which are always the most striking) it seems the author intends to open here. The trope of opening a story with a dramatic scene rather than giving the story its context is familiar to us anyway from film, which often aims at grabbing the viewer's attention, only explaining what is going on later. It could be argued that the Song never moves into 'filling in the background' (as films usually do), but this very lacuna with respect to setting is what gives space for the imagination to enter in. Presented with dialogue alone the reader is drawn in to consider what is going on, rather than have it laid out for them. The author wants the reader to be actively involved, setting the scenes in their own mind.

Before we turn to look carefully through clues in the text at the human relationship revealed in this sacred idyll, one key question wells up throughout the Song, asked by Solomon:

- 'Who is she that goeth up over the desert as a slender rod of the smoke from aromatic (spices), of myrrh, and incense?' (3:6).
- 'Who is she, that advances as the dawn arising, beautiful

as the moon, all excelling as the sun, terrible as the camps
of an army ordained to battle?' (6:9).

- 'Who is this that cometh up from the desert abounding in
  delights, leaning upon her beloved?' (8:5).

Who is this maiden? Who is she, who seems to come from nowhere
and disappears, without a name, at the end of the Song, into nowhere?

The Song does not answer this, but does show that her love is
what the Gospels call 'the pearl of great price.' 'If a man should give
all the substance of his house for [such] love, he should despise it as
nothing' (Song 8:7). As after the exile from Eden humanity entered
a desert, so paradise is regained in the one who 'comes up from
the desert, abounding in delights' – Eden in Hebrew means 'delight'.
In the light of this we may quote the French novelist Leon Bloy:

> Woman can never be or believe herself anything but Love
> personified, and the Earthly Paradise, sought for so many
> centuries, by Don Juans of every grade, is her Miraculous
> Image … All women – wittingly or unwittingly – are persuad-
> ed that their bodies are Paradise. 'And God planted a garden
> in Eden, in which he placed the man he had formed' (Genesis
> 2:8). Consequently, no prayer, no penitence, no martyrdom,
> have an adequate efficacy as conferring a rightful claim for
> possession of that inestimable jewel, whose price could never
> be paid with the weight of the starry firmament in diamonds.
> Judge, therefore, of the immensity of the gift when women
> give themselves, it is no less than the gift of God.
>
> (Bloy 2015: 127–8)

God *is* love (1 John 4:8). But God's love in this poem as in most of
the Bible is revealed through the language and stories of human relations: parents and children (calling God 'Our Father'); landowners
and labourers (Matthew 20:1-16); betrothed lovers ('as a bridegroom

rejoices over his bride so shall your God rejoice over you'; Isaiah 62:5); married couples ('in that day, says the Lord, that you will call me "my husband", and no longer call me "my master"'; Hosea 2:16). Whether it is the actual intention of the author of the Song of Solomon to depict God's love in the language and story of the human relationship shown is unsure. In fact, it is unlikely: in the Bible, the allegories for God's love taken from human relations are clearly explicated, whereas in the Song, it is left to the inventive imaginations of later commentators. However, if the inspirational role of woman in the Song is made clear (and not circumvented by reading her through the lens of the cultural patriarchy) then her most likely symbolic meaning in relation to Solomon is as a personification of wisdom. To read the maiden of the Song as 'passive', 'lost' or 'dependant' in relation to the male figure is to miss *who she is*, both literally in the story and, if one looks for further significance, symbolically.

Humanly she is shown to be resourceful, emotionally intelligent and guided by a deep intuition. She fulfils Jesus' call to be 'wise as a serpent and gentle as a dove' (Matthew 10:16). Solomon in fact twice calls her 'my dove' (2:14 and 5:2) – the dove that in Jewish imagery brought the olive branch of renewal to Noah and mankind, and in Christian imagery hovered over the Son of Man in the Jordan (Genesis 8:11; Matthew 3:16). 'Wisdom is justified in all her children' (Luke 7:35); even as a literary figure the maiden in the Song can be seen as a child of wisdom as much as, if not more than, Solomon. There is no evidence she actually existed but she can be seen as a depiction of relational wisdom, or what we might call today emotional intelligence. 'Something greater than Solomon is here,' Jesus says (Matthew 12:42).

The opening lines

The poem starts with some 'introductory verses', which are hard to attribute or allocate with certainty: the *dramatis personae* and setting at this point are still opaque. From then on it becomes easier as the distinct characters of the lovers emerge. These introductory verses are, however, saturated with import both for the story and for its symbolic meaning. St Bernard devoted eight sermons to the interpretation of the first line alone! They provide a key to the 'closed garden' of the Song and it is worth trying to unravel them.

'Let him kiss me with the kisses of his mouth.' St Bernard gives some elaborate symbolic readings for 1a and yet grasps the importance of human affection as key to the characters in the romance. He recognises that a lowly maiden is requesting a personal relationship with a king:

> She does not resort as others do, to the arts of seduction, she makes no devious or fawning solicitations for the prize that she covets. There is no preamble, no attempt to conciliate favour. No, but with a spontaneous outburst from the abundance of her heart she is direct even to the point of boldness.
>
> (Bernard of Clairvaux 1971: 39–40)

And yet, St Bernard notes 'there is a certain modesty in the fact that she addresses that utterance of hers not to the Bridegroom himself but to others, as if he were absent.' St Bernard sees her indirect directness as the combination of 'becoming modesty' with 'passionate desire.' He explains this through a rather wily allegory: 'One who ardently seeks access to the interior of a great home does not push themselves forward to the door but goes round to the intimate friends or members of the household to attain what he desires' (ibid.).

St Bernard construes that this entire introductory episode presents the maiden chatting with the maids preparing her to meet the king. Certainly, this is one way of making sense of why she does not address the king directly. Certainly, it could be her sister concubines, who are trained in augmenting female beauty, who express their appreciation of her natural femininity as being 'more alluring' than the wine of the somewhat artificial cosmetic regimen (verses 1-2).[35] The third verse contains 'We will run' and 'We will be glad', implying that it is more than the king who is speaking (no 'royal plural': the king doesn't refer to himself as 'we' elsewhere in the poem or in Solomonic writing). It would suggest a separate group; that the girls are speaking collectively.

Verse 3b shows the maiden celebrating – or simply stating the fact – that the king has summoned her in his 'chambers'. Certainly the group designated as 'we' is rejoicing as if this was a great privilege. Not all the girls of the harem were granted this private introduction. She is especially chosen. In verses 4-5 the maiden clearly addresses the entourage of ladies accompanying her from the harem, 'ye daughters of Jerusalem'. It could be (as Bernard, in his very open-minded way, accepts is possible) that verses 1-5 are all a conversation between her and her handmaids. Instead of the more general 'inner chambers' of the Hebrew text, the Greek and the Latin has rather more humble 'storerooms' or 'cellars'. This could imply a 'waiting room' where the maidens are kept *before* being presented to the king (as wine is kept in a cellar before it is drunk). Therefore, the conversation may be taking place in a vestibule to the king's room in the harem, rather than in the presence of the king himself. Or the cellar could express the harem itself: as wine for the king, so women are 'fermented' in the cosmetic culture of the harem for up to a year before being 'drawn'. In 'The Wedding Feast at Cana', written hundreds of years after the Song, in John 2:8, 'Jesus said to the servants, now draw some wine out, and take it to the chief

---

35 Bernard continues with an allegorical reading: 'In my opinion the [attendants of the maiden] are the holy angels who wait on us to offer to God our petitions and desires as we pray' (Bernard of Clairvaux 1979: 207).

steward.' This may be an echo of verse 3 in the Song where the maiden *is* the wine. At the Last Supper Jesus also identifies himself with the wine; now not drawn by one person but 'poured out for many'. If the Gospel reflects the Song then the servants/handmaids draw the wine/maiden and take her to the chief steward/king. But the actual wedding, however, is between the bride and the bride-groom who, in the Gospel story, are not involved in, or aware of, what is going on. So the opening episode may be providing the wine for the romance of the Song, which only comes after, and the character of the king may not yet be present.

A reading of the opening episode as solely between the maiden and the handmaids, however, is not normative. Traditional commen-taries and more recent (less religious) 'meditations on the Song', presume the opening lines *do* express a private dialogue between the maiden and Solomon. The setting of the inner-chamber/storeroom can also, indeed, express the intimate and exclusively personal quality of a relationship. Storerooms and cooling cellars in the Middle East were indeed 'inner chambers' – rooms at the centre of the house without windows to the outside. Jesus spoke of the inner chamber or storeroom as the right place for a 'secret' personal relationship with God (Matthew 6:6). The image may imply that Solomon, from the very beginning, has brought her away from the opinions and expectations of the royal court, granting a meeting between him and her alone.

Many ancient commentaries read the whole section as spoken uniquely by the maiden to Solomon. It is clearly *his* kisses spoken of in the first verse but most commentators have taken the 'breasts', 'name' and 'ointments' that are praised as also his.[36] There are diffi-culties with breasts, as we have seen, avoided in most translations of the Masoretic as 'love'. However, there are good reasons why a king would have been known as anointed, as one who carries a name, and

---

36 In Hebrew there is an assonance between 'name' *shem* and 'perfume' *shemen*.

as perfumed. King David, in his last words, speaks of himself as 'the anointed one', marked permanently by the oil the prophet Samuel first poured on him (2 Samuel 23:1, 1 Samuel 16:13). Psalm 89 says, 'With my holy oil I have anointed my servant David.' On his coronation the king was made to carry the 'Name of God', which the High Priests wore every year in the ritual of Yom Kippur (Barker 2003: 129). The Song, however, speaks of a personal name – '*thy* name.' The very name of Solomon is attractive – meaning 'peaceful or gentle man'. The maiden in the Song has no name, divine or human. Solomon would also have been 'fragrant with the best ointments' especially through his sacerdotal role in the Temple. So, there are reasons why the opening verses could be her speaking of Solomon, or, at times, speaking as part of the group, the 'we' of the maidens.

However, there is another set of symbolism in the Bible with respect to oil, name and fragrance, centring not on the king but on the feminine figure of Wisdom. They could, therefore, apply to the maiden just as well. Proverbs, the earliest biblical wisdom text we have, sees Wisdom as the oil which was extracted from the tree of life (3:18). Sirach describes Wisdom as the anointing oil itself, a sweet perfume of myrrh, cinnamon and olive oil: the king was anointed on his head and 'between his eyelids', which may have symbolised the opening of the eyes to Wisdom (24:10). One of the early names of God in the Jewish tradition was El Shaddai, which with the plural *dd* contains the Hebrew consonants for 'breasts' (a Hebrew word for breasts is *shadayim*). In Genesis, El Shaddai is linked to fertility, fruitfulness and many children (Genesis 28:3, 35:11), particularly as 'giving blessings from the breasts and from the womb' (49:25) and promising sons who would be kings (17:16) (see Baile 1981: 240–56). The Book of Enoch, accepted as canonical before Jamnia, speaks of a tree 'whose fragrance was beyond all fragrance, and its fruit is beautiful and its fruit resembles the dates of a palm and its blooms very delightful in appearance' (1 Enoch 24:4-5; Enoch 1921: 50). Enoch is told (by the Archangel Michael) that its fragrance 'shall be given to the upright ones as Wisdom … and its fragrance shall be in their bones'.

Hebrew words, as we have seen, often have both a concrete and abstract meaning. If the context is the presentation of a girl to the king in the harem the concrete meaning of *dd* fits the narrative, and 1b is more likely to have been spoken by the king or the handmaids about the maiden. Two passages attributed to Solomon in Proverbs help explain the juxtaposition of breasts and inebriation, playing at the same time with the similarity between the word for breast and feminine love:

> Rejoice with the wife of thy youth.
> Let her be thy dearest hind,
> and the most agreeable fawn:
> let her breasts [*dãdayim*]
> inebriate you at all times,
> be thou delighted continually
> with her love [*dôdyim*].
> (Proverbs 5:18-19; *yim* being feminine possessive)

The second passage, in contrast, depicts a woman who is 'wily of heart' who invites a young man:

> I have perfumed my bed with myrrh, aloes and cinnamon.
> Come, let us be inebriated with the breasts [*dãd*],
> and let us enjoy the desired embraces till the day appear;
> let us delight ourselves with love [*dôd*].
> For my husband is not at home;
> he has gone on a long journey.
> (Proverbs 7:17-19)

The Song, however, distances itself from this scenario in saying that the maiden's breasts are '*better* than wine'.

But is it the king or handmaids who are speaking? At verse 2 in the Vulgate and Masoretic we have a singular subject and object and a plural indirect subject, 'Draw *me*: and *we* will run after *thee*.' This helps hone the picture: the handmaids (being plural) are not the ones here speaking to the maiden, which means that Solomon (here as either subject or as object) must be present in the opening episode. Solomon could still be the one speaking to the maiden here, or the maiden to Solomon. The Greek text has a slight variant here, which weighs the favour to the former: the Septuagint gives a statement of fact, 'they drew you' εἵλκυσάν σε, in the past historic tense, a single completed action, rather than a petition. As the most ancient text we have of the Song we have to consider this nuance. The maidens (in third person plural) are here the subject and, therefore, not the speakers. They have, indeed, drawn her to him, through the whole process of selecting her (as of especial beauty), speaking about her to him, and simply escorting her. The only real possibility here is that Solomon is saying to her, 'As they drew you to me (past historic), draw me, and them as well, to you!' He is saying, in effect: 'You take the lead! We will all run after you!' In this answer Solomon is turning the tables on his kingship and the expectation of the harem – he is giving her the initiative. Maybe he is, already, early in his reign, tired of the court and its expectations – a fragment of the Song in the Dead Sea Scrolls seems more urgently to say, 'Take me away! Let us hurry!' (6Q6, dated 50 CE; though there are some missing letters the double imperative is clear).

'A good answer is a kiss on the lips,' says Proverbs 24:26, and here the maiden has received what she asked for – a personal relationship where they are equal, and a response from him that he will *give himself* to her. As John of the Cross says, 'Love does not only make all things equal; it makes the lover subject to what is loved.' If this maiden is already in some way or unconsciously representing wisdom to Solomon, 'Draw me: and *we* will run' may also express his sense of his role as king, for Proverbs 8:16 says, 'When a man becomes wise, those of his household follow'; or Sirach 10:2, 'As the ruler of a city is, so are all its inhabitants'. 1a, spoken by the maiden, in its indirectness is a strange line if it is spoken to Solomon rather than to her handmaids. There is a middle way, though: here (and only here) the maiden addresses herself directly to the king *by way of an aside* to her maiden assistants. This could be, as Bernard says, a sign of modesty; one doesn't want to challenge the king or demand from him directly. Also, in addressing her handmaids she is already addressing the whole culture of the harem, challenging the cultivation of women for the 'intoxication' of kings. Yet hers is the protest of a lover not a critic. Her opening line in fact distances her from her maiden companions, and the institution they are expected to serve, in asking for a *personal* relationship with the king, and there is no doubt that the king is meant to overhear.

In this one line, she expresses her independence from the *others* and the uniqueness of the kiss she wants from the king. Though it seems as if she is not directly addressing him, he knows quite clearly it is a challenge to *him*. From his response in the following line we see he has indeed been jolted into the realisation that this whole woman in her body and soul *is* something different and incomparably *better* than the usual delights of the harem.

So we can conclude, with as much certainty as the text gives, that the women of the harem have drawn this one woman to the attention of the king, he has summoned her with the company of some handmaids, and she is meeting him. Origen Homily 1:5 has 'the Bridegroom' bringing her alone into the inner chamber with the others waiting outside; pointing out that 3b has 'he hath brought *me*', not *us*. Origen then has her returning to the handmaids to tell them what she alone has seen (a conversation not expressed in the Song), and then all of them entering after her in 3c (Origen 1966: 85). In the end we can safely say it is a bit of a dance, and yet the entanglement of the characters in the opening lines seems to be intended by the author, skilled poet as he/she is. In these opening verses, it is as if the maidens representing the harem generally are deeply involved in what is going on, so that it is hard to extract the personal voice of the lovers. They are in their very ways of talking as they are quite literally *in* the harem. The 'we' of 3c is probably spoken by Solomon but *as if* sharing in the viewpoint of the maidens. That it is a line spoken by Solomon rather than the maidens is hinted in the ending, which is distinctly 'Solomonic': 'the upright/righteous love thee.' Much more than the maidens, he of all people is ready to recognise wisdom in her. As Proverbs attributed to Solomon show: God 'stores up wisdom for the upright' (2:7), to be righteous in the commandments *is* to love wisdom (4:4-6), the fulfilment of desire and uprightness is 'the tree of life' (11:30, 13:12) which 1 Enoch says 'shall be given to the upright ones as Wisdom'. The opening words, anyway, tell us much already about the harem and the lovers: she is insisting on real love, and he recognising that to love wisely one needs to live wisely.

PART TWO

A Narrative-Spiritual Reading

Having illustrated the literal storyline within the Song, this second part does not intend to deny there are spiritual meanings but rather to set them on a firmer footing. One may quote the renowned Torah scholar and mystic Rabbi Abraham Isaac Kook (1865–1935):

> I always stress the importance of the profane and mundane things of this world as the basis of the holy. Holiness has to be built on the foundation of real situations in this world, for that is the material base to which holiness is the form. The firmer the material base the more important the form which it can bear. Sometimes the holy treats the mundane and profane in a harsh manner, so that the material base is depleted. A period inevitably follows in which the material world reclaims this maltreatment from the holy, and unholy arrogance increases in the world. In the end, however, the holy will subdue the profane not through arrogance or denial of the worldly but through the absorption of the profane within the holy. For the power of holiness is so much stronger it can work with even the most scandalous facts of history.
>
> (Unterman 1976: 84–5)[1]

Rabbi Kook makes no reference to the Song but recent 'secular love song' interpretations have dismissed spiritual symbolism as suppressing the Song's natural meaning. My aim here is to weave back

---

1 By 'scandalous facts used by God' Rabbi Kook gives the appropriation of the covenant by Israel/Jacob through pretending to be his older brother.

together the clear narrative context of the Song with its mystical associations. God in the end is the *coincidentia oppositorum* (the integration of opposites), and we, as humans, are not liberated by leaving something behind, but only by fulfilling our task as *mixta composita*. The Song is the record of the joyous and painful weaving together of spirit and flesh within two human lovers.

The meeting

FIRST EPISODE
Introductory verses – 'The meeting' (chapter 1, verses 1–5)

Shulamite: (Aside to her maiden companions) 1. *'Let him kiss me with the kiss of his mouth.'*

Solomon: (Echoing what the maiden companions have said previously about her) *'… because thy breasts are better than wine.*

2. *Fragrant with the best ointments: thy name is an oil poured out: therefore, have the maidens loved thee.*

3. *Draw me: we will run after thee to the odour of thy ointments.'*

Shulamite: *'The King hath brought me into his store rooms (inner chambers).'*

Solomon: (Expressing what the maidens had said) *'We will be glad and rejoice in thee, remembering thy breasts above wine: the upright love thee.'*

Shulamite: (Aside to her maiden companions) 4. *'I am dark but shapely, O ye daughters of Jerusalem, as the tents of Kedar, as the skin-shields of Solomon.*

5. *Look not closely upon me because I am brown, for the sun hath discoloured me: the sons of my mother contended against me, they set me as keeper over the vineyards: my own vineyard have I not defended.'*

Simeon Solomon, *The Desire of the Lovers*, from *Eight Designs on the Song of Songs* (1878)

At the literal level, we are led into a scene in which a new woman in the harem is presented to the king and it seems that her breasts are bared by the handmaids or attendants, 'to show her beauty'. The custom of revealing the maiden's breasts would have been routine for those familiar with the harem – like the exhibiting of choice merchandise – but it startles or discomposes *this* woman. Her opening line asks for a personal relationship, not the impersonal 'use' of the harem. She challenges the king, albeit indirectly as an aside to others, 'Let him kiss me with the kiss of his mouth.' She will be to him not merely an odalisque or a concubine. The king for his part, looking at her intensely, recognises from her words the unusualness of her character. That she is very beautiful goes without saying: the system or method by which women are chosen in the first place for the royal harem would alone assure that. But the king sees, in addition to her beauty, strong personal qualities, which he will have to respect.

The maiden in the Song has undergone the elaborate perfumery regimen of the harem so that her body is saturated with sweet scent. As Esther indicates this could have taken twelve months prior to meeting the king. There is here, however, no question of such a period, it would have been some weeks at the most; at her presentation, she is still tanned by the sun. She is a recent arrival: she has not the pale skin which was also part of the regimen for beauty. Her skin, we learn, is darkened because she has had to 'go out at midday' 'to guard the vineyards' prior to her selection for the harem.

The fact that the regimen was shortened must have meant that the king's interest in her was awakened early, probably because her exceptional 'natural' appearance had been praised. She is recognised and recommended by the leading women of the harem as a woman of particular beauty. Certainly the handmaids play the role, in this opening episode, as vehicles of communication between the lovers (St Bernard reads them as angels). It would be commonplace within the social network of the harem that a word of appreciation about women of particular beauty would reach the ear of the king. Her name is mentioned. Later in the Song at 6:8 her lover remembers how 'The daughters saw her and declared her most blessed: the queens and concubines – and they praised her.' When arriving in the harem, long before she becomes queen, we are told that 'Esther was admired by all who saw her'. The opening lines of the Song show this was the same with the maiden. In a profession which was geared toward the cultivation of beauty the handmaids would have celebrated 'a good piece of work'. All this seems to be expressed in the opening lines. The king refers to the maiden's breasts as 'better than wine' twice afterwards in his personal dialogue with her – if the handmaids use this expression about her here, maybe it was what was first mentioned to him about her.

Her words require from him a kiss. Surely, he does kiss her now. How? Most obviously with a kiss on the lips, however, in the light of the request she has made for a personal love *not* influenced by the expectations of the harem, could he not have fulfilled that demand with a kiss on the cheek or her brow, showing that, to him, she is not a concubine but an equal, a familiar, as one of his family? Throughout the Septuagint the maiden's preferred name for her beloved is 'my kinsman' (ἀδελφιδός μου) as if for her this expresses their equality (across any social divide); at 4:1 it has 'neighbour' (πλησίον). The real response, at this moment, is a kiss of solicitude rather than of desire. They are to be *friend* to one another – the only relational term in the Song that they both use for the other. Such a kiss would indeed be surprising, not what is expected for a concubine, not what maybe she expected, probably not what she wanted – she is a fully human woman in the Song. His first words are, as it were, an explanation: [I kiss you thus] 'because thy breasts are *better* than wine.' He shows that her love (undoubtedly including a sexual longing) is much more delightful to him than as intoxication or entertainment. In 1b he is distancing himself from the impersonal sexual usage of the harem. Her feminine nature is much more than feminine attractiveness. Her womanly love is a much greater blessing.

There is no need here to imply a divide between physical attraction and real love; all the senses are included in these opening verses: touch, taste, smell, sight, and (as conversation) hearing. The poem is avowedly sensual, and also erotic in the sense that both physical attraction and longing for communion has its roots in a desire to transcend the confines of the self for the sake of intimacy with the other. Sexual love provides for many their first experience of ecstasy, which literally means 'standing outside oneself.' That is why *eros* leads to *agape* (the highest form of selfless love). From the beginning the relationship is one of soul-love and friendship (the terms of endearment used in the next episode) rather than only physical attraction.

Ultimately the beauty of the maiden of the Song lies in her character. It is this which makes her stand out among the beautiful. 'One is my dove' (6:8). An unpredictable kiss must be the answer to such an unexpected request as hers. And yet with this kiss he is brought right up to her: 'Fragrant with the best ointments' – he is drawn into her perfume, not as into intoxication but as expressing who she is: 'Thy *name* is an oil poured out.' In the biblical tradition names are not just labels; they carry the qualities and presence of a person. Abram became Abraham ('father of a multitude') when he responded to God's call. Simon became Petros (a play on the Greek word *petra* meaning 'rock') when he made his profession of faith. In Aramaic Jeshua (Jesus) means 'Yahweh saves' (Hebrew *Yah'shua*). The wearing of the name of God at Yom Kippur by the anointed High Priest meant they actually carried the power of God, starting the process of atonement and the restoration of creation (Exodus 39:30, Leviticus 16). The maiden's name is not given, just as the maiden who anointed Jesus' feet with precious ointment is remembered and praised but anonymous in Mark 14:9 and Matthew 26:13. This sense of the 'hidden name' unspoken may reflect the hiding of the wisdom tradition in the Deuteronomic editing of the Bible (a thesis argued by Barker 2003). However, in the case of the Song, it hints that she is both *everywoman* and yet has a real hidden identity, that of wisdom.

Simeon Solomon, *The Consecration of the King*, from *Eight Designs on the Song of Songs* (1878)

Already in the opening lines of the Song we find imagery that has strong resonances with other parts of Jewish scripture: wine and oil, tents and shields, vineyards and inner chambers and the hallowing of the name. Edmée Kingsmill sees the real meaning of the poem in the religious connotations of the images. The human love story for her, as for most commentators up until recently, is only a metaphor for divine–human relations. The use of religiously charged imagery, however, could just as well be read as lending a depth and richness to the human love encounter. In these lines, for example, the tents of Kedar and the skin-shields of Solomon carry biblical associations, which tend to set them in contrast. The Arabian tents were made from the wool of black goats, and these heavy, un-shapely tents are contrasted with the symmetric rising curves of Solomon's shields. The 'tents of Kedar' symbolise a fierce nomadic people in contrast with the artistry and peace of Solomon's kingdom. The Masoretic text gives 'curtains of Solomon' whereas the Vulgate has 'decorated skins' (Latin *pelles*, lit. 'with a showy outside'). In early civilisations animal hide was used for shields (rather than metal or wood). Solomon used emblematic hide-shields to decorate the walls of the Temple and they had general ornamental use in Jewish homes (see 1 Maccabees 4:57 and Ezekiel 27:10-11).

Solomon also, however, amassed a huge army of chariots, which would have been equipped with similar hide-shields, and throughout his reign he had to defend his kingdom from aggressors (2 Chronicles 1:14; 1 Kings 11:14-40).[2] So the 'skins' represent a dark side, emblematic of conflict; as the maiden's own tanned skin is a sign of her conflict with her 'mother's sons' who made her guard her vineyard. Both the shields of Solomon and her own skin are the result of the necessity of defence. A psalm (one the author of the Song would undoubtedly have known) laments:

---

2 Solomon extended his kingdom, however, more through political marriages with the families of local chieftains than through conquest.

Woe is me … that I must live among the tents of Kedar.
Too long have I been dwelling among those who hate peace.
I am for peace but when I speak they are for war.

(Psalm 120:5-7)

These images are linked, respectively one assumes, to the blackness
and the shapeliness of the maiden – 'dark as …', 'shapely as …'
Medieval and early modern commentators saw this contrast from a
moral view, pointing to the simultaneously sinful and redeemed
nature of the penitent soul (represented by the maiden). Such
readings are conditioned by medieval imagery – devils were depicted
as black, and beautiful women (like Mary of Magdalene) were only
acceptable if dressed in sackcloth. References to Kedar in the
Bible point not to personal sin but the suffering of the innocent and
peace-loving when faced with the contentiousness of others. This is
clearly the case in the Song: the maiden says her brothers 'contended
against me', also translated as 'were incensed, or angry, against me'
(see Kingsmill 2009: 111, n. 18). The juxtaposition of images does
not, therefore, imply redemption from personal sin but freeing from
oppressive and abusive relationships to one of peace.

The pastoral idyll

SECOND EPISODE
Part 1 – 'The pastoral idyll' (chapter 1, verses 6–16)

Shulamite: 6. *'Show me, O thou whom my soul loveth, where thou feedest,*
where thou liest in the mid-day, lest I begin to wander after
the flocks of thy companions.'
Solomon: (In the guise of a shepherd) 7. *'If thou know not thyself, O thou*
fairest, among the women go forth, and follow after the
traces of the flocks, and feed thy kids beside the tents of the
shepherds.'

(After an interval) 8. *To my mare among the chariots of Pharaoh have I likened thee, O my friend! 9. Thy cheeks are comely with circlets, thy neck with strings of beads. 10. We will make thee chains of gold, with studs of silver.'*

Shulamite: 11. *'While the king was reclining at table, my nard gave forth its perfume. 12. A bundle of myrrh is my beloved to me; he shall abide between my breasts. 13. A cluster of camphor my beloved is to me, in the vineyards of Engaddi.'*

Solomon: 14. *'Behold, thou art beautiful, O my friend! Behold, thou art beautiful … thine eyes of doves.'*

Shulamite: 15. *'Lo! thou (too) art fair, my beloved, pleasant indeed. Our bed is flowery: 16. Our house-beams are of cedar, our rafters of cypress.'*

Solomon, recognising the maiden's desire for a personal relationship, knows that the context of the harem is not the right one to explore this freedom undisturbed. The trappings of the royal palace tie him to his persona as king; he would be free of that, to meet her as just himself. It seems he has arranged to meet her in a pastoral setting, on her own ground 'in the country' – perhaps one of his royal gardens or hunting lodges near Jerusalem. The rural context of fruit, flowers, trees and fields, begins to shape the melody of the Song. He arranges for her to be taken there, with maybe the same maid companions, where, in the midst of a garden she makes herself at home in a small latticed wooden house. Later, maybe the next day even, he comes to meet her, without any of his royal pomp, but dressed simply, even as a country shepherd or farmer.

As he comes to meet her, she speaks in a way that is both deeply affectionate and also playful, even cheeky. As on their first meeting he had said, 'draw me and we will run after thee', so the first thing she says turns the tables back on him: 'show me where *you* are, for I might wander: as you need my help, so I need yours'. She is already quite free of the deference and etiquette of the royal court, already deeply in love. And she expresses it, asking not just to be given his evenings but to be let into the very centre of his life, 'at mid-day'. She is longing for real relationship, and says in effect, 'If you won't or can't then I'll be off. Don't think you're so special – just a country fellow – there are others!' Solomon plays along by challenging her back, as if to say, 'If you don't trust in my intentions, then you are more than free to meet someone else.' But he really points back to her, 'If thou do not know thyself, O thou fairest': he trusts her own innate wisdom to guide her instincts.

After this introductory sparring, the Masoretic text gives a second paragraph break, which fits with the sense of an unspoken period where all this testing playfulness is resolved to a deeper relatedness. It is as if, in that pause, they have let go of any lingering insecurities and already touched on the heart of their relationship – and this finds expression (paradoxically to modern ears which hear friendship as a lesser form of love) in the first of nine times in the poem when the male figure calls the female *amica mea* (Heb. *ra'yatî*), 'my friend'. With a friend one is safe. With friends, there is no need for pretence. The lover is now simply himself, Solomon, speaking of the horse he loved, maybe as a young boy, and had given to Pharaoh of Egypt as his most personal gift, to cement a political and trade alliance and an arranged marriage that involved the Pharaoh conquering and killing the inhabitants of the Canaanite city of Gezar and giving it to his daughter as a dowry, and Solomon building a separate palace for his new queen (1 Kings 3:1, 7:8-12, 9:16-17, 10:28-29). All bartering … in comparison with the simple love that he now has. Now he is with a real friend, not one for the sake of expediency. Like this mare among an army of foreign horses, he recognises *this* friend among the 'foreign women' he married, to be *his*, and the one he loves.[3]

The reference to a mare here, in the Song, is the one and only occurrence of a female horse in the Hebrew bible. As we have seen

---

3 1 Kings 11:1 says, 'King Solomon loved many foreign women besides Pharaoh's daughter – Moabites, Ammonites, Edomites, Sidonites and Hittites.' One might say he has now found his *one* 'Shulamite'!

in Part One, this image in likelihood goes back to a story from Egyptian history. He recognises already that the 'exclusiveness' and 'all-encompassing' nature of their relationship will cause disturbance in the harem as it does in his unconscious (as the Prince of Kadesh's mare drove the stallion chariots of Pharaoh wild and ungovernable). Upsetting the apple cart in the harem – as shown in the case of Rameses III – is politically dangerous.

However, the gauntlet is thrown down and Solomon picks it up. He knows he can no longer avoid the issue that he is king. He royally promises to augment the natural beauty of her cheeks and neck with gold and silver jewellery. The Masoretic gives a slightly different impression, of replacing her simple circlets and beads (as befitted the lower levels of the harem) with the gold and silver of a queen, as in Psalm 45:9. The reference to jewels and precious chains offered as adornment for her cheek and neck, however, is also an allusion to the bejewelled bridle and reins of a favoured king's mare – who was, maybe, Solomon's first love as a child. There is a shadow here of the mare's exile from the one to whom she belongs 'among the chariots of Pharaoh', a shadow that will fall across the maiden also at the end of the Song.

At this moment of recollection of early love, tinged with the regret that he 'gave it away' as he got older, the king draws the maiden to himself, as if to say, 'you I will not lose.' He is now resting with her (from the weariness of the role he has to play as king). Despite his willingness to meet her in the country without the trappings of kingship, their relationship is not based on make-believe; in her next words she names the fact that he is king. The Masoretic and Vulgate has him 'reclining at table'. It could also be that she is the table and he has let his head rest on her bosom or shoulder (that she is tall becomes clear from later imagery in the poem); however, in the ancient world people did 'recline at table' on divans. They seem, indeed, to be sharing some simple food she has prepared, maybe sitting outside in the early evening. John of the Cross in his Spiritual

Canticle speaks of 'the supper which refreshes, and deepens love' (John of the Cross 1987: 223). We can picture them there with the evening sun slanting over the garden, and the birds singing. Here, in a shared meal, the perfume of her love arises. Literally, the fragrances that the regimen of the harem has instilled in her – nard, myrrh, camphor – in giving forth their odour express her *self* as a gift to him.

It is nard that is first mentioned as her fragrant response to his tiredness and the hint of foreboding that came with his memory about the mare. Nard, though used in cosmetic perfumery, was also used as a preservative balm: the antidote to loss, decaying, passing away. The link of supper and nard is echoed, many years later, in the Gospels: Mark 14:3, 'As he reclined at table, a woman came with an alabaster jar of ointment, pure nard, very costly'; John 12:3, 'There they made him a supper … Mary took a pound of costly ointment, pure nard … and the house was filled with the fragrance of the ointment.' Jesus recognises this as an act of loving *compassion*, anointing his body so that it may be preserved.

The emphasis on fragrance in the Song (the word itself occurs eight times alongside many names of spices) is understandable given the harem context through which the maiden passed. This need not mean, however, that fragrance (and specific spices) may not have allegorical or spiritual meaning, or that the fragrance of the maiden need be only of a cosmetic or applied nature. She speaks here of '*my* nard', and the bundles or clusters of myrrh and camphor used in perfumery (as shown in Esther 2:12) become the expression of what 'my beloved [is] to me.' At this point he is, firstly, 'a bundle of myrrh'. The word for 'bundle' here in the Masoretic is *sĕrôr*, literally 'something bound up.' It is the sachets containing spices, which were worn in the harem to saturate the skin with scent. However, *as him* it implies one 'bound up' in political marriages. The Sufi Jalaluddin Rumi was one who knew: 'King Solomon grew weary and embittered of his reign' (Rumi 1957–67: 2). In Hebrew myrrh means 'bitter': she experiences the bitterness of what it is for him to be king, and she holds him in compassion, 'between [her] breasts.' Myrrh like nard was also used for embalming and preserving (as in John 19:39). The third spice that she likens to Solomon, *'eskôl kōper* in Hebrew, is usually translated 'a cluster of cypress': but neither the resin nor fruit of cypress was regarded as particularly aromatic and there is no record of its use in cosmetic perfumery. The closest oil that was used as cosmetic and for embalming is *kopher*, camphor.

The link to vineyards in the next line led Origen to propose it referred to a 'cluster of grapes', which the lovers may have been sharing at their meal. However, camphor can also be drunk mixed with water or wine and acts as a stimulant. The Qu'ran says of the righteous, 'they shall drink a cup (of wine) mixed with camphor' (76:5). Camphor oil is made by distilling the leaves, roots or stems of the *Cinnamomum camphora* tree, which (for a simple infusion) would have been bound in clusters in the liquid. Origen admits that Engaddi – the mountainous part of Judea, rising fifteen hundred feet above the Dead Sea – did not produce vines, but doesn't note it was well known for its date palms (Genesis 14:7; 2 Chronicles 20:1).[4] So, literally, we have camphor-infused date wine. But how is *he* this *to her*? Later in the Song the very term 'cluster' is used to speak of the fruit of the date tree, which he likens to the maiden's breasts (7:8). This is echoed in Sirach 24:14 when Wisdom says, 'I grew tall like a date-palm tree in Engaddi.' What the image actually invokes in the Song is that she stands up from table to her full height and holds him close to her, enfolds him to her bosom, as the sprigs of the camphor firs (him) are held in the wine (her).

In these lines fragrance is both given and received; the aroma and stimulus of the camphor pervades the wine. Christian mystics often describe being filled with a sweet perfume. Teresa of Ávila writes that in deep prayer, 'The whole creature, both body and soul, is enraptured *as if* some very fragrant ointment, resembling a

---

4 The very term 'cluster' is used to speak of the fruit of the date tree later in the Song (7:7-8).

delicious perfume, had been infused into the very centre of the being [marrow], or as if we had suddenly entered a place redolent with scents coming from not one, but from many objects … although it entirely pervades our being' (Teresa of Ávila 1913: 158). This seems to echo the experience of the maiden in the Song. Also, the fact that she feels she is actually *receiving* these fragrances from her beloved is echoed in Augustine's Confessions 10:27: 'Thou didst send forth thy fragrance, and I drew in my breath' (Kingsmill 2009: 234).

It is no coincidence that nard, myrrh and camphor are spices used for embalming. The maiden has intuited Solomon's grief that in this life he will never be free from his role as king – made even more poignant by his recent short-lived attempt to step outside royal identity by playing a shepherd. She has responded compassionately, but she has also challenged him *to let that role die* – to be *himself*. Camphor is yet more evidence of an Egyptian context in the background of the Song. It is a spice not mentioned anywhere else in the Bible but was a much-used ingredient for the mummification process in Egypt. In Egyptian belief the attempt to preserve bodies was to allow the transition of the whole person from one life to the next. At a human level, this is exactly what is going on here in the Song. It is as her lover, and not as king, that she receives him. There is a dying to the past and an opening to the possibility of a new life, but in the transmutation, *he* has been preserved – the whole person that he is. At this point she stands back and looks at him, smiling: this is *him*. And in her looking he sees her in the real beauty of who she *is*.

There is an old saying, 'It is only the beauty of the angels that keeps them from coupling'; when they approach each other they always want to stand back and gaze at each other:

> But in the strange intensity
> Of the life which is to come
> Copulation will be as rare
> As the eggs of the Great Auk –

Comparatively!
It will be a desperate agony
For a man and woman to come together.
The beauty of their profiles
Will hold them away.

(Turner 1925: 46)

Indeed, the lovers in the poem have moved from scent to sight: 'Behold,' says Solomon, 'thou art beautiful, O my friend! Behold, thou art beautiful … thine eyes [looking at me are] of doves,' and the maiden replies, 'Lo! thou (too) art fair, my beloved, pleasant indeed.' Like calling to like.[5]

The Hebrew word *nā'îm*, translated here as 'pleasant', can also mean 'befitting'. David as a young man 'was ruddy, and had beautiful eyes, and was handsome' and still, in his old age, calls himself 'the *pleasant* psalmist of Israel' (1 Samuel 16:12; 2 Samuel 23:1). That David's son (and son also of the great beauty Bathsheba) should be 'fair' indeed befits his background. It is a fairness that is natural and human, 'pleasant', rather than regal and majestic.

From the next line, we can see that they have come back to each other's arms and are reclining together, either on the same couch or on the soft ground at their feet. 'Our bed,' she says, 'is among the flowers: our house-beams are of the cedars, our rafters of cypress trees (above)' (1:16-17). Solomon had built his temple 'lining the walls on the inside with boards of cedar; from the floor of the house to the rafters of the ceiling and he covered the floor of the house with boards of cypress' (1 Kings 6:15). But she makes comment that their house, their real home, their temple, *is* nature: cedars around them like the pillars of a house, looking up at a cypress arching above them, the floor a carpet of moss and flowers. There are small variations in the opening of this line in ancient texts: the Vulgate has

---

5 As Rumi says, 'Borrow the beloved's eyes, / Look through those, and you'll see the beloved's face / Everywhere' (Rumi 2011: 175).

'Our bed is flowery' (*floridus*); the Septuagint, 'Our bed is thickly shaded' (σύσκιος), which further confirms they are under the trees; the Masoretic, 'Our couch is luxuriant, fresh and green' (all possible meanings of *ra'ānan*). The prophet Hosea (in the eighth century BCE) described God as an 'evergreen cypress' (*bērôs ra'ānan*), and yet condemns those who 'worship under oak and poplar and terebinth because their shade is good' (Hosea 14:8 and 4:13). In the Song, they seem to be under the tree of God, the cypress, known in Genesis also as the tree of life. In the Garden of Eden there was no need for a temple as the garden itself was the place 'where the Lord walked at the time of the evening breeze' (Genesis 3:8). Here, at the close of evening, they are in that original temple.

Under the trees

SECOND EPISODE
Part 2 – 'Under the trees' (chapter 2, verses 1–7)

Shulamite: 1. '*I am a flower of the field, a lily of the valley.*'
Solomon: 2. '*As a lily among thorns, so is my friend among the daughters.*'
Shulamite: 3. '*As the apple tree among the wood of the forests, so is my beloved among the sons.*

I sat under his shadow, whom I desired, and his fruit was sweet to my taste.

4. *He brought me into the place of stored wine, he set in order the deep love within me.*

5. *Stay me with flowers, compass me about with apples: because I faint away with love.*

6. *His left hand is beneath my head, and his right hand shall encircle me.*'

Solomon: 7. '*I adjure you, O ye daughters of Jerusalem, by the roes and the harts of the fields, that you stir not up, nor make the beloved to awake until she herself please.*'

Ancient versions of the Song give a chapter break here – the setting, however, has not changed, but one can imagine that in this break the lovers have gathered themselves in each other's arms (as is clear from 2:6). They lie together among the flowers on the soft ground. This is where they belong; for the maiden's next words are 'I am a flower of the field, a lily of the valley.'[6]

The fact that there is a chapter break and yet no change in setting suggests the possibility that the curtains have been lowered temporarily on the intimacy of this couple. The question is often raised as to whether the poem expresses actual sexual intercourse at any point. Middle Eastern erotic poetry is usually not so oblique and veiled when presenting sexual intercourse – as something that has to be left 'off the scene', as in a Victorian novel. But here the lovers are hidden from our eyes. The reader is free to fill in the gap as they deem fit. Certainly, this is the point where they really come together but the nature of that union can be read at many levels – as with all things in the poem.

As Solomon foresaw, this rustic setting allows the maiden to be herself. She is no hot-house ornamental plant of the harem or palace. The Hebrew text reveals that the maiden does not, in fact, identify herself with two types of flowers (rose and lily) but simply with the lily – firstly in bud and then in bloom (see Kingsmill 2009: 101, 237).[7] But they are in different locations, the bud is in *sārôn* – which means 'plain' or 'straight' (though there is an assonance with the place name Sharon in Judea which was a place of pasture). The full-grown lily is in *'amāqîm* – 'valleys'. There are many interpretations but at a

6 Jewish commentators have always interpreted this line as spoken by the maiden; Origen read the motion of descent 'to the ground' in this and the previous line as expressing the Incarnation, and therefore interpreted them as spoken by the Bridegroom who for him symbolised the Word (who at this point in the Song becomes flesh). Most Christian commentators followed him, but it is another example of how symbolism often does not fit the natural sense of the text.

7 The lily in Palestine is a wild flower of the fields, unlike the cultivated garden rose; and yet their unmanicured and effortless beauty Jesus sees as more splendid than 'even Solomon in all his glory' (Matthew 7:29).

literal level the phrase expresses her growth from a young girl, plain and with straight chest, to the curves and valleys of womanhood. And yet, in the maiden's statement *both* are in the present tense: she is *still* the child she was. *Sôsanâ*, lily in Hebrew, expresses innocence in Jewish and Christian symbolism, and yet for the Jews it also expressed a full 'embodiment' of Israel.

There is a whole story about a personified *sôsanâ* in the Septuagint version of the Book of Daniel.[8] Susanna (the Greek transliteration) used to walk every day in her husband's garden and was spied on by two ruling judges of Israel. One hot day she decides to bathe in the garden and sends her maids away: 'Bring me olive oil and ointments, and shut the garden doors so that I can bathe.' When she undresses the judges come from their hiding and say:

> Look, the garden doors are shut, and no one can see us. We are burning with desire for you; so, give your consent, and lie with us. If you refuse, we will testify against you that a young man was with you, and this was why you sent your maids away.
>
> (Daniel 13:20-21)

She refuses them and raises the alarm. They testify against her. As high judges, they are believed and the lily is condemned to death. But when she is led off to execution 'God stirs up the holy spirit of a young lad named Daniel' and this boy tests the judges by separating them and asking each: 'If you really saw this woman [with a man], tell me this: under what tree did you see them being intimate with each other?' They name different trees: the first a terebinth, the second an evergreen oak. They are caught out. They didn't in fact see anything except their own lustful desires. Susanna 'was found

---

8 Though not included in the Jewish *Tanakh*, this story was Scripture to the Jews in Egypt and is as old as most of the other parts of Daniel which most scholars date to the early second century BCE.

innocent of a shameful deed.' The moral of the tale is that this 'lily' is a true embodiment of Israel rather than its official judges.

When the maiden in the Song calls herself 'a lily' (*sôsanâ*) – expressing the fact that *in her womanly attractiveness she is as innocent as a child* – could the author of the Song be evoking the story of Susanna, whose attractiveness prompted the wrong kind of looks and intentions? Interestingly the judges, in their imaginations, present two of the types of trees under whose shade idolatrous worship was condemned by Hosea. The lovers in the Song are lying under cypress, symbolising God. If there is a reason for the chapter break in the Song just at this point it seems that the author is giving space for the reader's imagination, but then challenging the reader with the story of *sôsanâ*, that we may not see this maiden as the judges saw her, but that in her beauty 'she is truly a daughter of Israel', as Daniel says of Susanna (13:48).

Solomon responds as if recognising this: 'As a lily among thorns, so is my friend among the daughters.' Instead of the judges in Daniel's story of Susanna, the thorns are the other 'daughters', the women of the harem.[9] With some experience of those hot-house plants he knows they will construe the maiden's intentions in the wrong way – as a concubine who, in wanting an exclusive relationship with Solomon, is aiming way above herself. In the end these thorns will try to stifle and undermine his 'friend'.

But she replies in laughter, 'As the apple tree among the wood of the forests, so is my beloved among the sons.' Surrounded by his palace guards – picked as they were for their stature – Solomon may well have looked – and it may have been a harem joke – like an apple tree among the wood of the forest. It is notable that his father King David was not known for his height in comparison with his brothers

---

9 Rumi, in the *Masnavi* (verses 374–6), reflects on institutions which pamper rather than restrain carnal nature: 'Man's animal-soul is a pyramidal thorn-structure / No matter how it is arranged it pierces whatever it touches / Burn these thorns (with the renunciation of sensual passion) and stay close to the friend' (Rumi 2000: 84).

(1 Samuel 16). But still the maiden sits under the shadow of the one whom she desires, and she discovers that what sets the apple tree apart from the large trees is really its fruitfulness (and also, maybe, its rarity: apples are not a cultivated fruit in Palestine). 'His fruit was sweet to my palate', literally 'throat'. In the very name of the apple tree that satisfaction is expressed: the Hebrew word *tappûah* implies aroma *pûah*, a variation of *rûjh*, breath. Hence, Jerome's use of respiratory 'throat' rather than gustatory 'taste' (as in modern translations) fits the fact that the apple was known rather more for its fragrance than for its savour. The apple tree bears flowers in spring and fruits in the autumn, unlike the 'wood' of the forest it never seems hard or dead. Apples are referred to four times in the Song, and nowhere else in the Bible. Later tradition, however, has seen it as the fruit of the bitter tree of the Garden of Eden, that set the teeth of the woman against the man and the man against the woman. Even if this is taken into account, here, in this new garden, the 'fruit is sweet' and that relationship is restored.

The question of 'which tree are they lying under?' is taken away from the old dualism of 'idolatry versus the God of Israel' (Hosea) or 'lust versus innocence' (Daniel) by the maiden's simple statement of relationship: 'I sat under *his* shadow.' As if to say, 'Do not judge our relationship from anything outside or above us – we are a law unto ourselves.' The bud of the lily is also the fully sexual woman, for she has found for herself the tree of life, 'whom I desired, and *his* fruit was sweet to my taste'.

The maiden's next words are nearly exactly an echo of 1:3, and yet now, explicitly, the inner chamber or storeroom *is for wine*. In contrast to the previous 'I am', 'so is', 'I sat' (2:1-3), 2:4 implies movement (dative): 'he brought me', so here, if anywhere, there is a change of setting, but as there is no Masoretic paragraph break or obvious change in the dialogue, the episode continues.

In the garden, one presumes, there is a house for the maiden's lodging. The garden, as we find out later in the Song, contains a vineyard (2:13, 6:10). So it may well be that this wooden house also served the function as a store-place for the new wine. The evening is getting late, the king must return to his palace, the maiden must be brought to the house where she can dwell, separate from the harem. So, literally, he brings her 'into the place of stored wine,' where a comfortable room has been prepared for her.

No doubt there are a legion of allegorical meanings here – which need not concern us in this narrative interpretation. Most of them talk about inebriation with God. However, the maiden's experience (in the Septuagint and Vulgate) is that 'he set in order the deep love within me' – an experience rather of 'settling' than intoxication.[10] The Hebrew (in the Masoretic) uses a noun *degel* which can mean 'concern, intention, look, or covering'; its concrete meaning is 'banner' which is why this line has been translated 'his banner over me is love.' Literally, the house that Solomon has provided for her, away from the eye of the harem, is a sign of his love, his concern, and also his cover for their relationship, his intention that they meet 'away from all that.' Also, in a practical sense, as a covering from 'the dew of the night' (which she mentions at 5:2). She needs this shelter physically, but also so that she has the peace to assimilate and compose the 'deep love' which has arisen within her.

She needs this protection for she is, by now, *deeply* in love. 'Support me with flowers,' she says, 'compass me about, surround me with apples: because I faint away with love.' She is in a dream of flowers and apples, as a child, tired from an excess of joy, she rests in his arms as he leads her to the bed and lies down with her. 'His left hand is beneath my head, and his right hand shall encircle me.' Supporting, protecting. And the maiden falls asleep in his arms.

At this point, we can see the king leaving. His intention is to spend time with her but he is concerned to avoid the insinuations of the court and harem that he is abandoning them to find his life and his

---

10 This form of intoxication must be resolved into what Jewish and Christian mystics have called 'a sober drunkenness'.

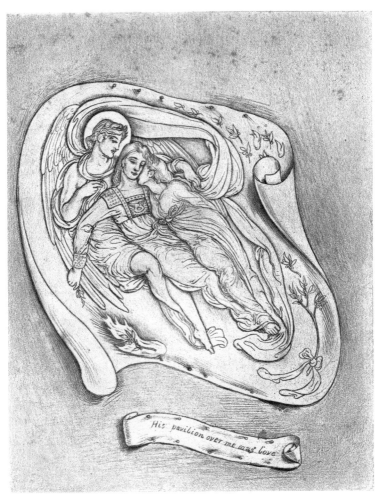

Simeon Solomon, *The Wedding Night*, from *Eight Designs*
on the Song of Songs (1878)

love elsewhere. He has decided it is wisest to return to his palace at night. She carefully gets up; in the light of the moon through the lattices of the garden house he looks one more time at the sleeping maid, and draws himself away, closing the door behind him. He makes his way across the fields to another small store-house where the maiden companions have had a room and living quarters prepared. He calls to them from outside, 'I adjure you, O ye daughters of Jerusalem, by the roes and the harts of the fields, that you stir not up, nor make the beloved to awake until she herself please.' The friendship of the maiden with these others (as has been seen in the opening episode) must give space now for her rest, not for enquiry as to what had happened.

For Solomon, this is serious enough for him to give a very solemn and earnest request; none of the ancient versions say that he 'orders' them – something one would expect from a king. Nor does he 'demand it' on the authority of his own kingship, or even of the God which he, as king, represents. Rather he 'urges' as one who doesn't have authority in himself to tell them what to do. Invoking the spirits of nature, appealing to their natural sense as women – to give another woman the peace and privacy she needs. It may be that, so worried is he about 'news' getting back to the harem and of their influence on the maiden, that he has arranged things so that *they do not know* it is the king who is visiting this maiden. For all they *know* this has all been prepared for the sake of some favoured courtier. Why would the king bother to leave his harem to meet a concubine? No, this has – in their eyes – been arranged so that a courtier can 'enjoy' a royal concubine. But Solomon does not want the maiden to have to pretend to them, he wants her to be left in peace. He also recognises that she, at some interval soon, will *need* someone to talk to, so they are only urged to leave her 'until she herself please'.

This is the first of four adjurations in the Song (also 3:5, 5:8, 8:4). Commentators have seen the evocation of wild animals (rather than God) as guarantors of an oath as signs of pagan influence (see Keel

1994: 92). However, the Song is divine poetry, it is not a poetic expression of Jewish theology. The female roes and harts of the field are perfect poetic images here; these shy and easily frightened creatures evoke the need for peace and distance that the king urges. Their nascent love must be carefully cultivated in this peaceful sanctuary. But these animals are also fleet and sure-footed in the high places as he knows this maiden is, with the deep things she is experiencing, with the possibilities of going where no one has gone before.

The invocation of roes and harts also reflect Proverbs supposedly written by Solomon:

> Let your fountain be blessed,
> Rejoice on account of the wife of your youth.
> A loving hind and a gracious doe,
> Let her breasts fill you at all times,
> That with her love you may be intoxicated continually.
>
> (Proverbs 5:18-19)

These wild but gentle animals came to the mind of Solomon when he took his last look at this maiden as he had to leave, with the intoxication of her love brimming in his heart. At that moment this mysterious maiden, who seemed to come from nowhere, seemed to him Lady Wisdom who, as a young man, he had devoted his life to. He recognises, at this point in the Song, the fount of wisdom that has given him this woman, and that she herself is this fountain. She is a child of Wisdom.

Springtime

THIRD EPISODE
'Springtime' (chapter 2, verses 8–17)

Shulamite: (Soliloquy on awakening) 8. *'The voice of my beloved, behold he cometh leaping over the mountains, springing across the hills.*

9. *My beloved is like a roe and a young hart. Lo! He himself standeth behind our wall, looking through the windows, watching (me) through the lattices.*

10. *Lo! My beloved speaketh to me: Arise, hasten, my friend, my dove, my fair one, and come!*

11. *For winter has now passed over, the rain has subsided and gone away.*

12. *The flowers have appeared in our land; the time of singing is come: the voice of the turtledove is heard in our land:*
13. *The fig tree hath brought forth her green figs: the vines in blossom yield up their sweet odour.*

Arise, my friend, my beautiful one, and come!'

(After an interval) 14. *'My dove in the clefts of the rock, in the hollow places of the wall, show me thy face, let thy voice sound in my ears: for thy voice is sweet, and thy face is comely.*

15. *Catch for us the little foxes that destroy the vines, for our vineyard hath flowered.*

16. *My beloved to me, and I to him, who feedeth among the lilies.*

17. *Until the mid-day approach, and the shadows decline.*

Come back again! Be, O my beloved, like to the roe and to the young hart upon the mountain of Bether.'

Picture a little house in a small clearing, perhaps in a thickly wooded valley, with the tree-clad slopes of the hills rising near at hand. Country-bred as she is, the maiden has probably awakened with the dawn. Onto the awakening of nature, she projects a dream of her lover's return. Her soul yearns for the one she loves, and in her imagination, she hears him and sees him like the sounds and sights of spring. This part of the Song became known in the Provençal tradition as an *alba*-song, a morning *raga* in Indian music.

It is clear by now that the encounter is in springtime – whenever plants are mentioned in the Song they are in their budding or first flowering, expressing the blossoming of love. The consistency of this speaks again of the unity of the text, from chapter 2, 'The fig tree hath brought forth her green figs,' to chapter 7 where mandrakes are 'giving up their fragrance.' Fig trees in the Holy Land produce unripened figs in May (when Jesus curses the unproductive fig tree as he goes up for Passover in April it was a symbolic gesture, the tree itself could not be blamed as figs are not edible until June). Likewise, the mandrake is a rhizome (whose root is used as an aphrodisiac), which produces a scented fruit above ground only for a brief period in late spring. May, whose zodiacal sign is the house of Venus, and also Our Lady's month: an appropriate month for a song that celebrates the feminine.

The maiden imagines her lover's voice summoning her into the new paradise that *is* their relationship. She likens him to exactly those fleet and sure-footed animals which he had evoked the evening before, as if her sleep had been impressed by these graceful symbols of wisdom. On waking she wishes her beloved back. In a half-dream, she pictures him moving swiftly over the Judean hills that separate this garden from the city, him arriving at the wall that surrounds the garden – 'our wall', as the maiden companions also dwell within – then, in her imagination, he is there outside *her* house, peering through the wooden screen at the door. All these are the Wisdom motifs: 'Happy is the man who watches at her [wisdom's] doors,' says Proverbs 8:34. Sirach says, 'Happy the man who peeps in at her [wisdom's] windows' (14:23). In her reverie, she imagines being as joyful as one who searches for wisdom. She even hears him speaking, bubbling over with that joy, summoning her forth, encouraging her, consoling her after the 'winter' of her troubles.

Simeon Solomon, *The Invitation to the Bride*, from *Eight Designs on the Song of Songs* (1878)

'Arise, my friend, my beautiful one, and come!' But the scene, we have inferred, does not take place in his real presence, and, after 2:13, there is a pause, a reality check, and she comes out of her dream. The Masoretic text gives here a paragraph division implying just such a pause. Maybe she even rises from her bed to open the door and look for him, but he is not there, and there is no sign of his approach. A shadow falls, reminding her of the obstacles that hold them apart, how obligations to the realm prevent his coming to meet her again so soon: as king, he cannot come in the morning, she can only expect him in the evening. Her next words, 'O my dove …', express her longing. She remembers his gentle sweetness with her the evening before, but also that he is the leader of Israel. He is not there because he is up in the royal palace on Mount Zion.

'My dove in the clefts of the rock, in the hollow places of the wall': as we have seen, that most un-dovelike leader of Israel, Samson, had 'hidden in the cleft of the rock' after the loss of his wife (Judges 15:8). But before him another leader, Moses, had dwelt 'in the clefts of the rock' on Sinai (Exodus 33:22). The maiden's dove is rather in Zion, which means 'fortress' but was also known as 'the rock'. The Septuagint has in the 'protection' (σκέπη) of the rock. Septuagint and Vulgate locate this rock as 'close by the walls' or 'in the curve/hollow of the wall.' The palace of David was indeed built on the perimeter of the old city walls of Jerusalem. Within the walls of his castle this present leader is withheld by the task of his regal duties. Yearning, the maiden poetically petitions him from the far distance of her pastoral sanctuary, beckoning for him to come to the clefts/openings/windows of his 'rock' to let her witness him, bidding him speak to her from 'the hollow places of the wall', which also imply the aperture of a window.

This short verse has a paragraph break after it as well, as if, in recognising his distance, she has paused again to think. If he, Solomon, is at his royal duties then let him do what he has to do to protect and preserve their love. 'Catch for us,' she says, 'the foxes, the

little foxes that destroy the vines, for our vineyard hath flowered.'
Stop, in other words, the gossip and rumours that will already be
circulating in the palace about them, which, left ungoverned, might
'*destroy the vines*' of their ripening love. The wily women will never
understand that, quite simply and exclusively, 'my beloved is mine,
and I am his.' She knows that the taboos, prescriptions and conventions of harem life and the burdens of royal duties are the big foxes
which may indeed inhibit her lover's freedom to embrace the love
they have for one another. For his sake he must overcome them, for,
she knows, he is not one who will be nourished by the pomp and
structures of the palace, not 'he who feedeth among the lilies'.

She is willing to wait 'until the day approaches and the shadows
[created by the rising sun] decline'. Their blossoming love will have
troubles, but the midday will come, they will be reunited once more.
'Come back again! Be, O my beloved' she implores in eulogy across
the hills, 'like to the roe and to the young hart upon the mountain
of Bether'. The mountain of Bether means, literally, mountain of
separation or cutting – from the Hebrew *beter*. It refers to no geographical space but speaks of their having to be apart for most of
the day. Bether also evokes the covenant between them – a covenant
in Hebrew is *cut*, not made, in memory of Abraham's sacrifices in
which animals were 'cut' (Genesis 15:10). Their very separation shows
that the union between them is unbreakable (as in a covenant), for
they live in each other's hearts. This does not mean, however, that
she does not feel the pain of separation. In this whole episode she
is alone, longing for his return.

A tenacious maiden

FOURTH EPISODE
Part 1 – 'A tenacious maiden' (chapter 3, verses 1–5)

Shulamite: (Soliloquy as night falls) 1. *'In my bed by night I sought him whom my soul loveth: I sought him and I found him not.*

                2. *I will rise, and will go about the city: by the quarters and the streets will I seek him whom my soul loveth.'*

                (In the city): *'I sought him, and I found him not.'*

                (After an interval) 3. *'The watchmen who keep the city found me: Have you seen him whom my soul loveth?*

                4. *Even as I had a little passed by them, I found him whom my soul loveth: I held him.*

                I will not let him go, till I shall bring him into my mother's house, and into the bed-place of her that brought me forth.'

Solomon: (On returning to the Garden) 5. *'I adjure you, O ye daughters of Jerusalem, by the roes and the harts of the fields, that you stir not up, nor awake the beloved till she herself please.'*

The maiden has, in fact, been waiting all day, and lovers' hours are an eternity. The king had made no intimation as to when he would come back; but evening has come and still no sign. His duties have detained him, no doubt, but in his absence, she is beginning to lose any sense of his presence with her. Is he really the faithful man she imagines him to be? She retires to her bed in a state of loss: 'In my bed by night I sought him whom my soul loveth: I sought him and I found him not.' It may be supposed that she did, at first, fall into a light sleep: filled perhaps with dreams in which she seemed to be still in the company of her lover. These may have been so vivid that, in suddenly awakening, she is unable, for the moment, to realise that he is not with her – instinctively reaching forth her hands in the darkness, groping in the emptiness: then with a quick pain and a sinking of heart, realising that she is indeed alone. The maiden by this time is deeply and irrevocably in love: her entire being – her soul – is given over to this love. 'The one whom my soul loves' is repeated four times in this short episode. The gifted writer of the Song is willing to sacrifice elegance here, repeating a phrase to emphasise the *fixed intent* of the maiden's love: a choice deep and permanent in her soul.

She responds to his absence with a strange, steady, half-dreaming purpose to go to the city to find him, a purpose which in fully awak-ened everyday consciousness would seem hopeless. It is too much to be held in a state of suspension, not knowing when he will next come to her: she decides to take the initiative and go to the city and see if she can find a back-way into his guarded palace. Reaching the city, she repeats the words she had uttered on her bed – 'I sought him but found him not' – but with a growing weariness, realising the impos-sibility of her attempt, perhaps even with the beginnings of despair.

However, her lover the king had already foreseen just such an occurrence – could it be that his absence, as mystical commentators through the generations have said, was precisely intended to prompt her response in 'seeking him'?

> At first she sought but could not find, but when she per-severed it happened that she found what she was looking for. When our desires are not satisfied, they grow stronger, and becoming stronger they take hold of their object.
>
> (Gregory the Great 1971: 34)

Anyway, his royal command has allowed her to pass unmolested and unharmed through the city walls and watches (cf. Isaiah 62:6: 'Upon your walls, O Jerusalem, I have set watchmen; all the day and all the night'). By this time the king is also deeply missing his maiden. The Zohar, a classic text of medieval Kabbalah which will be assessed in Part Three, commentating on this part of the Song, notes just his state of mind and affirms also our reading of the 'rock' as the palace in Zion:

When the Holy King begins to yearn for the Queen
He climbs up on roofs, runs down stairs, scales walls;
He peers through the holes in walls just to see if she comes!
When he catches a glimpse of her he raises the cry.

(Moses de Leon 1983: 157)

She is watched on her walk from the royal garden on the outskirts, through the 'streets and the quarters' towards the palace, until she is met by the watchmen themselves, and behind them their master – 'him whom (her) soul loves'. 'I found him,' she says, 'I held him. I will not let him go.'

Throughout the whole of this episode, as the maiden's words bring it before our eyes, there is nowhere any suggestion of apprehension, or sense of danger on her part: this girl is completely fearless. She does not collapse into his arms like an incoherent and sorely frightened child. Instead, there is probably the sudden pause in her slow walk, as the dark figure looms suddenly a few paces before her: then a low, glad cry as she steps swiftly forward and almost fiercely gathers him to her, with fully as much force in her embrace as in his embrace of her. The intensity of her purpose and steadiness of her will is revealed in her words.

Her lover, having foreseen the crisis and prepared for it, now lets her take the initiative – one thing is for sure, she will lead him away from the palace. She leads him through the city seeking a place where they can be alone together. In the past, her mother's bed-place was often her only refuge from the hostility and insolence of 'her mother's sons' (reawakened now in the foreboding she has about the royal court). The memory of this peaceful place arises in her mind along with the necessity to cement their relationship. 'Her mother's bedroom' in this context represents the structure of Jewish betrothal rites, which are governed by the female line through whom family descent is traced. Solomon, a few lines later in the Song, recognises this in his memory that it was Bathsheba who had 'crowned him in the day of his espousals' rather than priest or lord of the realm. It is unlikely she leads him to her mother's house: her mother has died and her brothers have *that* house. Where can she – who, unlike the 'foxes … has nowhere to lay her head' – lead him (cf. Matthew 8:20; Luke 9:58)? To the house of Wisdom:

> Wisdom has built herself a house …
> and proclaimed from the city heights:
> 'Who is ignorant?' Let him step this way.
> (Proverbs 9:1, 3-4)

Solomon, recognising that he has spent the day away from her at so-called 'important business' that is but *ignorance*, follows her. She is a child of Wisdom and 'Wisdom is justified in all her children'; he lets *her* take the lead (cf. Luke 7:35). Why should it be necessary for him to leave her, merely because night has fallen? Why need they ever be separated, when it is pure bliss simply to be together? All his self-important business is but trifles, 'vanity of vanities, all man's toil under the sun … what of all his laborious days, cares of office, his restless nights? This, too, is vanity' (Ecclesiastes 2:22-23). But there is a wisdom that is real: it is no coincidence that the famous example of Solomon's wisdom given in the Bible is his insight into the nature of motherhood (1 Kings 3:16-28).

Having left the house of her upbringing where does the maiden lead him? Back to the house close to which they had spent their time the day before. All her hopes and thoughts of privacy, intimacy, security, permanence, remoteness from disturbance (comforts associated in the mind of the child with her mother's own room) are now transferred to the private room and bed that he has procured for her. This will be Wisdom's house. She 'will hold (her lover), and will not let him go' until she has drawn him to be with her, even there. It is to be noted that from this point forward in the poem, the initiative and the leadership in all the action passes from the lover to the maiden – from the man to the woman – and remains with her until the end. So, she leads him back, over the hill on the outskirts of Jerusalem, up to the walls of the enclosed royal garden, and past the house of the handmaids towards the small dwelling of the maiden, and *her* bed. Having found 'him whom her soul loveth' and having brought him there, all is well. Laid down together with him, in peace, she may yield to the accumulated physical fatigue – she abandons herself to her rest, supported in her lover's arms, her head upon his chest.

All the king knows, already late at night, is that he does not want them to be disturbed by the ministrations of the handmaids. So, either as they pass the handmaid's house he calls out once again his solemn adjuration, or, in the early morning, after no great lapse of time, when her handmaids come to wake her they are startled at once into silence by those same words, heard before (but two short days ago), of solemn warning. They have nothing to do but withdraw in silence. In the Masoretic text, there is a paragraph break here, and so we can leave the lovers together for a while adding with our own imagination whatever relations *we* feel are fitting for them. At this point, however, the movement of the sacred idyll may be said to have reached a certain climax: the achievement by and between the lovers of a condition of perfect equipoise. If it be true that the Song of Songs is to be considered and read as one of the Sapiential Books, it is in the point of *rest* that the power and presence of divine wisdom may be said to brood most closely and intensely over the human protagonists. These lovers, in their achievement of this state of still equipoise and peace, have themselves become the foothold or abiding place of Wisdom herself: according to Wisdom's own words: 'In all things I have sought *rest*' (Sirach 24:11).

The bridal chamber

FOURTH EPISODE
Part 2 – 'The bridal chamber' (chapter 3, verses 6–11)

Solomon: (Soliloquy at night) 6. *'Who is she that goeth up over the*
desert as a slender rod of the smoke from aromatic (spices),
of myrrh, and incense, and all powders together of the
perfumer?'

(After a pause) 7. *'Lo! Threescore valiant, of the most valiant*
of Israel, surround the bed of Solomon: 8. all possessing
swords, and most experienced in war: every one hath his
sword upon his thigh because of fears in the night.

9. *King Solomon made himself a litter of the woods of Lebanon:*
10. He made its pillars of silver, its support of gold, the
reclining place of purple (cushions): the interior he filled
with love, on account of the daughters of Jerusalem.

11. *Go forth, O ye daughters of Zion, and behold King Solomon in*
the diadem wherewith his mother hath crowned him in the
day of his espousals, in the day of the joy of his heart.'

Masoretic paragraph breaks mark not a change in setting but in the
mode of dialogue. Here, we sense that the maiden is sleeping peace-
fully in his arms, and Solomon is given his first soliloquy. Just as
during dawn in Chapter Two, we have been given a window onto
the maiden's reveries, so here, late in the night of the same day, we
are introduced to the inner world of the male lover.

By the first utterance, then, it is to be seen that it is into something
like a state of vision that the royal lover has now been intromitted
in his vigil over the sleeping maiden. He speaks to himself in the half-
darkness (or the words of the poem may be an embodiment of his
thought). He expresses a state of wonderment bordering on stupe-
faction (a state transcending all normal mental processes), in which
he finds himself after the events of the night. Uppermost on his

mind, as the first word indicates, is wonder: 'Who is she?' *Who – or what – is this girl, who can act in this astonishing fashion?* His outward mind remains in darkness, he makes no attempt to answer his question, makes no futile guesses at the identity of a mystery. To answer himself would be in some way to compare her to 'the others', by using the memories and impressions of them as a reservoir of composite material from which to extract (or rather 'abstract') various qualities and characteristics to be re-combined into a new material image, signifying *her*. But this girl escapes all comparison with other women: to whom, among them all, is she for a moment to be likened? Who, among them all, is in any way to be compared to *her*? No: there is no point of resemblance, except in a common womanhood. And his mind returns in half-dreaming recollection upon his memories – or rather, its confused impressions – of 'the others', by whom he has sometimes lain in a half-darkness just like this.

By long subjection to the regimen of the royal harem, the flesh of these women had become literally saturated with the perfumed unguents and aromatic essences with which it had been deemed fitting and necessary to prepare their bodies for the royal bed. It is but natural, therefore, that the strongest and most prevailing of all the vague and generalised sense-impressions remaining in the mind of the king – that one which should have come to epitomise for him the whole of his experience of women – should be just this: of a warm perfume – of a perfumed warmth. The importance of perfume in this sacred poem cannot be overemphasised and must be borne continually in mind. The strength of the impression of *perfume* in the mind of the king is a basic factor in the poem's very structure. It is most of all under the image of perfume that the closeness of the beloved to the lover is signified.

Thus it is, then, that dreaming alone in the gloom, with the warm body of the sleeping woman supported upon him, it is above all by her perfume that his sense is pervaded and his imagination of her suffused. It being dark, at least so far as the outward and sensory consciousness is concerned there remains this one all-embracing and dominating impression. But in the altogether new and strange mood of exaltation now possessing him, that consciousness is found no longer to exist in isolation from the deeper, inward conscious-ness – what the mystics have called the 'spiritual senses'. Body is no longer autonomous and independent of spirit – spirit no longer abides remotely, in a withdrawn inwardness, from the body; but, for the time being at least, the two are one. Thus, it is that there comes to be induced within him, out of the perfumed closeness of bodily contact, a sharpened sense of the maiden as an intensely *living* being, yet in a unique and exquisitely tender and intimate relation to himself. A sense which might have moved Adam on first awaken-ing to the touch of Eve – Eve meaning 'the living one'. It is only out of this condition of acute 'psycho-physical' awareness of her as a dynamically living personality that the state of wonderment – almost of awe – now supervenes within his mind concerning her: *Who* is she? *Who* can she be? (as Adam might also have asked). At last, out of the complex of shifting impressions, arises that strange, lonely image of a slender column – a mounting, aspiring trail of aroma; like a sign rising from afar in the desert, some remote and secret sacrifice turning all the most precious perfumes conceivable to man into this rare incense.

Picture a desert: a featureless, flat vacuity – an infinite succes-sion of repetitions, an unbroken horizontality. This image points forward to his ensuing reflections on the normal and ordinary relations with 'the others' – with the 'daughters of Jerusalem'. One is exactly like another – all his experiences with them have followed an identical course – all have arrived at a similar consummation – physical – apparently with no particular manifestation of the will by either party. This royal prerogative stretching out before and behind him must have felt like the repetitive monotony of the desert. But out of the midst of this desert now appears in his mind the image of a slender column of aromatic smoke. The *perfume* of this girl, now resting on him in sleep, arises in his nostrils a new sense of exquisite and penetrating sweetness – piercing ever upwards, a spiritualised sense, the steady, resistless *verticality* of something infinitely subtle. And his mind experiences the delighted, vicarious thrill of an almost ecstatic vertigo. As smoke rises infinitely, so his sense of the mystery of this girl seems to expand into heaven: she has become for him at this moment a sacrament of heaven, an outward sign of the full – the unlimited – life of heaven, a sign which carries with it the very taste, smell and touch of heaven.

Already the king had sensed this maiden as not just the 'female' of his own species but a soulmate, the feminine counterpart of his own personality. Now he realises her in a clear state of personal distinction as unique in herself, *other* than himself, not *owned* as part of his cohort. On this night, he has realised her forever on the heights of his own being. She is a 'child of Wisdom' – she manifests wisdom to him. If the Song of Solomon is a 'wisdom text' – as its placing in the Septuagint infers – then it is through the medium of incense and aromatic spices that the path to wisdom is expressed. The encounter with wisdom involves raising the senses to transcendent grace, where fragrance is the manifestation of love.

From these rare altitudes, his attention returns to more accustomed levels and he begins to reflect in general terms upon the two sharply opposed aspects of his now irretrievably divided *double* life: on the one hand as King of Israel, on the other the lover of this maiden. His mind having been raised to Wisdom is now able to survey with heightened perception the other, now almost inconceivably remote, aspect of his life. He muses upon the state of a king in those of its features that are in analogy with his present circumstances; he reflects on the royal bed. He does so, however, with a critical, even cynical, clarity, tinctured with a definite bitterness.

In a marked sense, the whole third chapter of the Song is characterised by the image of the *bed*. It is with this word the chapter begins, and the whole of the maiden's ensuing action arises from the fact that her lover is not with her *in her bed*, and her need to bring him to be with her in it. She finds him and leads him into 'the bed place' of Wisdom. The next five verses are occupied with Solomon's meditations on how *this* bed of hers contrasts with his own bed of state, and then also his own royal travelling bed, or litter.

The elaborate pomp – the posting of guards in the royal bed-chamber, around the central curtained enclosure – viewed from the simplicity of where he now is lying, seems to him ludicrous and bizarre. All those precautions of weaponry because the king is not safe in his bed! Here, quite unguarded, there is no fear. Guards needing to protect him from his own harem – compared to this love!

The first faint light of dawn may be breaking and Solomon, gazing into the darkness above the bed, begins to see the roof of the small wooden house in which they dwell. No fortress, it reminds him rather of the travelling palanquin 'King Solomon made for himself from the wood of Lebanon.' This litter with 'pillars of silver, the support of gold, the reclining place with purple cushions' seems to have been his own construction: made to be borne upon the shoulders of slaves during the royal progressions (undertaken in the fair seasons of the year, to various parts of his dominions). He speaks in the third person, as though of the concerns of another altogether remote from himself. It is almost as though King Solomon has become for him a total stranger – one whom he has never met – with whose mind and motives he has neither sympathy nor acquaintance – whose doings and possessions he views now from afar, with a certain detached and puzzled curiosity not unmingled with contempt. The description of the palanquin (especially in the Masoretic which speaks of 'inlayed stones') resembles the tent bed of the Assyrian general during the siege of Jerusalem described in the Book of Judith: 'Holofernes was resting on his bed under a canopy of purple and gold studded with emeralds and precious stones' (10:21). That Holofernes was Israel's enemy and was, indeed, *not* safe in the night (because of Judith) shows that Solomon may even be regarding *his* royal palanquin with something of horror or at least distaste.[11]

On journeys Solomon would be accompanied by a number of the women of the harem who would share with him in turn, on successive nights, the royal litter when it was set down in a pavilion as a way-station. The Hebrew for the cushioned reclining place used in the Song is *merkāb*, which literally means 'saddle', expressing that this is a travelling seat. The word is found only once elsewhere in the Bible, among the cultic prohibitions of Leviticus, forbidding those with gonorrhoea to take part in Temple liturgy. The use of this particular word, which has only one other place in the Torah, serves as a clue. It shows an association in Solomon's mind, revealing that his reveries are, in the light of his present situation, distasteful and disturbing to him as if he is one contaminated by what happened:

> Every bed on which the one with the discharge lies shall be unclean, and everything on which he sits shall be unclean … Any *merkāb* (saddle) on which the one with the discharge rides shall be unclean. All who touch anything that was under him shall be unclean until the evening, and all who carry such a thing shall wash their clothes … Moreover anything made of cloth on which semen falls shall be washed with water, and be unclean until the evening.
>
> (Leviticus 15:4, 9, 17)[12]

---

11 This would, of course, be a poetic and literary association made by the author of the Song and *read back* into Solomon's sensibility, for the siege was 370 years *after* Solomon's death. Though the Book of Judith can be dated to just over 100 BCE many of the stories may well have gone back to the era in which the Song author was writing.

12 This would not have been a literal situation for Solomon; every measure was taken so that the king would not have to fall under proscription from playing his ceremonial role in the Temple. The harem women would have had to keep the purity laws strictly (especially the prohibition of relations outside the harem); though monitoring their behaviour was never completely foolproof despite the custodianship of the harem eunuchs. For Solomon it is more 'a fear in the night', an association with possible though unlikely dangers coming from the harem, a fear which likewise with *this* maiden needs no 'guards' because of her exclusive and real love for him.

This puts the next line in a different light: 'The interior he be-strewed/ covered with love on account of the daughters of Jerusalem' (3:9-10). Jerome's Vulgate has *contravere*, literally 'spread over', and the Masoretic has a passive participle of the verb *rispâ* – 'to receive ornamentation', to be 'inlaid' like stones in plaster to make a mosaic, remembering how he was 'fitted together' there with the daughters of Jerusalem in lovemaking. The reference to the daughters here led some Victorian commentators to see them as a sort of pious 'sewing-party', busily embroidering a bed-cover as a token of their love and esteem for their king, much as ladies of Paris might cross-stitch slippers for the curate! Another example of how the literal meaning was too shocking and unthinkable for commentators to even *see it*.

Solomon is here remembering his impressions of those nights with a certain bitterness in contrast with this one. In his thoughts, he seems to apostrophise these 'daughters of Jerusalem', bred and nurtured as they have been to the seductive techniques of the harem, on account of whom he 'ornamented with (so-called) love' that covered space. In comparison with what he has now this was no real love, no personal intimacy, in fact was *so impersonal*, he can only think of it now as something that had happened to someone else! A gulf separates such 'love' and what he shares with this companion in the bed where he is now. It would be anachronous to read a moral shame or regret into Solomon's reveries of his past amorous associations, and certainly contempt for the women who provided the services of the harem. The habitual 'use' of the harem would have been seen as entirely normal, indeed indispensable, to the kingly status.

Solomon's sense of alienation from normal usage and tradition, which is depicted here, serves to highlight the mental and moral gulf that separates him from all his previous experience. Has it ever been heard or known – within his own knowledge or that of his fathers – that a woman has taken the initiative in sexual relations (and in such a way as this one), not merely taking him, the king, with her, but purposely drawing him to her own bed? This was not the case between his father and his mother (though nobly wed, Bathsheba was simply *taken* by David). How much more unexpected would it be for a woman to take the initiative in the royal harem? The harem, as a department of the royal household, was completely under *his* direction. The queens and concubines had invariably been 'taken' to *his* bed. Here Solomon has found his spiritual bride, his 'lily among thorns.' Here, in the total absence of any protection, in the simple bed of this extraordinary woman – herself in fearless sleep, in a complete peace – the fantastic contrast closes upon him so that he seems almost to lose the sense of his own identity as the king, speaking as of something foreign and remote – completely 'objectified' before his present consciousness – of 'the bed of Solomon' as of a thing which might never have concerned him. 'In love there can be no fear, but fear is driven out by perfect love' (1 John 4:18); here in this simple bed in the country he is in the ambiance of perfect love (quite unlike the drunken Holofernes!). Solomon has been concerned to raise *this relationship* beyond basic 'desires of the flesh'. 'As soon as Spirit is posited,' Søren Kierkegaard says, 'dread is annulled' (Kierkegaard 1946: 73).

The muted anxiety that lies in the background of Solomon's reveries, however, is that as king he is shackled by his appointed role in life, unable to embrace the freedom offered by this maiden's simple existence. Among the 'does and the harts of the fields' there are no attractions for palace, wealth and status: *she* cannot be one of his concubines, she who seeks the true love of one to one. But the strictures and protocol of his palace place a portcullis in the way of such love: he could hardly dismiss his numerous queens for the sake of a humble girl from the country without political trouble: those marriages cemented alliances, and if they were flouted the state itself would be in danger. The exclusive and all-consuming love this maiden demands challenges the social conventions of the time, placing him in an unprecedented situation, from which no previous experience offered a solution. Why even the patriarchs Abraham and Jacob had, respectively, a concubine and a spare wife. Could he, King of Israel, be expected to be monogamous? The conflict he finds himself faced with, here, makes him weigh up his royal position.

The altogether unprecedented situation he finds himself in awakens Solomon to what is going on spiritually: he is being led and taught by Wisdom. This explains the last lines of this episode in which he repudiates his former relations with the 'daughters', those associates of his past nights, of whom, and from whom, he has learnt so little – and yet so much that he would now forget. He would have them behold him now as he is crowned by Wisdom in a true marriage of his heart. Not in order to 'show them up' but *to help them see what they could be.* Like this maiden he is with, they could also be led by Wisdom (rather than the conventions of the harem). He refers to them no longer as 'daughters of Jerusalem' but 'daughters of Zion.' The phrase is so reminiscent of Psalm 87 (possibly written by Solomon), where 'Zion shall be called mother, for all shall be her children.' Who is this mother? She who has brought him to this 'crowning', to these espousals, she who has set upon his brow this invisible but more than kingly diadem – she whom he calls his 'mother' is none but the divine wisdom itself.[13]

> Go forth, oh you daughters of Zion, and behold King Solomon in the diadem with which his mother has crowned him in the day of his espousals, in the day of the joy of his heart.
>
> (Song 3:11)

Here, with the love of this unknown but unparalleled being, he is truly crowned more regally than with the crown of Israel. One could

---

13 Kingsmill is right when she says: 'The "mother" in the Song points to Wisdom, especially since it was with wisdom that Solomon was crowned in consequence of his request for it' (Kingsmill 2009: 251–2). Except that Wisdom for Solomon was never an 'it', but always a 'she': a mother to him and a wife as these lines in the Song express.

hear Solomon speaking of this nameless and matchless maiden as the possibility for the whole of the daughters of Zion in the words of Isaiah:

> About Zion I will not be silent, about Jerusalem I will not grow weary, until her integrity shines out like the dawn and her salvation flames like a torch. Nations will see your integrity, all the kings your glory, and you will be called by a new name, one which the mouth of Yahweh will confer. You will be a crown of splendour in the hand of your Lord, and princely diadem in the hand of your God; no longer are you to be named 'Forsaken' and your land 'Abandoned' but you shall be called 'My delight' and your land 'The Wedded'; for Yahweh delights in you and your land will have its wedding.
>
> (Isaiah 62:1-4)[14]

This 'mother' is also the one of whom the beloved maiden, on her part, has spoken unconsciously – into whose 'house' and 'bed' she has indeed brought her royal lover; and where – with her pure and unerring intention accomplished – she now rests with him in peace. Thus are the espousals of King Solomon with this maiden fulfilled by divine wisdom, and it is Wisdom who stands guard over them in the stillness, enfolding them with her wings from the terrors of the night, sanctifying their rest. This is an espousal where passion is resolved in a superfine delight. For Wisdom herself said, 'My delights were to be with the children of men' (Proverbs 8:31).

If the handmaids had come early in the morning (which they had been adjured not to do) they would indeed have beheld the bridal chamber in this small wooden cottage. A late Christian Gospel of Philip says that 'those who are united in the bridal chamber shall no longer be separated', and yet, 'no one will be able to see the

---

14 Although the prophet Isaiah lived in the eight century BCE, later chapters (40–66) are probably written in or around the time of the Babylonian exile.

bridegroom and the bride unless they become like them' (Analogues 79, 122; Welburn 1994: 295, 311).

> [Indeed] many of the servants do not behold [for] though the mysteries of the truth are revealed as types and images, the bed-chamber is hidden … Spiritual love is wine and fragrance, all enjoy it who will anoint themselves with it, they also enjoy it who stand apart from them as long as the anointed ones remain there … For the holy of holies has been revealed, and the bed-chamber has invited us in. Even when it is hidden evil is brought to naught … But when it is revealed, then the perfect light will pour out upon everyone, and all those who are in it will receive the anointing. Then the servants will also be free. Those who are separated will be united and will be filled. And all who enter into the bed-chamber will kindle the light … and no one will be able to molest such a one even if they live in the world.
>
> (Analogues 111, 124, 125, 126, 127; Welburn 1994: 305–15)

And yet in the dispensation of the Old Testament the time is not yet ripe for opening the bridal chamber to the view of the world. The last words (or expressions of the unspoken thoughts) of the royal lover were concerning *espousals*. And yet this is a love-relationship of an entirely uncommon and until now unheard-of kind. Solomon imagines the maidservants coming as witnesses to this espousal, but earlier that night they were in fact urged not to come. For the lovers, whether they are affianced in the eyes of others or society is hardly relevant. Their love, and their manner of loving, is entirely their own, *personal* to themselves. The maiden has broken the codes of the harem by coming to him of her own volition and the king has not only permitted this act of audacity, he clearly welcomes her courage. There is no longer any question of a nightly separation.

The primacy of *personhood* even in the bridal chamber is a classic example of how the human and the divine aspects of the poem are intricately linked. 'The Divine Sophia and the creaturely Sophia are not two but one,' writes the theologian Sergei Bulgakov, 'although in two modes of being' (Bulgakov 2002: 61).[15] The young king is being taught wisdom through human love. In the later extrapolation of Christian theology Solomon's prayer for wisdom is answered in the Incarnation: 'Christ Jesus has become for us wisdom from God,' writes St Paul (1 Corinthians 1:30). In this episode, Solomon also speaks 'of what he has seen, heard with his own ears, touched with his hands' (cf. 1 John 1:1). If Wisdom became flesh in Jesus, in the Song she reaches her fullest literary personification in the Hebrew Bible. The allegory has been missed through the centuries because of the Jewish fear that too strong a personification of God's wisdom jeopardises monotheism, and because the specific gender of Christ's incarnation favoured a representation through the male figure in the Song in Christian exegesis. The great gift of the Song, however, is that the maiden is fully human, the Shekhinah has been brought down to earth. This is still within the dispensation of story rather than history, a prefiguration yet 'of one who is to come' – the wisdom of God, open and manifest to all (cf. 1 Corinthians 1:24).

The maiden described

FIFTH EPISODE
Part 1 – 'The maiden described' (chapter 4, verses 1–7)

Solomon: 1. *'How beautiful thou art, oh my friend, how beautiful thou art!*
Thy eyes as of doves were it not for that which lies hidden within them.
Thy hair as a flock of goats, which come up from Mount Gilead.

---

15 Fr Bulgakov (1871–1944) is known for his study of divine wisdom in Christianity.

> *2. Thy teeth as flocks (of ewes), which come up from the washing;*
> *all bearing twins, and there is none barren among*
> *them.*
> *3. Like a thread of scarlet are thy lips: and sweet thy speech.*
> *As a piece of pomegranate, thus are thy cheeks, apart from that*
> *which lies hidden within.*
> *4. As the tower of David is thy neck, which is built with ramparts,*
> *on which hang a thousand shields, all the armour of*
> *valiant men.*
> *5. Thy two breasts are like two young roes, twins of a gazelle, that*
> *feed among the lilies.*
> *6. Until the mid-day approach, and the shadows fall away,*
> *I will go to the mountain of myrrh, and to the hill*
> *of incense.*
> *7. Thou are wholly beautiful, my friend, and there is no blemish*
> *in thee.'*

In the slow gradation of light that is dawn (through which he first saw the wooden rafters of the house) Solomon sits up and now gazes at the maiden. 'How beautiful thou art, O my friend, how beautiful thou art!' The words are spoken slowly, almost as if to himself, giving immediate and unpremeditated utterance to something that has been forming in his mind as he watched her features appear from the dark, and which he now speaks as he sees her eyes open. The epithet 'friend' is heightened later in the Song to 'sister-bride'.[16] As *friends* there is for them no ordinance, no custom, human or divine, to forbid their remaining uninterruptedly together – by night as well as by day. 'What God has joined together let not man [and the conventions of human society] put asunder'

---

16   In the Vulgate it is 'sister-bride', implying one epithet, rather than 'my sister, my bride' as in modern translations. Sister-bride is of course strictly taboo according to the conventions of society. The relationship of this Song also bypasses all attempts of 'the world' to define it. Friendship may be the best way of giving space to the unique working out of a relationship between sexes *according to its own inner dynamic* rather than expectations of others (or ourselves).

(Mark 10:9). In any case, this woman, in the strength and integrity of her perfect innocence and simplicity, would, after the memorable events of that earlier night of separation, in no likelihood allow her lover to quit her side again: 'I will hold on to him and not let go.' At least he will stay with her 'until the breathing – that is the active life – of the day approaches, and the shadows [of morning] fall away' (4:6).

While gazing down on her upturned face, the king dwells with a lover's fondness upon each of her features. There is even (as in other similar scenes to be met with later in the Song) a certain precise sequence of the allusions, by which the direction, or movement, of the vision is indicated. In this present instance, it is downward. The first thing he speaks of are her eyes as they open to him after the night's sleep. Then after a space he continues, dwelling upon each of the separate features which, in their ensemble, make up her complex beauty: 'Thy eyes as of doves were it not for that which lies hidden within them.' The mysterious later part of this line we meet again in verse 3 and later in the Song at 6:6. The Masoretic version in all these verses (6:6 being 6:7 in the Masoretic) gives a more concrete meaning – 'behind your veil.' The Septuagint and Vulgate, however, imply not something hidden (as by a veil), but something hidden *within* which *contrasts* with the previous image. One guesses at a sort of power or strength, which qualifies somewhat the docility, beauty and charm of doves. This impression is all but confirmed in verse 9 (in the next episode) where the lover says that his heart has been 'wounded' by a glance of the beloved ('dove's eyes' do not commonly 'wound'!) It is as if he were saying: 'How is it that within thy eyes, which might be those of a dove for gentleness, so great a power lies hidden?' In a word, this woman is an amazement to him: and it is for this reason that so many of the images he finds for her various perfections can be seen as attempts to explain her fascinating but also bewildering nature to himself. At times even contradictory, he tries to describe her outward charms but stumbles as he realises what he is really encountering is an inner beauty and strength of character.

The metaphors the couple use throughout the poem to celebrate each other have cultural associations within this ancient Jewish society that can help reveal deeper layers of meaning. While gazing into her eyes, he is aware also of the 'night' of her dark and luxuriant hair, framing the face which her eyes illumine: and he says: 'Thy hair as a flock of goats, which come up from Mount Gilead.' The associations of Gilead come from a very early part of the Jewish story as the place where Jacob and Leban make a covenant of reconciliation (Genesis 31:48), where the words *gal* ('heap, wave, billow') and *ēd* ('witness') are put together (Kingsmill 2009: 253).[17] This simile may be compared with a later one at 7:6 where he likens her head to Mount Carmel. Carmel has always been a mountain covered with luxuriant and dark vegetation, oak, pine, olive, laurel, that made it a place to hide for prophets and hermits. Why goats? It took a visit to Palestine to realise; the goats there are dark. The dark hair of the maiden flows over the plane of her shoulders as a flock carrying the darkness of hill trees into the valley below.

With the simile of flocks and the resonance of Gilead still in his mind he continues: 'Your teeth as flocks (of ewes) which come up from the washing; all bearing twins, and there is none barren among them.' The Hebrew word for 'bearing twins' can also be translated 'existing as twins' which makes more sense: the rounded milk-white bodies of sheep new-shorn, passing side by side in even files from the washing-place.[18] However, the final image is one of fertility, as

---

17 The heap of round stones gathered by Jacob and Laban was the symbol of their reconciliation. The roundness of the stones gave a rolling and billowing effect, which may explain a little how it could be associated here with locks of hair.

18 Jewish as well as Greek aesthetics valued symmetry. In the Bible this is a sign of the beauty of God's creation; e.g. Sirach 33:15: 'Look at all the works of the Most High; they come in pairs, one opposite the other'; and Sirach 42:24-25: 'All things are twofold, one opposite the other, and He has made nothing incomplete. One confirms the good things of the other, and who can have enough of beholding His glory?'

if the big teeth (ewes) and little teeth (lambs) are all connected: for each big tooth, there are two little ones. Giving birth to twins was, for the ancient Hebrew culture, a sign of the womb's fecundity. It is a very pastoral image, the maiden's teeth bright clean but not sterile, perfectly pure ('up from the washing') and yet full of life. Even her teeth carry that quality of virginal intactness alongside that of maternal fecundity – *Virgo Deipara* – that is key to her unique character. And the fact that he sees her teeth means that she is smiling at him.

The Hebrew *ke-hût* for the maiden's mouth echoes a Jewish folk tradition, which has roots in the Kabbalah, of wearing scarlet or crimson threads to ward off the 'evil eye'. If this was a practice even at the time of the writing of the Song it implies that Solomon's gaze on the maiden's features is purely loving. Pure love here is also associated with fecundity: a scarlet thread tied about the wrist is mentioned in Genesis 38 when Tamar gives birth to twin boys. A scarlet band or ribbon was also worn on the horns of goats sacrificed at Yom Kippur – as in the famous painting by William Holman Hunt. The Song is full of what in modern literature is called 'free association' whereby in the stream of consciousness one image somehow leads onto another through links that are not always apparent as they come up but are always under the surface (James Joyce's *Ulysses* is the prime example of this, where motifs reoccur once they have been brought to consciousness). The goat image for the hair is likely to be associated in Solomon's memory with a practice of Yom Kippur, the main ritual of the temple he was dedicated to. A scarlet band – and the Latin word Jerome uses, *vitta*, implies band rather than thread – was also worn by priests in Solomon's temple as a badge of office and by vestals and brides as emblems of chastity.

The Hebrew *midhbâr* means 'instrument of speech', so the maiden's speech is sweet both in the *way* and in *what* she expresses. Her cheeks are compared to twin pieces of pomegranate 'apart from that which lies hidden within.' The initial associated link is with the 'sweetness' of her mouth, which lies between and inside her cheeks. But there are other associations: pomegranates were known in ancient Israel as the fruits the scouts brought to Moses to demonstrate the fertility of the 'promised land'. It is traditional even today to consume pomegranates on Rosh Hashana because, with its numerous seeds, it symbolises fruitfulness. It is this power of fertility which 'lies hidden within.' Pomegranate within the conventions of Eastern erotic poetry is an image of the female breast.[19] This accounts for the outer appearance (each piece half of the whole): the contrast between the smooth yellow skin like the surface of the pomegranate and the red blood-like seeds within.

Some rather prudish Jewish scholars believed the pomegranate was the forbidden fruit in the Garden of Eden. Some more legally minded ones corresponded the pomegranate's supposed 613 seeds with the 613 *mitzvot* or commandments of the Torah. The Kabbalah – slightly more fruity – speaks of mystical experience as entering the 'garden of pomegranates'.[20]

For Solomon, however, at the time the poem is set, the image would have Temple associations: Exodus 28:33-34 describes the *me'il* (robe of the ephod) worn by the high priest as having pomegranates embroidered on the hem. Solomon is said to have designed his own coronet based on the pomegranate's 'crown' (calyx). Most notably, 1 Kings 7:13-22 describes the capitals of the two pillars that stood at the entrance of Solomon's temple as engraved with pomegranates – two halves of the pomegranate that led to the inner mystery 'hidden within' the Temple. The body, likewise, is the temple of the soul 'which lies hidden within' (4:3).

Next in his descending vision Solomon describes the firm and

---

19 For Nizami of Ganja (1140–1209 CE), the greatest mystical erotic poet of Persian literature, the word is repeatedly used with this significance (cf. Nizami of Ganja 1924: p. 153 v. 5, p. 187 v. 18, p. 235 v. 6, p. 241 v. 12, p. 246 v. 1).
20 Cf. the book of that title; *Pardes Rimonim*, by the sixteenth-century mystic Moses ben Jacob Cordovero.

beautifully formed neck of the maiden, rising proudly 'as a tower of David' hung round with the shields of its defenders, above the sloping 'rampart' of her breast, a surprisingly martial image emphasising the strength, dignity and uprightness of her character apparent in the carriage of her head upon her shoulders. The complex nature of the impression this woman makes on him is evidenced by the change here from images which have been quite 'feminine' up until now to this markedly 'masculine' metaphor. Hers is a completely feminine beauty, yet he feels the need of masculine images to account for and describe a little of the *strength* he perceives in her – something he likens here to 'all the armour of valiant men.'

His glance travels still downward, and the rampart image dissolves into something soft and tender: 'Thy two breasts are like two young roes, twins of a gazelle, that feed among the lilies.' Here he gives a purely visual physical impression without the complex metaphors of the earlier images. Partly covered and veiled her breasts are in her white night tunic, like roes bending their heads behind the lilies (verse 11 makes clear she is wearing a garment). After the strength of the previous image this one is full of modesty, a reserve, which seems to be so much part of her character. This is a half-playful image, with none of the enigmas of his earlier impressions: shy, retiring creatures, yet full of delicate charm. The image is quite the opposite of the cold exposure of when she was initially 'unveiled' before him. Here her breasts are only partially, and then no more than transiently, visible.

Verse 5 gives the last visual image. From now onward (until verse 6 of chapter 5) the character of the imagery becomes either more generalised and abstract or, when of a concrete nature, only of an olfactory impression. From here, until the sun reaches the meridian and all shadows go, he says he *will make his way* (all versions give a future tense) 'to the mountain of myrrh, and to the hill of incense.' So much of Solomon's praise of this maiden has been filled with binary images – reminiscent of the saying in Ben Sirach: 'Look at the works of the Most High, they come in pairs, one opposite another' (33:15). Literally, the reference is to Solomon's last visual impression: the maiden's breasts, hidden from sight but experienced now as fragrance. Vision involves distance; here Solomon expresses his intention to come to a new closeness to her. An erotic image, and yet the spices are of Temple usage. Figuratively, St John of the Cross links the mountain of myrrh and the hill of incense to 'faith and love [which] are the two guides of the blind; they will lead you, by a way you know not, into the bridal chamber of God' (John of the Cross 1987: 38). Solomon may have been reminded of the day of the dedication of his temple when the priests could no longer see what they were doing because of the incense and he exclaimed, 'Yahweh has chosen to dwell in the thick cloud' (1 Kings 8:11-12). Incense, in ritual use, is a conduit between the earthly and the spiritual worlds, the sense medium through which the transcendent is evoked. As readers, we too can no longer observe the lover and maiden as they lie in each other's arms. Incense does not encourage imagination: in the spiritual life no images pertain to immediate contact with God.

From his next words we see that in this experience Solomon comes to a complete awareness not of any particular characteristic of the maiden's beauty but of her whole self as beauty personified. He beholds her inwardly with the lover's vision as – for him – the one unique embodiment of all beauty, and it is this interior vision which he tries, in his next words, to express: 'Thou art beautiful, O my friend, and blemish is not in thee.' It is his awareness that his arms hold the comprehensible sum of all possible beauty – hidden indeed from the eyes, perceived but confusedly by the scent and contact, but clear and incandescent to the inward consciousness – that speaks in these words.

'Out of Zion's perfect beauty God shines,' the psalmist sings (Psalm 49(50):2). One of the Song's essential themes is this expression of a *transcendent* quality of beauty. Beauty is not a matter of outward appearance but a quality of *being* itself. The transition from the visual to the complete experience – ending in Solomon's final statement – shows that the maiden in the Song is much more than one who looks beautiful, she *is* beautiful. Beauty is no mere appearance: it is both personal (fundamentally *of character*) and interpersonal (the fruit *of relationship*). The love of beauty asks of us as much courage and decision as the search for truth or the practice of goodness.[21] We *choose* beauty: to bow down to the other person as the image of God. As Solomon perceives the maiden appear with the gradual dawning of day, another emerges before a loving gaze. To hear 'You are precious in my eyes and honoured and I love you' (Isaiah 43:4) frees us from shame. To know we are beloved is to be empowered to look with the same love at others. We owe our very being to this vision: 'We all, with unveiled faces, beholding the glory of the Lord, are being transformed into the same image from one degree of glory to another' (2 Corinthians 3:18). The vision of beauty is to see others as God sees them.

'The world will be saved by beauty! I maintain,' says Prince Myshkin in Fyodor Dostoevsky's *The Idiot*, 'that the reason he has such playful ideas is that he is in love' (Dostoevsky 1986: 394). It is exactly the same with Solomon in his Song. Pope St John Paul II comments that in the Song the appreciation of beauty is a mode of love: 'The words of the bridegroom [*sic*] are a language about love and at the same time a language about the femininity of the bride [*sic*], which 'appears' on account of love, so worthy of amazement and admiration.' Beauty is, in other words, *in the love* of the beholder. John Paul notes that 'the bridegroom expresses more directly the beauty of the bride and her attractiveness, being aware of it above all with the *eyes of the body*; the bride by contrast looks rather with the *eyes of the heart* through her affection' (John Paul II 2006: 560). Certainly in this part of the Song it is the lover who looks and speaks,

---

21 As Hans Urs Von Balthasar says, 'She [beauty] will not allow herself to be separated and banned from her two sisters, truth and goodness' (Balthasar 1982: 18).

but this is no monologue, as the maiden responds with the silent language of love expressed through her body, and welcomes him to 'make his way' to the heights of her mystery.

The sister-bride

FIFTH EPISODE
Part 2 – 'The sister-bride' (chapter 4, verses 8–11)

Solomon: 8. *'Come from Lebanon, my bride, come from Lebanon, come; thou shalt be crowned from the top of Amana, from the summit of Senir and Hermon; from the dens of lions, from the mountains of the leopards.*

9. *Thou hast wounded my heart, my sister-bride, thou hast wounded my heart from one glance of thy eyes and one curl of thy neck.*

10. *How beautiful are thy breasts, my sister-bride! More beautiful are thy breasts than wine and the odour of your ointments above all aromatics.*

11. *A honeycomb distilling sweetness are thy lips, (my) bride: honey and milk abide beneath thy tongue, and the perfume of your garments as the incense of Lebanon.'*

There is a paragraph break in the Masoretic text at the beginning and end of this section and it does give a distinct episode framed by the word 'Lebanon' in the first and last line. The sense of tall Lebanon cedars gives the impression that the maiden and Solomon are now standing, and he is struck again by her height.[22]

The mountains mentioned are parts of the Lebanon range, and

---

22 A fragment of the Song in the Dead Sea Scrolls gives a slight variant here from other versions in having a statement of fact rather than an imperative. The fragment states twice, 'You come from Lebanon', the request, in the next line, is 'Look down from the top of …' The emphasis is that she is already one who dwells on the heights. 4Q107 Canticles manuscript, the scroll from Qumran Cave 49, dates from the first century BCE.

carry associations evoked by the moral strength and beauty of this maiden: *Amana* means 'firm' or 'constant', *Senir* is an Amorite word meaning 'coat of mail' or 'breastplate', *Hermon* means 'the high place' and has associations of divine consecration (the dew of Hermon of Psalm 42). It is the virtues who 'dwell on the heights' (Isaiah 33:15-16). Likewise the wild aloofness of mountain lions and leopards; an image prompted by the supple strength and loneliness he perceives in the maiden. The lover repeatedly urges her to come '*from*' there. In her descent to the valley of human possibility she will be crowned *from the place from where she has come.* Isaiah 57:15 says, 'This is what the high and exalted One says – he who lives forever and whose name is holy – 'I live in a high and holy place, but also with the one who is contrite and lowly in spirit.' Solomon may half hope she may accept the highest mark of honour *he* can give, to be his bride, his queen, his royal counterpart at the court (O what scandal it would cause!). But this, he knows, would involve a descent for her from a much higher and more innate nobility.

With each encounter Solomon is becoming progressively more entranced by this maiden, and is now in a state of deep transport. The yearning in his speech takes on something of a frenzied flight of imagination. He calls the maiden 'my bride' though nowhere in the poem is a marriage in the eyes of the world implied. The woods and perfumes 'of Lebanon' echo again the Temple: cedar of Lebanon was used especially in the Holy of Holies (1 Kings 6, 16; Isaiah 60:13). At the centre and yet distinct from the rest of the Temple this sanctuary was what made the whole Temple holy. So, the union of hearts of these two lovers is what makes all true marriages. Lebanon is mentioned six times in the Song (three in this present episode). In each case the reference expresses a supreme standard of value, the ultimate fineness, rarity, preciousness. Hence, here the king seems to beseech the maiden to descend from the heights of her perfection to a nearness to him. As the High Priest on the feast of Yom Kippur processed '*from*' the Holy of Holies (associated with the heights of mountains) to imbue the body of the Temple (symbolising the world where people actually lived) with holiness.

The symphony of mountain imagery in the last three verses shows the lover is under the spell of heights. One feels he suffers under the recognition that in being together they have entered the Holy of Holies (which the High Priest does only by *giving up his life* – carrying the blood of the sacrificed goat as *his* blood). Can Solomon really be expected to lay down his *whole* life for her? 'Thou hast wounded my heart, my sister-bride, thou hast wounded my heart from one glance of thy eyes and one curl of thy neck.'

The momentary sense of possession by which the lover seemed to hold within his embrace the living essence of beauty now leaves the wound of longing. He reaches out offering to her all that is humanly possible, but realises that this is a beauty way beyond what this world can grasp. As the Sufi mystic Ibn al-Arabi centuries later said in his *Tarjuman al-Ashwaq* (2:7), 'Wild is she, none can make her his friend.' Or another Sufi, Manjhan, concerning the eponymous princess in the sixteenth-century *Madhumālatī*:

> Just as the day grew radiant when she revealed her face, the day darkened as she let down her locks. They were not tresses but the sorrows of lovers become the adornments of her head. Whoever in this world saw her locks, lost all awareness of his own condition. When this blessed virgin let loose her hair, the world was shrouded in darkness, the God of love spread out his net to snare the souls of grieving lovers. Did you know why the world was filled with such sweet fragrance? Did the musk deer open its pod? Or did Madhumālatī let loose her hair?
>
> (Manjhan 2000: 34)

And yet she is turned to him. This high beauty is not abstract but a vital figure who stands with him. It is not his *eyes* that are wounded as if by an inaccessible aesthetic but his *heart* by the excess of love brought forth by specific instantiations of her loveliness. There is a real woman behind this vision, and no question of coldness from her. Instead of keeping him at a distance (as in the unattainable beauty and aloofness of the *femmes fatales* of courtly love literature) she clasps him to herself as she would a lost child, holds him to her bosom. A protective gesture, not so much to console her lover but to communicate strength to him, an instinctive response that comes from the depth of her femininity, of her capacity for empathy, knowing as her Maker did before her that 'it is not good that man should be alone' (Genesis 2:18).

Just at the point when his love is *too much for him* and he bows his head, having to avert his eyes (that have been the doorway to his heart), a quick, maternal, sheltering impulse from the depth of the maiden's being gathers him to her. As if she would recall her lover from that plunge of the spirit's eye, of which she herself has been the innocent occasion, into the unfathomable gulf that separates the creature from its creator – the pain of the human eye when faced with a beauty not of this world. Back into the warmth and safety of close communion with herself – with his 'helpmate' – she seeks to shut out the void in the most natural of ways, simply by smothering his eyes upon her breasts. As if she were to say, 'Here, where you have already learned to find peace, now again find it – and find here also strength and healing.'

The lover's next words seem to indicate a returning calm: even though still, perhaps, as of a child hushed and pacified. He uses words very similar to his earlier awareness at the opening of the poem: 'How beautiful are thy breasts, my sister-bride! More beautiful are thy breasts than wine and the odour of your ointments above all aromatics.' The Septuagint has, at this point, rather a question: τί ἐκαλλιώθησαν μαστοί σου – 'Wherefore (or for what reason) have thy breasts been made beautiful?' The main verb is in the past passive. This shows a new awareness in the lover of what we might call the *source* of the maiden's beauty, or its *telos*, its end, purpose or goal.

'Who made thee *thus*, and why?' The answer seems to be 'For him.'

Now the vision of the depths or heights of divine beauty is felt (through the two senses of smell and touch) to be close, and warm, an incarnate and humanised beauty communicated through a living and breathing person. Again, the impression comes to prevail in him of a beauty far sweeter, yet far more penetrating and nearer to tears, than any a simply sensuous passion or inebriation could induce. This is no delirium of the blood but, as the mystical interpreters of the Song have intuited, a state of contemplation, finding the creator *in* the creation, the source of beauty *in* what is beautiful.

In the verses that follow we are allowed to see that the maiden now lavishes upon her lover still further marks of her love. We may think of her taking his face between her hands and lifting it to her own, and as pressing her lips long and firmly upon his, for he says: 'A honeycomb distilling sweetness are thy lips, (my) bride: honey and milk abide beneath thy tongue'.

And now having strengthened and revived him (as with milk and honey) the maiden makes a further gesture conveyed to us by the concluding words of this same verse: gently disengaging herself from his arms, she steps back a pace; and, letting fall her night-vesture to the floor, stands now before him in her unveiled simplicity. For the next words are these: '… and the perfume of your garments as the incense of Lebanon' – as the waves of fragrance rise up to him upon the air disturbed as it might be by the sudden rustling fall of her nightrobe about her feet, as we hear some verses later her statement, 'I have put off my tunic' (5:3).

This gesture of hers is not in response to any plea or suggestion of her lover: he has nowhere been seen to convey by word, sign or even mute entreaty that it is in his mind to expect *this* token of her love. Here, as in so many places in the romance, the maiden takes the initiative in unexpected ways (something lost in most religious commentaries tied as they are to models of male guidance and leadership). Nor is this the calculated gesture of the courtesan – the character of this woman as we have already seen is innocent of any desire to play the games of the harem. It is her own deliberate will and act to undress before him, an inspiration that comes from deep within *her*. It gives back to him the experience of her as a whole *but within the mode of vision*, which before could only take in particular aspects of beauty. The image of burning cedar sticks, used outside the Holy of Holies in the Temple, points again to a moment of *apophasis*, where a vision is both given and hidden within a cloud of incense.

The closed garden

FIFTH EPISODE
Part 3 – 'The closed garden' (chapter 4, verses 12–16)

Solomon: 12. *'A garden closed up is my sister-bride, a closed garden, a fountain sealed.*
13. *Oh the perfumes sent forth from thee … a paradise of pomegranates … with the fruits of fruit trees … camphor with nard … 14. nard and saffron … sweet cane and cinnamon … with all the woods of Lebanon; myrrh and aloe … with all the most noble ointments.*
15. *O fountain of the gardens: O well of the living waters, which flow out with vigour from Lebanon.*
16. *Arise, O north wind, and come O south wind, blow over my garden and let flow the aromas thereof.'*

The paragraph break here, as elsewhere in the Masoretic text, implies a space in the action, which the reader is free to fill, or leave, as their imagination please. However, the implication of the next line is that the cloud of incense is no smokescreen for 'normal' sexual relations: 'A garden closed up is my sister-bride, a closed garden, a fountain sealed.' In this 'gap' we might, however, picture the royal lover absorbing the impact of the subtle yet powerful magnetisms that flow out from the force of this maiden's love, from the unveiled body standing before him. And it may well be that after a long pause he speaks these new words. His utterance, when at last the words come forth, is hushed and slow – almost as if he were attempting to formulate to himself perceptions too deep, delicate and remote for words. He speaks in a low voice, iterating and reiterating the words, which are the central line of the Song. St John Paul recognises the image of the sister-bride as 'a garden closed up ... a fountain sealed' has a 'key significance in the poem as a whole', for in them 'the bride presents herself to the eyes of the man as the master of her own mystery' (John Paul II 2006: 570).

The maiden is impenetrable according to most of the senses – one cannot see into or touch the garden, or drink the water within. However, the sense faculty in which this encounter is now happening (as the previous line made clear) is that of scent, and through the olfactic mode the garden can be entered and experienced. It is scientifically proven that with the elimination of the other senses the one surviving sense faculty is greatly enhanced and aroma here dominates the lover's impression of the maiden as specifically a fruit garden. He is able to distinguish particular scents as he did the visual instantiations of her beauty: 'Oh the perfumes sent forth from thee ... a paradise of pomegranates ... with the fruits of fruit trees ... etc.' The list emphasises again, in the words of Solovyov, that 'the object of true love is not simple, but twofold': 'camphor with nard ... nard and saffron ... sweet cane and cinnamon ... myrrh and aloe.' As Ben Sirach said, 'the works of the Most High, they come in pairs.' 'All the most noble ointments', delicate fragrances diffused from her, from the living warmth of her body.

The lover distinguishes a mixture of natural scents – reminiscent of a garden – and cultivated ointments evocative of the 'noble' or royal perfumery of the harem. The garden and the woman are breathed together as a living *symbol*. The Greek, *sym-ballein*, means

Simeon Solomon, *The Guarding of the Bride*, from *Eight Designs
on the Song of Songs* (1878)

'throwing together' two things so that we see their similarity and access a larger whole. This putting together of the closed garden and woman is expressed visually in much medieval art, most famously the early sixteenth-century Flanders 'Lady and the Unicorn' tapestries which depict the five senses – taste, hearing, sight, smell and touch – and a sixth entitled 'My only desire' (see Plate 5 in the coloured plate section). The unicorn (often accompanied by a lion) represents the masculine dimension in relation to the garden and the female figure. 'My only desire' shows the sense of 'sight' through which the unicorn comes to self-knowledge in the maiden's arms – being able to see himself through his relation to her. According to myth only a pure virgin (the enclosed garden symbolising her virginal womb) could capture a unicorn. Often the garden had a fountain. Both of these are often associated with the Virgin Mary. A painting by Stefano da Verona (1435) of *The Madonna of the Rose Garden* (see Plate 6) shows both the perimeter of the garden and the fountain to the right of Mary as guarded by angels. From her womb, however, the Christ child comes forth like a spring of living water.

It is notable that among the list of scents given by the lover are new ones – saffron, sweet cane, cinnamon, aloe. These all have links with medicinal or culinary use. These are juxtaposed with scents with 'sacral' associations – camphor, nard, cedar and myrrh. The very scent of this maiden is, in other words, for him, a mixture between the homely and the holy, the body and the spirit. She is sweet to his taste, a balm to his soul, and health to his limbs.

We have, in these lines, a haunting echo of the lost paradise. Earthly beauty is not that paradise, for it fades and dies with age, and yet the dream of all cosmetic culture is of the incorrupt and immortal body. For the lover, at this moment, this maiden is that original garden now 'closed', for long ago 'God drove out the man; and he placed at the east of the garden of Eden cherubim and a flaming sword, turning every way, to guard the way of the tree of life' (Genesis 3:24). Before him now stands that very tree. The sequence of interrelated images growing naturally out of each other is one of the hallmarks of the Song (and key to its interpretation). In the *flow* of her perfumes to him, a new image arises in the lover's mind: the waters flowing from the tree of life making all that dwells in the garden alive: 'O fountain of the gardens,' he says in a half-dreaming voice, 'O well of the living waters, which flow out with vigour from Lebanon.' In the shifting images of dreams the maiden is now associated less with 'the garden', than with a deep and hidden principle internal to the garden.

The maiden is now to her lover the 'fountain' – the 'guarded or sealed fountain' of 'gardens', that is, of nature cultivated for human delight and usage. He recognises now that her essential beauty is something 'guarded' and 'sealed' from the artificial 'culture' of the harem. This beauty is not something that can be controlled, modified and directed for man's delight and use. And yet here is the living source of all that is sweet, healthful, refreshing and delightful in all gardens or – equally – in women. This fountain or 'essence of womanhood' flowing directly from her Creator is not defined by anything in this world and yet is the life of all that is. Eve in Hebrew means 'to breathe, or to give life' (cf. Genesis 3:20).

A new and original association arises in his mind: these living waters, that are for the health and wholeness of the world, find their source in the woods of Lebanon, the only wood that Solomon felt worthy for building the Temple of Yahweh. These cut woods were 'floated down by sea from Joppa' (Ezra 3:7). Essentially chosen for their fragrance, it was contact with water which made this cedar aromatic. Solomon's temple was built to express (in decoration and architecture) the seven days of creation that went into the making of the Garden of Eden, culminating in the last creation, that of Eve. In herself Eve summed up and contained the living essence of that garden, *life*. She is the embodiment in human form of God's Shekhinah, a feminine word in Rabbinic Hebrew meaning 'dwelling' or 'settling'. Solomon had built the Temple to be the place where

God dwells. Here, in front of him, was a temple not made by human hands, a dwelling place for Wisdom (that feminine aspect of God) for which he had always prayed.

The combination of streams of living water and currents of scented air merge in a new image of the wind: 'Arise, O north wind, and come O south wind, blow over my garden and let flow the aromas thereof.' Here Solomon is at his most hieratic, like Jesus in the Gospels 'he commands even the winds and the water and they obey him' (Luke 8:25; Matthew 8:27). The Qur'an narrates that the wind was made subservient to Solomon, saying, 'it flows by his order towards the land which God has blessed' (21:81; see also Qur'an, 34:12, 38:36, 54:12). Here, Solomon bids the winds to flow over – now using the possessive case – 'my garden,' that its fragrance may flow out to him yet more powerfully. *Ruah*, wind in Hebrew, is another word for breath (by which the scent of the garden is inhaled). The coincidence of opposite winds also points to the Spirit (also *ruah*) who does not correspond to our ideas of 'where it comes from or where it is going' (John 3:8). It is also Wisdom, 'a breath of the power of God, a pure influence flowing from the almighty' (Book of Wisdom 7:25). This garden is the place where the winds meet, the heart of creation where breath and form are united. Solomon, whose one desire was for Wisdom, recognises her, embodied in a new temple standing before him.

Eating the fruits

FIFTH EPISODE
Part 4 – 'Eating the fruits' (chapter 5, verse 1)

Shulamite: 1. *'Let my beloved come into his garden, and eat the fruits of its*
                    fruit trees.'

Solomon: *'I have come into my garden, O my sister-bride, I have gathered my*
                    myrrh with my aromatics: I have eaten the honeycomb with
                    my honey.
                    I have drunk my wine with my milk: eat, O friends, and drink, and
                    be inebriated, dearest ones.'

In the Masoretic text there is a paragraph break *after* 5:1 suggesting
this verse should be linked together with the previous chapter and
episode, as the evident continuity of imagery supports. But it is
only now, with the opening of chapter 5, that the voice of this incomparable maiden is heard again: almost as if she had been waiting
to hear certain words – or a single word – from her lover's lips, as a
sign, or even a 'cue', waiting for her lover to speak of this *garden* as
belonging to him (as he does in 4:16 – 'my garden', not some poetic
image for womanhood as a whole). In her own mind she *is* his. The
possessive case reassures her of the personal nature of this relationship. She responds, takes up his imagery as applied to herself, and
invites him into 'his garden'.

   The echo is of Eden 'with all manner of trees, fair to behold, and
pleasant to eat of' (Genesis 2:9). The 'new Eve' invites fallen man to
return to paradise, the garden that has been closed, guarded and
sealed by the cherubim with flaming swords. He has already realised
that she is that garden. It is only after some lapse of time that we
hear again the voice of the lover in the words which follow next:
'… I have come into my garden, O my sister-bride, I have gathered
my myrrh with my aromatics: I have eaten the honeycomb with my

honey. I have drunk my wine with my milk: eat, O friends, and drink, and be inebriated, dearest ones' ('in like manner as I am', he may well have added).

The maiden, having heard her lover compare her to 'a closed garden' and 'a sealed fountain', has given over her body to his hands and lips in complete assurance and confidence that his enjoyment of her is no merely sensual ravishing. All the images in these words of his are indeed tactile and gustatory; he is gathering in the harvest, absorbing, drinking in *his* garden as she is wholly given unto him. Both the Septuagint and the Vulgate assume that the four verbs (came, gathered, ate, drank) refer to past time; but in the Hebrew (where present, past and future verb forms cannot be distinguished) this is uncertain. The verbs do, however, shift in the final line into an imperative – which can only be applied with a future sense, as something that he urges 'to be done'. The imperative is linked to that at 4:8 for the maiden to 'come down'. In this line, as then, he is wishing to share her with others in the world.

In the excess of this whole verse there is a noticeable touch of delirium: as though, far from having become inwardly united to her in a union of souls, he has become partially removed and alienated from her. His mind wanders from the sole thought of her to that of others, of his 'friends', his 'dearest ones' (all ancient versions have the plural). For, having first spoken to her alone, the 'closed garden' of their solitude is, as it were, broken in his summoning of others to enter who, in fact, cannot do so. In trying to throw open and make public what has been granted to himself alone he has lost the awareness of the unique person and relationship of his beloved, making her, as it were, 'mother-nature' to all, rather than his own 'sister-spouse'. As though carried away by the overflowing fullness of the delights of *his* garden he has not recognised that it is her personal gift *to him*.

One has to remember that the relationship, so far, has not taken into account what we have called the 'social dimension' of human love. His loyalty has now turned back to the collective: *they* have become what is 'dearest' to him. Who are these 'friends'? The court? Neither is this maiden known to them, and the danger to the political alliances cemented by Solomon's *many* marriages means her 'demands on the king' would be regarded as a threat. The harem? Though the maiden is known and appreciated for her beauty there is no expectation that she will be raised to the level of the 'royal counterpart' – her background means that she should remain at the level of the concubines. Solomon has invited this maiden to 'come down' but to what? He has met her away from everything, as if he was poor. Would their love be accepted back in his privileged world? A proverb attributed to Solomon may express his hidden fear that 'Wealth multiplies "friends", but the one friend the poor man has is taken from him!' (Proverbs 19:4).

It would seem from what is to follow that this 'delirium' is an increasing one, growing upon him, clouding over his perception of the uniqueness of what he has before him. His 'wisdom' now seems to have forsaken him. He has wholly forgotten those words of his at the opening of the poem, that these breasts 'are *better* than wine'. Now, with the garden open to his touch and taste, he takes them as an inebriant after all. No longer does he follow his advice in Proverbs 7:4: 'Say to wisdom, "You are my sister", and to insight, "You are my relative".' Though he still calls her 'my beloved', part of him gives her away to be 'eaten and drunk' by others.[23] Part of him wishes *her* to 'be inebriated' and lose *her* better judgement, for, as Ben Sirach said, 'wine makes even the wise lose their way' (19:2).

The invitation to 'eat, O friends, and drink, and be inebriated, dearest ones' is a premonition of the voice of Holofernes in the Book of Judith. Though this book is probably later than the Song, dated to around 140 BCE, the figure of Judith (like that of Susanna in Daniel)

---

23 A reflection at the human and psychological level, maybe, of Solomon's wavering and near abandonment of the 'unique' relationship with the God of *his* temple when he 'turned his heart away after *other* Gods' (1 Kings 11:4).

contains echoes of the Shulamite.[24] Judith, whose name in Hebrew means 'praised', 'was very beautiful, and charming to see', but she was also gifted with wisdom, an honest heart and devout Jewish faith (Judith 8:7, 29). Those who saw her 'were lost in the admiration of her beauty' (10:7). As Jerusalem is besieged by the Assyrians she leaves the city and enters the enemy camp where, likewise, 'the beauty of her face astonished them all' (10:20). After some days of her staying in the camp the general Holofernes gives a banquet 'inviting his chief staff' and persuades Judith 'to come and join us and eat and drink in our company', promising 'she shall occupy the seat of honour next to me, drink the joyful wine with us and be treated like one of the Assyrian princesses in the palace' (12:11-13). The narrator continues:

> Judith entered and took her place. The heart of Holofernes was ravished at the sight; his very soul was stirred. He was seized by a violent desire to sleep with her; and indeed since the first day he saw her, he had been waiting for an opportunity to seduce her. 'Drink, drink!' Holofernes said, 'Enjoy yourself with us!'
>
> (Judith 12:16-17)

These lines are the echo from the Song, but the point of the story is that (to quote): 'Holofernes was so enchanted with her that he drank far more wine than he had drunk on any other day in his life.' (Judith 12:20). In fact, all his friends 'went to their beds wearied with all their drinking.' The maiden, who had her own drinks prepared by her maid, is sober, and alone with 'Holofernes who had collapsed wine-sodden on his bed' (13:1-2). His inebriation meant he lost his head, metaphorically, and when Judith finds his scimitar, literally.

Some modern commentators (e.g. Block and Block 2006: 4) see at this point in the Song a physical consummation of the relationship.

---

24 Judith is deuterocanonical, that is, part of the Septuagint but not of the later Hebrew collation of scripture.

The text, however, shows that, at least, the lovers are at this moment not quite singing from the same hymn sheet. The paragraph break after 5:1 gives room (as it were between the lines) for actual love-making, and the words of 5:1 can rightly be read as an expression of the lover's yearning for a complete relationship – personal, social and physical. But it does not seem they are there, yet. Certainly, the maiden, by the beginning of chapter 5, has been brought by her lover's kisses and caresses to a quiet, dreaming, semi-ecstatic condition, in which, secure in her confidence, she leaves him to manifest his love entirely as he wills. But the question remains 'what is possible and what is not possible in the context of their relationship?' Though they have been together in the bridal chamber, in the eyes of the world they are not married. In fact, in the shadow of her place as 'one of the concubines' their relationship would be construed simply as such. Solomon's expressed intention from the opening verses is that the attraction they feel for each other be not muddied by any such association. However, 'sensuousness is not sinfulness' (Kierkegaard 1946: 55). For the maiden the involvement of the senses in their relationship is an expression of their love of each other and she is oblivious of any further 'intentions' welling up in her lover as his passions move out of his control. Her love is active and awake within a state of sensual rest: 'I sleep,' she says, 'but my heart is awake.' She is by no means unconscious or indifferent to what is going on and yet, it seems, she does not interpret his caresses in the way he, in his abandon, seems to be lavishing them. It is to this drama that the next episode speaks.

To sum up: we have seen in the episode (which covers chapter 4 of the Song) a movement within Solomon from admiration of this maiden from a distance, worship from afar, towards an acceptance of her as *his*, as united to him. And yet such a union requires selflessness, loss of self – all that they were, or think they are – into the *greater reality* of the relationship. This maiden becomes his muse and guide to the wisdom of love, a calling beyond that of being king. She herself is also on a journey of discovery, for in the union each finds the other and in finding the other discovers their own essential personhood. Gradually Solomon and his Shulamite discover *who they are*. They experience themselves as known, loved, cherished and cared for but union has its demands as well. At the end of this episode, as morning passes into day, we have seen Solomon's thoughts return to his duties and role as king and the expectations of his so-called 'friends'. He is divided as to how to integrate the protocols of court and harem with the freedom of this newfound love. If she is his muse, can she not be also a guide to them as well? And yet the love she shows seems to point away from the traditions and trappings of royalty. In all likelihood she would be seen by the people as a seductress leading the king astray. The very opposite of what she is! In his inner conflict he seeks refuge in her, he presses ever closer to union, to losing himself in her, to shed the burdens that weigh on his mind.

The importunate lover

SIXTH EPISODE
Part 1 – 'The importunate lover' (chapter 5, verses 2–3)

Shulamite: 2. *'I sleep, but my heart wakes …*
It is the voice of my beloved knocking (or 'who knocks'): Open to me, my sister, my friend, my dove, my stainless one, for my head is filled with dew, and my locks with the drops of the night …
3. *I have put off my tunic, how shall I put it on? I have washed my feet, how shall I defile them?'*

Though in terms of setting this episode continues on directly from the last, the Masoretic paragraph break at 5:2 rightly notes a shift in emphasis. While the narrative of chapter 4 opened up the awareness of the masculine figure in the poem (with the narration mostly his),

Simeon Solomon, *The Calling of the Bride*, from *Eight Designs
on the Song of Songs* (1878)

here in chapter 5 the subject is the maiden's awareness and the narration completely hers. Even when she recounts the words of her lover they are presented in a reflective sense, as echoing within her.

At the opening, the maiden's outward senses are lulled to a partial slumber; but her heart, the motivating power of her love – remains wide awake. As an early medieval commentary (c.1160) on the Song by the Benedictine nuns of Admont says:

> Whenever I sleep, then he leads
> my soul, as if in a dream, into the fruitful meadow
> of the Holy Spirit,
> and my inner spirit into the brightness
> of heavenly wisdom.
>   (Quoted by Bernard McGinn 1994: 351)

For it is by her own conscious outflowing love that she would respond to that of her lover. And yet her heart and soul is present in the periphery of her being in response to every contact of her lover's hands or lips. Her senses are awakened by a sound. Commentaries here have introduced an actual door between the pair on which the lover knocks, but verse 5:1 acts as a bridge between the previous episode through which the action of chapter 4 is carried into chapter 5.

During this morning of their love there is no sign that they have been separated physically so that he has to 'return'. The 'knocking' is rather of the lover's voice onto the maiden's sleeping senses. Jerome's use of the verb *pulso* means literally 'pushing or pressing against' but also 'agitating, disturbing, or causing disquiet'. The morning has turned towards midday and the 'shadows are declining' – there is a sense of urgency in the lover's voice as he seeks a resolution, or an escape, from the conflict between his duties 'in the world' and his love for this maiden. 'Open to me, my sister, my friend' – the sense of wonder at the maiden's inner mystery as a secret closed garden has now become a growing sense of frustration and separation.

The maiden begins to be aware of a change in the manifestations of the king's love; the fire of his heart and soul so longer burns so clearly behind the physical caresses he gives, swept along as he is by a desire to bring things to *some sort* of resolution. Is it the sense of touch – the hardest to experience without wanting more – that, in the arms of this naked girl, awakens a new impulse in the lover? Or is it the need to somehow cement their relationship so that it will 'fit' in the world of the court and harem to which his thoughts in the clear and cold light of day are turning? Was this impulse part of the lover's original intention? His concern, so far, was that unlike the harem this was to be a relationship guided by love rather than instinctual drives and, unlike the court, one based on freedom rather than social norms. And yet, though he 'knocks' his words seem to express fear and alienation rather than desire. This is a state Kierkegaard finely observes as 'the dread in bashfulness.' The lover is struggling against 'the will of the flesh and the desire of man' – that is, the instinctual and natural drive towards sex and the patriarchal drive *to be in control.*

As this double impulse arises as it were impersonally, outside of his conscious mind there is no explicit intention on the lover's part to *get* sexual pleasure or to dominate. The weariness he already feels about harem and court means he knows that love brings much more happiness than sex, freedom and self-expression more reward than conformity.[25] Yet, like St Paul in Romans 7, he is swept along by something out of his control, which, in his better mind, he does not want. It is experienced by the male lover rather as a form of *dread*, of estrangement not only from the woman as his beloved, but also from his own deeper motivation. His intention to be guided by personal love breaks down.

In conflict with himself he comes across like a lost child – shut out from the light and warmth of all things beloved and familiar,

---

25 Something realised by Etty Hillesum, who was far from repressed; see her diary entry for 8 October 1942 (Hillesum 1999).

newly alienated from his companion who he had loved so tenderly just moments before. Separated from his close personal friend he feels 'outside'. 'My head is filled with dew' – his thoughts have, somehow, become soppy and wet – and, as a child, he moans about the dampness of his 'locks with the drops of the night.'

The lover has created his own separation. His feelings do not correspond to reality – it is close to midday and a woman who deeply and overwhelmingly loves him is by his side. He is absorbed in his inner conflicts and contradictions, which he cannot manage. What he wants from her is refuge from them. His desire for her is not *for her* but for a sheltering enclosure to which entrance must be gained at all costs. It is as if, unconsciously, he is calling on the maternal instinct in this woman, though now it could be any woman who might give him shelter. In his neediness, he has regressed to the state of an infant trying to blot out that feeling of separation, pressing to return to the womb.[26] The 'night' he experiences is his own unconscious desire for blindness at the daunting threshold of this relationship, one which has opened up such possibilities for love, but also such dissatisfaction with his life as it is. He dreads as much to look as to leap. As Kierkegaard points out,

> The reason for dread is just as much in his own eye as it is the precipice. For suppose he had not looked down! Thus, dread is the dizziness of human freedom ... looking down into its own possibility.
>
> (Kierkegaard 1946: 55)

The very real human characterisation of the Song means that the inner life of the soul is depicted and laid bare. If, at this point in the Song, this is true in the nuanced and deep psychological portrayal

---

26 Kierkegaard again says, 'In childish bashfulness ... the individual suddenly leaps away and instead of penetrating to the roots of sexual difference, the spirit grasps at separation', just as the lover indeed does soon 'run away' (Kierkegaard 1946: 62).

of the lover, so it is also in the inner world of the maiden. Fully conscious and enjoying his caresses she is not *thinking about herself*. 'I – that is the ego – sleeps'; 'my heart – that is the love I have for my beloved – wakes'. Kierkegaard (ibid.) makes a distinction between 'the sexual impulse – which is not simply an instinct, for it has an end and an aim, which is propagation – and the state of repose, of non-striving, which *is* love, the pure erotic.' The maiden experience is purely erotic in that it is aware only of an innocent delight arising from her lover's caresses, and does not, herself, desire anything more than these.

She hears the knocking of his appeal though. Her next words show her to us as at first confused and to some extent troubled by this new and unexpected approach of her lover. Secure until now in her own innocent delight, she has only a vague inkling of what it is that he is now requiring of her. Moreover, she has no idea whatsoever of the dark terrors slowly overwhelming him; and her words seem to convey a certain sense of bewilderment: she seems as though disappointed in him, as though she had not been expecting *this*. 'I have put off my tunic, how shall I put it on? I have washed my feet; how shall I defile them?'

She divines that in some way – she does not clearly know how, or why – her lover has suffered a certain change, and *feels himself* to be 'outside' when before he had felt he was united with her. Whether what has erupted into the love-relationship is the generative impulse or the need for some sort of position agreed between them vis-à-vis his 'ordinary' life, she doesn't know. For her this is something unforeseen and it is this, rather than tardiness – or even reluctance – of response that lies behind her question. Is it in the unformulated hope that this 'trouble' will pass way from her lover – that he will once more realise that he is *always with her* – that the maiden is now seen temporising with him?

She accepts the figurative imagery in which the terms of his appeal are cast – that he is 'outside' – that there is some barrier between them – answering him 'according to his folly' (in both senses of the word). She has, indeed, at 4:11, taken off her night garment or tunic. She now says, 'Will I really put it on again to let you in?' She has left the ways of the outside world (court and harem): 'I have washed my feet, how shall I defile them by going back?' She gently expostulates with him – 'Do you really want me *there* and in *those ways*?' Carnal relations, at this point, would be like putting on clothes, not taking them off. *Merely* physical sex would, in effect, be a covering up of their intimacy.

That most mystical of the Church Fathers, Gregory of Nyssa, in his *Homilies on the Song* refers to this tunic as of the 'garments of animal skin' with which Adam and Eve were invested after the Fall (Genesis 3:21). For Gregory these garments signify the covering of the paradisal body due to the fear of death, the body as orientated towards survival. The sexual impulse, which was orientated towards relation and love, unwittingly takes on the instinct to perpetuate the species. It is this mortal carnality of 'the flesh' which Gregory would have us understand the maiden has 'put way from her' when she revealed herself as the paradisal body (4:11). The *perfume* of the discarded night-robe, which comes to him upon the waves of the air (disturbed by its fall), is described as 'incense' – 'the odour of sacrifice' in the Temple (Leviticus 2:2).[27] St Paul later speaks of 'presenting our bodies as a living sacrifice' by 'not conforming to the patterns of this fallen world' (Romans 12:1-2). St Gregory speaks of throwing off the 'heavy vestment' and rediscovering our original body:

> As a spider spins out that which is within it in weightless and luminous silk, we too, in going out from and leaving behind our gross carnal nature, are clothed from our head down to the extremity of the feet in the aerial tunic spun from the soul.
>
> (Gregory of Nyssa 1955: 124–6)

27 A ritual Solomon inaugurated in the Temple (2 Chronicles 4).

If, as her lover discerned, this maiden is truly the garden of the vanished Eden then she reveals the body as a complete expression of the soul that was the creation of Adam and Eve before shame and fear made them put on the skins of animals. There, in Eden, as William Blake saw in 'Jerusalem: The Emanation of the Giant Albion', 'Embracings are Cominglings from the Head even to the Feet, and not a pompous High Priest [or king] entering by a Secret Place' (Blake 2008: 223). The maiden in the Song, at least since 4:11, is totally open and given to her lover. In this state it is no wonder she is baffled at the character of the new approach of her lover, and what he seems now to be asking of her. How shall she put *on* that 'tunic' which is 'but dust' and 'will return to dust' (Genesis 3:19)? Moses in Genesis 3:5 could come no nearer to the holy ground until he had taken off his animal-skin sandals; so the maiden knows that the robe of the flesh does not allow a full union. As W. B. Yeats writes of the lovers in 'Ribh at the Tomb of Baile and Aillinn':

> Transfigured to pure substance what had once
> Been bone and sinew; when such bodies join
> There is no touching here, nor touching there,
> Nor straining joy, but whole is joined to whole;
> For the intercourse of angels is a light
> Where for its moment both seem lost, consumed.
>
> (Yeats 1989: 402)

As, in the end, only perfumes can commingle completely, being of the nature of air, must she enclose again the perfume of her garden in the hermetic confines of 'the flesh'? Implicit in the flesh are 'the patterns of this world': must she now as 'a favoured concubine of the harem' jostle for her position at court? She has washed her feet; must she now soil them with the dust of the earth?

The desertion

SIXTH EPISODE
Part 2 – 'The desertion' (chapter 5, verses 4–6)

Shulamite: 4. '… *My beloved let pass his hand over the opening, and my*
inward parts/entrails trembled at his touch …

5. *I arose that I might open to my beloved: my hands distilled*
myrrh, and my fingers were abounding in quintessential
myrrh …

6. *I unclosed the bolt of my door to my beloved …*
But he had turned aside, and has passed by.
My soul melted while he spoke: I sought him, and I found him not;
I called, and he answered me not.'

The hiatus of the maiden's gentle resistance is brought to an end by
an unconscious gesture of her lover. That his action was unintended
is implied in both the Vulgate and Septuagint: Jerome uses *misit*
rather than *posuit* – his hand is 'sent', rather than 'put' – 'loosed, let go
of' rather than directed intentionally somewhere (like the 'pompous
High Priest' of Blake's poem). The Greek catches the movement as
it passes beyond the 'secret place' – 'My kinsman *let pass* his hand
away from (ἀπέστειλεν χεῖρα αὐτοῦ ἀπὸ) the hole (or opening).'
Though this bodily movement expresses the conflicted intentions
within him, one can also infer he is no longer master of his actions.
The immediate effect, in any case, is an awakening of the dormant
'love-longing' of the maiden. The impact is in her solar plexus.
The Hebrew *mēʿîm*, 'bowels, belly', and *hāmâ*, 'murmur, growl, to be
moved', are used together in Isaiah 16:11 and Jeremiah 31:20 to evoke
the intense and visceral compassion and longing of God. Though
the hand brushes the sexual organs the arousal is expressed as 'a
churning of the guts', at her deepest physical centre.

Deep compassion and longing for him make her want to open
to him at all levels, including the physical. His touch is amplified a

hundredfold in her very intentional response – she is all hands and fingers, reaching out to one who had felt he was 'outside' to bring him in. A tactile and sensual awakening expressed in myrrh, that is, as an offering of her body, sacrificing her transcendence for him.

This is the most erotic passage of the Song and it is here the perennial divide between humanist/secular and religious readings is most evident. The feelings she evokes do resonate on many levels. Her passion certainly expresses sexual desire, but also a self-giving that fully accepts the consequences of desire, a self-giving that knows the sacrifice involved. The stirring and awakening of the latent energies of the maiden's libido are expressed in her two words: 'I arose.' But what may be noted also is a new consciousness of *power in her hands*. Even as she is aware of a very definite magnetism in the caressing hands of her lover, she recognises in herself a capacity to distil and express the *very essence* of self-gift (which she likens to myrrh).

It is as if at this point any reluctance is set aside and, with all the strength of a new intention, the maiden lets go. She opens herself to the consequences of human life, to the generative act, and full physical relations with her lover. In doing this she is also conscious that she is embracing suffering – myrrh is bitter as well as fragrant (*murr* in Aramaic means 'bitter'). There is a bitter sweet suffering that comes with childbearing and motherhood. Children are born in anguish and delight. The maiden chooses out of love for her beloved to put on the tunic of mortal life.[28] With her desire will come her need to follow him where *he* chooses to be (cf. Genesis 3:16). She is by nature a 'garden closed, a fountain sealed' and yet in the next line she says, 'I unclosed the bolt of my door to my beloved.' She is still

---

28 It can be argued that only when the reproductive impulse is fully accepted, consciously willed and freely consented to by *both* parties, are its arising and exercise not attended by a sense of fear and misgiving. Certainly Christian morality has often insisted on the presence of such an intent (often called 'openness to life') in rendering the reproductive impulse fully personal.

speaking within the figurative convention: not of any literal door. In the conventions of Persian erotic poetry 'door' and 'bolt' refer to the woman's body.[29] The course seems to be set whereby this relationship would continue to sexual intimacy in a way that would seem 'normal' with respect to the vast majority of its kind. But the maiden's next words show a definite dislocation of such a 'natural' and apparently inevitable course. The uncalculated touch of the lover's hand has produced such a visceral shock upon the maiden that she appears to have been unaware of his departure, until she suddenly finds that he has already left her.

> But he had turned aside, and has passed by. My soul melted while he spoke: I sought him, and I found him not; I called, and he answered me not.

What would seem to be unavoidable and imminent has not, in fact, come to pass. As it was the strength of the lover's instinctual desire, which had brought the relationship to this critical stage, it is also his action which brings this crisis or opportunity to an abrupt end by withdrawing. She reached out to him, but he is gone. Her soul had melted like snow on the heights of the mountains and had flown down to him to meet him where he wanted. But in the passion of her *kenosis* (self-emptying) she is left only with her love – as it were boiling within her – for the object of that love has gone.

How can one explain this? It seems clear that the first manifestations of reluctance on the part of the maiden may have not, after all, failed of their effect: her pause in response reawakening him to the sense of her personality. At the same moment as he reaches the depth of his weakness, with that ungoverned touch of the hand, the floodgate of the simply physical impulse is checked. Awakening again to personal love the shame under which he laboured comes

---

29 Cf. Nizami of Ganja 1924: 134–42, a teasing Sufi poem where the maiden keeps 'the door and bolt closed' to instil the value of deferred gratification in the spiritual life!

into awareness. In the end he only finds enough strength to take by now the only course possible: to hold off an inevitable sexual coupling he rises and leaves her.

Another reading could be that the king's avoidance of physical union at this point with his 'friend' arises through a sense of consideration for her; that she may be the one to choose it, not simply as a response to him in his moment of need – had his own advice not been to 'awaken *not* love until *she* pleases'? His desertion could be seen as the reassertion within him of his clear intention that this relationship should be led by personal love and not by the need expressed, and yet never assuaged, by the harem. Or, it could be through a fear of commitment – especially as it has not been made clear between them *how* their life together will unfold. Physical union would *bind* them together in a way, which would make the possibility of separation yet more painful. They both stand tremulous on the point of awakening, but it is not yet clear *to what*. The couple, at this point, cannot contain the love they have for each other, he may think it safest, simply, 'to cool down'.

Noting that at points in the Song when (as it were) the temperature rises there is no consummation, one commentator has read the Song as a whole as 'a tease' (Carr 2003: 115–16; maybe predictably, a male commentator)! But there are, as we see, many ways to judge the action of the lover here, or the *anticipatory nature* of the love depicted in the Song. Most of all there is no 'obvious sense' to the Song: even at the narrative human level it needs interpreting, let alone at the symbolic level. We are dealing with psychologically real characters: the poem invites us into their 'inner world' and it is in the light of what is going on within them that the words make sense. But emotions lead to actions, and in this case the lover's abrupt departure is very hard on the maiden. Adding shock upon shock, it seems to drive her near out of her mind (as the next episode testifies).

It is perhaps the measure of the lover's failure, at this point, that –

despite the solemn terms of his two adjurations to the 'daughters of Jerusalem' not to 'stir up or awaken her' against her will – it has fallen to no one other than himself actually to do this. Such is the significance of all the imagery of 'knocking at a bolted door' – stirring up or awakening someone against their will. On top of that the energy which had been liberated in her with the laying aside of her own will in sacrifice to his, her movement of desire, now returns upon her in a reflex of frustration. For by now the same unforeseen impulse, which had first awakened in the lover, has passed to the maiden, an overwhelming sense of her need to retain him with her at all costs. The feeling that *she* is separate from him, lost and outside, the very thing she could not understand in his experience, is now hers.

From 'the delights of love' this *alba*-song or morning-raga has ended in a near-desperate sense of loss and of longing – longing to regain a union touched at but then shattered, and a loss intensified beyond endurance by the discovery that *he has left her*. We picture her wrapping herself quickly in her mantle and going out of the garden house. It is now midday and the heat of her feeling is echoed in nature – but, for her, the very sap of life has gone from the garden: 'I sought him, and I found him not; I called, and he answered me not.'

Vulnerability

SEVENTH EPISODE
Part 1 – 'Vulnerability' (chapter 5, verses 7–9)

Shulamite: 7. *'The Watchmen that go about the city found me: they struck me and they wounded me: those that keep the walls took away from me my mantle.*

8. *I adjure you, O daughters of Jerusalem, if you should find my beloved, that you make it known to him, that I faint with love.'*

Daughters of Jerusalem: 9. '*Of what manner is thy beloved from among the beloved, O thou most beautiful of women? After what manner is thy beloved from among all the many beloved, for that thou hast so adjured us?*'

A gap in the narrative occurs at this point (though there is no new chapter or paragraph break in the Masoretic text). The setting is still the same, for the maiden is back in the garden speaking to the handmaids there, but from what she says there has been an 'off-stage drama'. We hear of her response to the lover's disappearance. The assumption that the Song in its literal sense is just 'a happy love poem' ignores the fact that there is a full, and near-operatic, tragedy also being played out before our eyes. We have to picture the maiden, in her distress, after calling in the garden for her lover, assuming that he has gone back to Jerusalem. Was he not worried about the neglect of his kingly duties? But such is the passion of her love that, much less even than the evening before, she cannot remain collected in herself waiting for his return. Had she not given herself away? So she follows the same route she took the evening before, but now in the full heat of day, to the city in the hope of finding him.

The maiden is distraught, distracted from her usual equanimity, in a state maybe of near hysteria, and it is no surprise that, at this point, a certain silence falls. She gives us no words to bear witness to her state of mind or the unfolding of what happens, until we hear of something that has already occurred, yet she sketches for us a complete episode: 'The Watchmen that go about the city found me: they struck me and they wounded me: those that keep the walls took away from me my mantle.' She speaks these words in the past tense, from the regained security of her chamber, and we are left to picture for ourselves the terrors and dangers from which she has just escaped. Her encounter with the watchmen in 3:3 is repeated but with quite different consequences.

Why? We hear later at 6:1 that Solomon has, in fact, not gone to the city when he left her, only further into the valley at the bottom of the garden in order to reflect and be by himself, to face his dilemma and come to his own conclusion as to what he should do vis-à-vis this maiden and his 'ordinary life'. In his absorption, he had no pre-vision of what would happen – he left with the impression that she had no desire to put on cloak or shoes, let alone go into the city. In his rural retreat, he gives no instructions to the city guards. His ability to 'make provision for her' has, as it were, deserted him. Nor is she guided by the serene intuition, the inner light and exaltation, of the previous night but feels abandoned and in a state of panic. All is unforeseen, every action is improvised convulsively on the spur of the moment. He has gone … she has lost him … to find him … somehow … she must. John of the Cross gives the sense of what she is feeling in the opening lines of his Spiritual Canticle:

> Where have you hidden,
> Beloved, and left me moaning?
> You fled like a stag
> After wounding me;
> I went out calling you, and you were gone.
>   (John of the Cross 1987: 221)

John depicts 'the bride' seeking her love among the mountains and watersides, the woods and green meadows. However, what would be more natural in her present misery than that the memory should return of that other night and its daring expedient *to go into the city* – crowned as it was with its blissful and triumphant reunion – and the wild hope that this night may repeat it? The consequences, however, as her words describe, are such as might seem inevitable: the city watch have had no instructions on this occasion and come suddenly at some turn of the street upon a lone wanderer in the full heat of the day 'when people are resting and only mad dogs and burglars go about'. They probably take her at sight for a 'strange woman' (described in Proverbs 6:5-27, 12:14, 23:17-8). Even if they were the same guards, there is all too little in the demeanour of this distraught girl to recall to them the self-possessed and dignified figure of the former night that they should dream the two to be identical.

She is roughly handled by them, pushed around, jeered at. 'They struck me,' she says, 'and they wounded me.' Since there is no further allusion to a physical wound, it is likely that, highly sensitive and emotionally exposed as she is, the lewd accusations are what hurt her deeply. Her sense of loss is what dominates: her experience echoes that of the virgin daughter faced with the destruction of Jerusalem in Jeremiah 14:17-19, 'smitten with a great wound, with a very grievous blow.' Falling from the idyll of love to the harsh reality of injustice is a cause for endless tears: here is one who 'looked for peace, but no good came; for a time of healing, but beheld terror' (Jeremiah 8:15). Having been the butt of their threats and mockery she is told to 'go home' and this time, passing them by, she finds *no one*. She has no home except him whom she loves.

Weeping she heads back to the walls of the city – the Song uses different words for the 'watchmen' and the 'keepers of the walls' that reflect maybe the civil police and the soldiery. The city guards had not noticed her coming in (during their midday snooze) but they do on her attempt to exit. They abuse her, in pre-figuration of one who later (traversing the city from the abuse of the Praetorium to the violence of Golgotha) 'also suffered outside the city gate' (Hebrews 13:12). They grab her. Shaking free in terrified flight she leaves her garment in their grasp. Maybe, in her haste and desperation to find her lover (it being, anyway, midday in the Judean heat) she had but worn the linen dress that had fallen at her feet. Like the young man in Mark 14:51-52 she may have 'left the linen cloth' in the hands of those who tried to hold her 'and fled from them naked'.[30]

---

30 This may be one of the sought-after echoes of the Song in the New Testament involving a change of gender, as the figure of Wisdom in the Gospels also takes a male form.

The Masoretic Hebrew has *redîd* 'covering' (probably why Jerome used 'mantle'). *Redîd* can mean 'linen garment' (as used in Isaiah 3:23); such a meaning in the Song is backed up by the Septuagint, which has θέριστρον – 'a thin outer garment'. Other translations of the Song give 'veil'; unlikely, as in ancient times the veil was adopted only at formal occasions, as an ornament rather than a covering, e.g. at weddings (Genesis 24:65). However, Genesis 38:14-15 shows a veil was also used by prostitutes for the purposes of concealment. There may be an allusion here in the Song, that such is her position that outside the harem she is merely a loose woman, but it seems unlikely she would chose to dress as such at this moment, having no identity in the city to conceal. It is true though that she seems to be mocked as a prostitute.

The whole scene, with its anguish and terror, is brought vividly before us by the few bare and broken words of the desolate girl. It is like a nightmare sequence. The garment she had let fall for her lover in the peace and privacy of the garden house is 'taken away' in front of lewd soldiers. The nakedness she had revealed as a gift for her lover is now exposed to leering eyes. We picture her fleeing way into the country, trying to hide herself. Luckily, at that time of day, there are not many about. But more than fearing for her own safety she is in despair of finding her love. She returns to the garden, and the small house – the only place she can call home – and after weeping and re-clothing herself she goes to see the handmaids who are still keeping the adjuration they were given, not to disturb her until she requested them. Naturally seeking human comfort after a traumatic experience, she tells them what has just happened in the city and appeals for their help in the one and only thing that *really* matters for her: 'I adjure you, O daughters of Jerusalem, if you should find my beloved, that you make it known to him, that I faint with love.' How would they possibly find him if she could not? Because they would be going back to the harem to their usual work – she has resolved that she will never go back *there*. They may well see *him* there whereas she would never.

She is, indeed, in a very weak state (some translations have 'sick' or 'languishing' because of love). She uses the same words of address to these maids as her lover had done but forgets that on the first occasion of his visit – the evening before – he had spoken to them only as he was *leaving*, when it was already dark. He had returned that night – last night – with her and adjured them again but only in passing the hut where, already late in the night, they were resting. In neither visit past their house had they seen his face. As Moses with God, they would only have seen him fleetingly from behind as he passed by (Exodus 33:23). And on his first visit he had come in the guise of a shepherd. Their commission from the harem was to tend this girl and not bother the visitor. The visitor, for reasons we well know by now, did not want this relationship to be gossiped about back in the harem. Her lover is to them unknown – *seemed like a country fellow, probably a favourite of the king for him to be given a choice woman from the harem* … such might have been their surmises. However, now – with this request 'if you should find him' – their curiosity is redoubled. They take their chance to ask from one who, again like Moses with God, *had* known him 'face to face.' They had seen this maiden's face shine with love after she had spent time with him, as Moses' face had shone (Exodus 33:11). At the invitation of the maiden their pent-up curiosity tumbles out, twice:

Of what manner is thy beloved from among the beloved, O thou most beautiful of women? After what manner is thy beloved from among all the many beloved, for that thou hast so adjured us?

It is only now that the maiden realises that they do not know (or rather by now have their ideas but want to 'have it from the horse's mouth') who her visitor *is*. 'Among all the many beloved' who could he be? She cannot just say, 'Why! The king!' For it was not *thus* or in that mode that she had loved him, for she had loved him for himself and that they would not see. To them it would only be the scandalous news of the king relating with a woman *outside* of his harem. Sitting on one of the beds in the handmaids' house brings the maiden to some measure of composure, enough to describe the nature of the one whom her soul loves, *without saying* who he is.

The lover described

SEVENTH EPISODE
Part 2 – 'The lover described' (chapter 5, verses 10–17; chapter 6, verses 1–2)

Shulamite: 10. *'My beloved is white and ruddy, chosen out of thousands.*

11. *His head as the finest gold: his locks as crests of the palm trees, black as the raven.*

12. *His eyes as doves over rivulets of waters, which are bathed in milk, and dwell hard by the most plentiful streams.*

13. *His cheeks like unto beds of aromatics planted by the perfumers. His lips as lilies distilling choice myrrh.*

14. *His hands as of lathe-turned gold, filled with hyacinths. The front of his body as of ivory adorned with sapphires.*

15. *His legs as columns of marble, which are set upon golden bases. His semblance as of Lebanus, excellent as the cedars.*

16. *His throat most sweet; and wholly worthy of desire is he … such is my beloved, and he – even he – is my friend, O ye daughters of Jerusalem.'*

Daughters of Jerusalem: 17. *'Whither has thy beloved gone, O thou most beautiful of women? Whither is thy beloved turned aside, and we will seek him with thee?'*

Shulamite: 1. *'My beloved is gone down into his garden, to the bed of aromatics, to feed in the gardens, and to gather lilies.*

2. *I to my beloved, and my beloved to me, who feedeth among the lilies.'*

It is to be noted of this richly decorative description that it is largely composed of impressions of a tactile nature. The maiden seems to lay particular emphasis upon those parts of the lover's body which she has *touched*. For example, his hands – compared to the fine *turnings*, the lathe-work of goldsmiths – have a delicate and precious touch as hyacinths (maybe both the stones *and* the flowers are signified). If importance of touch may shape feminine aesthetic sentiment in particular, then the Song corroborates this.[31] The lover's praise of the maiden in Chapter 4 is a *visual portrait* of head, neck and torso, using densely symbolic imagery. The maiden's description of her lover is at once much simpler – as touch is a more primary sense than sight – and is full-length; her appreciation of him is fully embodied. In terms of art her depiction is more like sculpture than painting – evidently tactile. In fact, in the context of Jewish prohibition of graven images, these lines offer the only licit form of statuary – a 'verbal statuary'. They are also reminiscent of Daniel 2:31-33; the maiden's description mirrors the description of the statue of Nebuchadnezzar's dream which also starts with the 'head made of fine gold.' However, her description of her lover does not deteriorate in value, strength and worth as it goes down the body (as does the one of Nebuchadnezzar's dream). In marked contrast to the image of fallible kingship depicted in Daniel, *this* figure's feet are 'golden bases' to the whole, not vulnerable clay. *This* figure is 'wholly worthy of desire.' Also the imagery is not just of metals but of organic, living materials. In fact her description echoes the physical perfection of the first living man: 'You were a model of perfection, full of wisdom, perfect in beauty; in Eden, the garden of God' (Ezekiel 28:12-13).

This 'new Adam' is the mirror and echo of her beauty. As he had said, 'your eyes are as doves' (1:4, 4:1) she mirrors back 'his eyes as

---

31 Ellis (1933: 36) gives statistical evidence, with case studies, that 'the tactile element is indeed specially prominent in the emotional life, and notably the sexual life, of women'.

doves' (5:12). As he had said 'your speech is sweet' (4:3) she echoes back (with the more tactile instantiation) 'his throat [is] most sweet.'[32]

She remembers his voice, that most distinct quality of a person. She remembers … 'Such is my beloved, and he – even he – is my friend, O ye daughters of Jerusalem.' And yet who could hope to recognise an individual, mortal man by characteristics and lineaments more appropriate to an angel? This is hardly a 'Missing Persons' ID! One might be prepared for the quaint 'flatness', the almost comic futility, of the response from the listening group. They had tried 'Who is he?', now another tack, 'Where is he?' Surely she might give him away! 'Whither has thy beloved gone, O thou most beautiful of women? Whither is thy beloved turned aside, and we will seek him with thee?' One mention of the palace and they'd know it *was* indeed *him*.

However, she appears now to have begun to feel less urgently the need of their support. In all probability, through speaking at such length of her lover she has both regained her composure and a full and perfect belief in him. This is not the king of Nebuchadnezzar's dream – of whom the more one gets to know him the more disappointed one would be – down to the feet of clay. *Her* beloved is not one to be knocked over so easily. Dereliction begins to leave her: she feels instead that she possesses his image – that of the new Adam – so securely in her heart, that he cannot in reality have left her. Her loving intuition of who this man is for her rises again in all its strength – *bone of my bone, flesh of my flesh* – flooding her soul with comfort. So that, once more completely mistress of herself, she deflates the whole search by saying to the handmaids that she already knows where he is: 'My beloved is gone down into his garden, to the bed of aromatics, to feed in the gardens, and to gather lilies.'

These words answer their questions with a purposely vague statement, and close the incident for the handmaids. However, the

---

32 Reading at a theological level, one might say; from the beauty of created things we know the creator.

words are also deeply true – if she – body, heart and soul, *is* 'his garden' fragrant with lilies of the valley, she *has* now found her lover, in herself. She has reconnected with the inseparability of their relation: he will always be 'with her'.[33] She knows, too, *where* and in what *manner* her lover would wish to be *were* he actually to return to her. She knows that he will indeed return in the manner of a gentle deer 'to feed in the gardens'. Most of all, she knows, in what way *she*, on her part, will receive him.

The maiden's words are an affirmation of her continued faith in her beloved, but also express an intuition as to *where* he now *actually* is. Metaphor and literal sense are, as always in the Song, linked. Had she remained in command of herself she might have guessed that he did not leave her to 'go back to his duties as king'; he left only because he needed space to assimilate the deep emotions of his love, to 'cool his passion' and make sense of what he was feeling. In the heat of midday he would have wanted shade: he would be down in the same garden where they had spent those first two days together, only in some secluded spot in the valley below the vineyards, where cool water ran.

At the end of this episode we hear her clear statement of the turning of her heart and his, and the turning of her feet out of the handmaid's house: 'I to my beloved, and my beloved to me, who feedeth among the lilies.' We have heard these words before (2:16) but there is a now a change in their order. On the former occasion, it was: 'My beloved to me, and I to him …' now, it is 'I to my beloved, and my beloved to me …', for at this point it is *she* who originates the action ('to' being direction as well as intent).

---

33 'You in me and I in you, together we make one undivided being' (anonymous second-century Easter Homily, speaking of Christ and Adam).

Simeon Solomon, *The Nuptials*, from *Eight Designs on the Song of Songs* (1878)

The overwhelming reunion

EIGHTH EPISODE
Part 1 – 'The overwhelming reunion' (chapter 6, verses 3–9)

Solomon: 3. *Thou art beautiful, O my friend, sweet and comely as Jerusalem: yet terrible as the camps of an army ordained to battle …*

4. *Turn away thine eyes from me, for they have made me flee away …*

Thy hair is as a flock of goats, that appear from Gilead.

5. *Thy teeth as a flock of sheep that come up from the washing, all with twins, and there is none sterile among them …*

6. *As the rind of a pomegranate, so are thy cheeks, apart from thy hiddennesses …*

7. *Threescore are the queens, and fourscore the concubines, and numberless are the young maidens.*

8. *One is my dove, my perfect one, the only one of her mother, the elect of her that bare her. The daughters saw her and declared her most blessed: the queens and concubines – and they praised her …*

9. *Who is she, that advances as the dawn arising, beautiful as the moon, all excelling as the sun, terrible as the camps of an army ordained to battle?'*

A new episode opens; the last had been spoken in the handmaid's house (though partly of what had happened to her in the city). There is a paragraph break in the Masoretic text after 6:2 and, indeed, the scene has changed and the speaker is again Solomon.[34]

---

34 Commentators have found chapter 6 the most difficult part of the Song to make sense of: 'Its bits do not hang together well, and we do not know who is speaker to, or about, who', says Richard Norris (2003: 242). 'It seems to be made up of different sorts of fragments from a variety of sources', says the *Navarre Bible* (Navarre Bible 2003: 510). Both assessments are wrong, but, as it is a complex chapter, I have broken it up into five episodes (with some guidance from the Masoretic paragraph breaks) to show that it has a cohesive narrative sense.

Here, again, the poem gives no indication of the lapse of time but we are still in the afternoon of this one dramatic day. It would appear from what follows that, putting on her shoes, the maiden has gone down to the valley (7:2 speaks of the 'steps' of the beloved 'in [her] shoes'). There she finds him, maybe already coming up from the valley to meet her again. Raising his eyes and gazing upon her for some moments he says: 'Thou art beautiful, O my friend, sweet and comely as Jerusalem: yet terrible as the camps of an army ordained to battle.' Let us note that he says here, 'my friend', as in the earlier stages of their relationship – expressing as it does the highest level of equality (undoing of the consequences of the Fall whereby it was said the husband will 'rule over' the wife; Genesis 3:16). Yet here there is also an unprecedented sense of the *strength* that dwells in this woman's character. The king wonders at her: so touching and human and yet dazzling and formidable as an army![35] He is in a state of awe of something as it were *more than human*. We could remember the words of the great Russian philosopher of love, Vladimir Solovyov (1853–1900):

> In virtue of the *ecstasy of love* man sees his natural complement, his material other – the woman – not as she appears to external observation, not as others see her, but gains insight into her true essence or idea. He sees her as she was from the first destined to be, as God saw her from all eternity and as she shall be in the end. Material nature in its highest individual expression – the woman – is here recognised as possessed of absolute worth; she is affirmed as an end in herself, an entity capable of spiritualisation and 'deification'.
>
> (Solovyev 1940: 416)

---

35 Here, and in verse 10 following, 'terrible' (the Hebrew of the Masoretic is *ayummah*) means 'attractive yet daunting', *formidable* in French. Or as Dante says of Beatrice, 'She struck my eyes with such radiance, that I could not bear the sight, my mind all but failed' (*Paradiso* 3:128–30).

We must remember the state, which had overcome him, in which we have found indications of Kierkegaard's diagnosis of the state of dread imposed by bashfulness. Faced with the reality of sexual difference, he has split himself off from her, gone, one might say, 'on retreat'.[36] Such an 'abandonment' of his love at this point may have been cowardly but it was the only way he could remain true to a relationship which was intrinsically different from the impersonal sexual gratification institutionalised in the harem. Still, the fact that she had been left at the time when their love was in full flower was her first 'wound' – one that had baffled her so much it nearly drove her out of her mind, compounded then by the second 'wound' of being treated by 'the watchmen of the city' as a 'temptress' or 'loose woman' (outside of the acceptable social convention of the harem). Though her lover had not given this second wound she had, in effect, suffered it through his difficulty in integrating the feminine in any other way than as an object of desire.

Facing all this – in the realisation of *who* this maiden really is to him – he takes his anguished retreat and needed time of solitude. Returning to her (maybe at the point some while ago when she has intuited 'my beloved *to* me') he effects that reconciliation within himself of the feminine *anima* so that he is ready to relate to his 'friend' in a way self-possessed enough to be able to 'kiss [her] with the kisses of his mouth' rather than so swept away that both she and he are lost. He has, indeed, gone back to the roots of sexual difference; the complementary otherness spoken of in Genesis 2:18: 'it is not good for man to be alone, I will make a companion who is suited to him.'

However, how will he be greeted by this maiden (coming to meet him now) who, without intention, he had *led on* and then *pushed away*?

---

36 'The individual suddenly leaps away and instead of penetrating [sexual difference] they ethically grasp an explanation drawn from the highest sphere of spirit – this is one side of the monastic view, whether characterized as ethical rigorism, or a life in which contemplation is predominant' (Kierkegaard 1946: 63-4).

His conscience portrays her as 'terrible as the camps of an army ordained to battle', the wrathful deity. And yet his first impression is the true one – she is 'sweet'. We can imagine that she comes smiling, draws him to her and folds him in her arms. Immediately the subtle magnetisms of their simple bodily contact begins to knit anew between them the imperceptible bonds of their deep inward union, just now so painfully torn. No words can express the still and speechless joy of their reunion. For him all shame and dread is gone. For her the words of Isaiah come to mind: 'You shall no more be termed "forsaken", and your land shall no more be termed "desolate"; but you shall be called "my delight is in her"' (62:4).

This woman has just gone through a sharp and fiery trial. But 'God's strength is made perfect in weakness' (2 Corinthians 12:9). The Book of Wisdom speaks of one 'tried like gold in the furnace' who 'at the time of their visitation will shine forth, running like sparks through the stubble, who will conquer nations and rule over peoples' (3:6-8). It is this impression of a new power within her forged in the crucible of her suffering which, at last, becomes too much for him. He takes himself from her arms and stands back, feeling again the slipping away of his consciousness and the loss of his will – not this time because of the rising up within him of an instinctual urge but from awe at the spiritual strength that seems to emanate from her. In all likelihood the maiden herself is quite unconscious of how she may be influencing him, as she wasn't aware previously. He hides his face and whispers: 'Turn away thine eyes from me, for they have made me flee away.'

Among the complexity of emotions sweeping over him there is also self-reproach at *having fled away* many hours ago now. As he had thought she could be 'conquered' in the assuaging of his desire, now he is faced with the other extreme, her 'unassailability'. Her calm, gentle and forgiving gaze yet intensifies that this woman is *beyond any expectations*. And yet, as he had lost the guiding sense of their friendship previously, he is now losing it again as she appears to him as too much *other* than himself.

In the psychological theories of Carl Jung, we could say that the man is in the grip of a positive *anima* projection: his beloved has taken on a numinous significance, and the relationship has moved from the 'personal' level, entering an archetypal arena which is in effect *as unconscious* as his previous instinctual desire. What is needed is not physical detachment but a withdrawal of psychological projection. The lover has to realise that she has come to represent something within his own soul which is unconscious (that is why he is overwhelmed by it). The psychological task is to bring the *anima* to awareness as *part of himself*. The *anima* then becomes the lens through which he sees the real woman before him rather than the image or mask he has placed on her. Once owned and integrated *as part of who he is*, the man's sense of the 'spiritual feminine' becomes the lens through which the beloved comes into focus in all her distinctiveness. She is no longer hidden by a projection, and the one seeing and loving deepens his own self-awareness. The art of romantic love – if it is not an illusion – is to create a lens that brings these two disparate realities (self-awareness and awareness of the other) into focus at once.

Returning to the Song: in the next lines we find the lover engaged in this work of trying to reconnect with the maiden as he had seen her, not as a divine figure but as a beautiful girl whom he loves. He repeats over again the succession of images for her distinct perfections, which he had praised in the early hours of this same day (chapter 4), as if trying to regain that *personal* connection with the aspects of her beauty that had been to him so human and individual before, but were all but lost in the wave of instinctual passion that had risen some hours ago. Now again they are in danger of being subsumed, this time in the awe of her spiritual (archetypal) significance. Predictably, he avoids the first comparison he had made (in chapter 4) concerning her eyes, for he had just said these 'windows of the soul' were too daunting for his gaze. Instead he repeats, ad verbatim, his second and third musings from that time on her hair and teeth. Maybe only now, this time round, he is aware that the fertility he perceives in this maiden is a statement of fact and not a wish, it expresses who she *is* rather than the intention of his relation with her.

In reiterating his previous appreciation of her one gets the impression that the lover, this time round, is not actually looking at the maiden. He is simply trying to summon up a previous experience of her in which he saw her unique qualities. In this mode of recollection he is not consistent with what he *had seen*. He misses out her lips – unapproachable as they now seem to him – moving to describe her cheeks with a slight and subtle difference from the terms used before. He now puts emphasis on the outer skin or 'rind' rather than the 'seeds' as previously, and multiplying the 'hiddennesses' or '*things* that are hidden' (*occultis*, plural), when previously it was only singular, '*that* which lies within'). The 'rind' is specifically *not* the fertile aspect of the pomegranate – he has now in his mind dissociated her from the reproductive urge, yet she has become more mysteriously fecund to him.

At this point he breaks off his attempt to regain his previous experience through the same litany of comparisons. It proves futile – time has moved on and, to him, she cannot be the same as she was before. From chapter 4 the next step would be to appraise her neck but his new sense of multiple depths *in* her is focused and balanced at this point by an overriding sense that *every smallest detail is her*. He is cognisant of the integrity of her person, the wholeness of who she is in every part. The Bride in St John of the Cross's Spiritual Canticle expresses well this state of how the particular becomes all-encompassing:

> You considered
> That one hair fluttering at my neck,
> You gazed at it upon my neck;
> And it captivated you;
> And one of my eyes wounded you.
>> (John of the Cross 1987: 226)

With the fluidity of unconscious association Solomon in the Song contrasts the *external* multiplicity of women (as he had seen his harem grow), with the wholeness and incomparability of this one:

> Threescore are the queens, and fourscore the concubines, and numberless are the young maidens. One is my dove, my perfect one, the only one of her mother, the elect of her that bare her. The daughters saw her and declared her most blessed: the queens and concubines – and they praised her.
>
> (Song 6:7-8)

Thus his mind reverts suddenly to the forgotten fact of his kingly status, and to the women of the royal harem. He remembers them only as numbers (not as persons), an undifferentiated concourse divided into three classes: but this conglomerated multitude is not to be compared with this *one*.

The 'mother' referred to here is not so much her earthly mother (as in verse 3:11) but is the maiden's (and Solomon's) spiritual mother, divine wisdom. 'Wisdom is justified in all her children' (Luke 7:35). 'I am the mother of fair love, and of fear, and of knowledge, and of holy hope,' says Wisdom in Sirach 24:24. An ancient Jewish Zoharic commentary on the Song argues that the Hebrew *tamathi* does not mean 'perfect one' but should be read *t'omathi* – 'my twin sister' (see Rosenroth 1912: 713). She is praised particularly by women: 'Wisdom tells of her glory in the midst of her people,' Sirach 24:1, that is, among those who embody her. This maiden is indeed a prefiguration of that *chosen vessel* who, in the New Testament, is thrice declared 'blessed among women' (Luke 1:28, 42, 11:27), and is later seen 'clothed with the sun, and the moon under her feet, and upon her head a crown of twelve stars' (Revelation 12:1). Maybe it is with such a vision of her significance that the words of his that follow are raised into prophesy: 'Who is she, that advances as the dawn arising, beautiful as the moon, all excelling as the sun, terrible as the camps of an army ordained to battle?'

It is with such images as these that the lover struggles with the sense of awe that threatens his conscious mind again: he falls back on the same similitude of an armed and unconquerable host. As if seeing the portent of something advancing towards him, he asks, 'Who is she?' He is aware that this day, which had indeed included the evening before (as Semitic days do), is drawing towards its evening, its serenade, but she will always be 'of the dawn'. On the symbolism of dawn, Jung's leading associate Marie Louise Von Franz writes:

> Psychologically [the dawn] denotes a state in which there is a growing awareness of the luminosity of the unconscious. It is not a concentrated light like the sun, but rather a diffused glow on the horizon, i.e. on the threshold of consciousness. The *anima* is this 'feminine' light of the unconscious bringing illumination, gnosis, or the realization of the self, whose emissary she is.
>
> (Von Franz 1966: 206)

The dawn is also a time where moon and sun can both be seen, and this is the second image he gives to her. Solomon draws as if unconsciously from the imagery of the wisdom psalms of the Temple: the dawn is the mother of the sun which 'cometh forth as a bridegroom cometh from his tent', the army camps will soon bring forth many 'a champion to run his course' (Psalm 19:5). What is so overwhelming for Solomon at this point, as for all seekers of wisdom, is when she suddenly appears to him in personal form. To borrow again from Von Franz (referring to Thomas Aquinas): 'For an intellectual it is a shattering experience when he discovers that what he was always seeking is not just an idea, but is psychically real in a far deeper sense (devastatingly real, actual, and palpably present in matter) and can come upon him like a thunderclap' (Von Franz 1966: 192).

Being hurled over

EIGHTH EPISODE
Part 2 – 'Being hurled over' (chapter 6, verses 10–12; chapter 7, verses 1–2a)

Solomon: 10. *'I went down into the garden of nuts, that I might see the fruits of the valleys, and that I might examine whether the vineyard should have blossomed, and the pomegranates should have budded.*

11. *I knew not: my soul confounded me (hurled me over) on account of the chariots of Aminadab …*

12. *Come back again, come back again, O Shulamite! Come back again, come back again, that we may look upon thee!'*

Shulamite: 1.*'What would thou see in thy Shulamite, unless it be the multitudes of Mahanaim? (unless it be between the armies drawn up for battle?'*

Solomon: 2a. *'How beautiful are thy steps in thy shoes, O thou prince's daughter!*

The lover now tries to bring to awareness and express in brief and figurative terms to his beloved what had happened to him during his time of solitude. To attribute this account to the maiden (as many in commentaries do, without reason) breaks any narrative sense in the poem as she had in fact gone *into the city*. Besides, having 'fled' from his relationship the displacement activities described here have a particular 'male' quality. As Emma Jung notes, 'A man by nature tends to relate to objects, to his work, or to some other field of interest; but what matters to the woman is personal relation' (Jung 1957: 81). Instead of going back to his royal duties as judge for the people he goes to inspect, examine and judge the nuts, fruits and vines of his garden in a proprietorial way, displacing from his mind that she is to him his real garden.

In his unconscious state he has, in fact, forgotten the time of year. He looks among a springtime garden of nuts, among what is hard, dry and bitter, for succulent fruits and grapes. He goes too deep into the valley – in such dark regions the vine and the pomegranate will not thrive and blossom. Psychologically he did indeed go 'down': his will and desire lost their sense of direction. Then, out of the bitterness and confusion that stifled his will, his next words attempt to bring forth something of the terrible impalpable black menace that grew about his soul. Aminadab may be intended to be *faceless* and unimaginable as in a dream. He may be the voice of his conscience vis-à-vis the maiden in the form of the soldier from ancient Egyptian history who stuck his sword into the belly of the female horse who was disturbing the stallions (examined in Part 1). It may be a reference to his own ancestor of that name, the last chief of the tribe of Judah in Egypt, before the exodus: the spectre of Solomon's ancestral patriarch rising now to remind him not to neglect his duties to the tribe and the race of Israel.

This ancestor may have had particular significance for the author of the Song if (as we have proposed) he/she was a Jew in Egypt. Also, it is notable that the tribal-chief who did lead Judah out of Egypt is always known in the Bible as the son of his father, Aminabad, as Solomon, who actually built the Temple, would always be known as the son of David (Numbers 1:7, 2:3, 7:12, 7:17, 10:14; cf. Proverbs 1:1).

The chariots – that is, the power – of his 'fathers' overwhelms the budding sense that he *might* just leave everything for this maiden. They *hold* and *carry* him, literally, as a chariot holds and carries its rider, towards his task, his duty, as king. The dream suggestion is rather of some terrifying rumbling, crashing and hurtling round in the darkness of the unseen chariots – a memory welling up perhaps of one of David's battles in Solomon's childhood. If the Song was written in Egypt then the chariot battle of Amenemhab in Kadesh is also evoked. If written in the early Hellenistic period then this image also hints at the story of Phaethon whose father was the sun god

Helios, a story which has its roots in Egypt and which an Egyptian priest recounted to Plato:

> There is a story that even you [Greeks] have preserved, that once upon a time Phaethon, the son of Helios, having yoked the steeds of his father's chariot, because he was not able to drive them in the path of his father, brought the fire of the sun down upon the earth and had to be thrown from the chariot by a thunderbolt from Zeus the father of the Gods.
>
> (Plato 1925: 24)

Solomon came to the throne young; his concern was how to rule well (1 Kings 3:9). He had inherited a fiery chariot that needed a steady hand.

The dilemma between love and the weight of royal expectations is expressed in the Sufi poem *Salámán and Absál* written by Nur ad-Din Rahman Jámi (1414–92). Salámán (the similarity to the name of our hero is no coincidence) is son of the Shah of Persia; however, he falls into an all-encompassing love with one of the maids of the Palace. There is only one way they can stay together:

> No Remedy but Flight;
> Day after day, Design upon Design,
> He turned the matter over in his Heart …
> To fly with Absál to the Desert;
> There by so remote a Fountain
> That, whichever way one travell'd
> League on League, one yet should never,
> Never meet the face of Man –
> There to pitch my Tent – for ever
> There to gaze upon my Belovéd;
> Gaze till Gazing out of Gazing
> Grew to Being Her I gaze on,

> She and I no more, but in One
> Undivided Being blended.
>
> (Jámi 1904: 34)

However, the Shah finds them and with council and entreaty wins his son back to his duty:

> The Throne under thy feet, the Crown upon thy Head,
> Oh Spurn them not behind Thee! Oh my Son,
> Wipe thou the Woman's Henna from thy Hand:
> Withdraw Thee from the Minion who from Thee
> Dominion draws; the Time is come to choose,
> Thy Mistress or the World to hold or lose?
>
> (Jámi 1904: 38)

It is the noise of just such counsels, entreaties and reproofs from his ancestors with which Solomon struggles as Salámán does in Jámi's story:

> Ah the poor lover! – In the changing Hands
> Of Day and Night no wretcheder than He!
> Wounded by Love – then wounded by Reproof
> Of Loving – and, scarce stauncht the Blood of Shame
> By flying from his Love – then, worst of all,
> Love's back-blow of Revenge for having fled!
> Salámán heard [his Father] – he rent the Robe of Peace –
> He came to loathe his Life, and long for Death.
>
> (Jámi 1904: 39)

While our Solomon goes over these moments of anguish, still standing before this beloved maiden, his face covered with his hands, he remembers that it is in the *sight* of her that he finds peace. He had lost his way when he had lost that vision. He calls aloud as if in despair but also in hope. Repeating as if in invocation: 'Come back again, come back again, O Shulamite! Come back again, come back again, that we may look upon thee!'

The Hebrew verb used in the Masoretic text for 'look' is *hāzâ*, which is used in the Bible in a special sense for the vision of God. The use of the plural 'we' does not imply that this is the chorus of hand-maids speaking but rather refers to his realisation that the vision he seeks was shared also with those who '*saw* her and declared her most blessed' (Song 6:8). The lover has for the first time used towards the maiden a name or specific designation. 'Shulamite', as we have seen, probably refers to his close identification with her as a soulmate or sister, being a female version of his own name (Hebrew *Shlomo*). It also refers to the 'peace' (*shalom*) he feels emanating from her. Its sudden use just here, however, points to a strong attempt on the part of the lover to fasten the whole of his attention upon the indivisible and unique personal identity of this beloved woman. He is concerned to regain a relation neither led by the amorphous promptings of carnal desire *or* the projection onto her of an archetypal symbol, or divine identity. He needs, at this moment, to see her as she really is.

This cry of his heart out of the interior darkness for the *sight* of her is met by an immediate response in one who has also suffered confusion and humiliation (though never his despair as she never had cause to feel herself guilty). She is empathetic to the extent of his need, though. As the poet Novalis put it: 'Few know the secret of love, feel its insatiability and eternal thirst.'[37] Standing as it may be close to him, she takes his head between her hands and turns his face upward, that his eyes might meet her own. She is quick to seize upon the name he has given her (it may have been with a joyful leap of her heart that she heard it). As she stands there, close to him in her soul she is savouring the sweetness of it. So it is, after a space, she renders it back to him. Half playful, yet maybe with a hint of

---

37 'Geistliche Leder', in Novalis 1987: 37

wistful resignation, she says: 'What would thou see in thy Shulamite, unless it be the multitudes of Mahanaim?'

The Vulgate has *castrorum* – camps, an accurate translation of the Hebrew Mahanaim. However, Mahanaim is also the place where Jacob, early in the morning had met the angels of God and called them 'camps' (Genesis 31:55, 32:1-2). The Shulamite knows that Solomon had encountered her advancing toward him 'as dawn arising, beautiful as the moon, all excelling as the sun, terrible as the camps of an army ordained to battle' (Song 6:9). We have seen the dazzled and stupefied state of mind in which the lover in the Song alludes to 'camps', which he uses as an image twice. Mahanaim literally means 'two camps' implying the two ways her lover has been overwhelmed, by desire firstly, and then by awe.

We have seen, at several points in the Song, the readiness of the maiden to grasp at once the personal application of all that her lover says (whether he is addressing her directly or speaking his thoughts aloud in her presence), most notably her self-appropriation of the image of garden and, here, the name 'Shulamite'. She is *his* garden, *his* Shulamite, but she does not quite accept his dual portrayal of her as 'camps'. She does not identify with being a 'multitude' when he had already in a moment of insight seen her as unique and 'one'. 'The camps of God' are like the archetypes of the *collective unconscious* identified by Jung, images that have their root in an inherited and pre-personal awareness, and which can overwhelm the ego identity. In her eyes, and in the directness and simplicity of her character, she sees it as essential in their relationship that they remain *equal* in their love. She doesn't want to be the stimulus for some sort of divine vision – even if it be the dazzling majesty and might of the Heavenly Hosts themselves! She questions his thirst for vision. It is as if she were saying to him: 'Will you never see thy Shulamite except as dancing between the armed camps of angels? Will you never see *me* among those multitudes?'

This response shows she is aware of exactly what is going on in him. In Jungian terms she does not want to be swamped by an *anima* projection, for she wants to be a *real person* to him, as she wants him to be simply who he is (neither king nor shepherd). He has already lifted his face to look at her, but she now realises that the very closeness of them is making a clear awareness of her as a whole and real person difficult.[38] So instead of allowing him to gaze indefinitely upon her face she now intends to be truly *seen*. She takes a few slow and graceful steps back so that they might truly recognise and salute each other. Maybe lifting her robe a little as she does so for the poem shows that he notices those 'dancing steps': 'How beautiful are thy steps in thy shoes, O thou prince's daughter!'

The Masoretic has, 'How beautiful are your feet in your sandals.' The notion that Solomon could see her feet may have echoes in later legends (in Arabic and Ethiopian texts) about Solomon placing a pool of water between him and the Queen of Sheba as she arrived to meet him. For Solomon had heard rumour that this 'Queen of the South' may be a demon. As demons have the hooves of goats, he made sure by a passage of water that she had to lift up her skirt as she approached him. He sees her feet *in her sandals* – they are not hooves![39]

The fact that he notices that she is wearing shoes may be an allusion to his consciousness of what she had gone though in searching for him in the city some hours past. Far from being deterred, still she has set out searching for him. She is indeed brave, undaunted by difficulties, indomitable, 'plucky', a 'prince's daughter!' *Bat-nābib* expresses her character, not her actual class. *Nābib* means 'generous' and 'willing' (as well as 'noble'): Solomon has some idea now of the act of self-giving she is about to perform.

---

38 'Relationship is only possible where there is a certain psychic distance', C. J. Jung wrote in 'Woman in Europe' (Jung 1945: 187).

39 The Ethiopian tradition, as we have seen, however, makes no link between Queen Bilquis and the Shulamite in the Song. Arabic sources do not refer to the Song at all.

Looking upon the beloved

EIGHTH EPISODE
Part 3 – 'Looking upon the beloved' (chapter 7, verses 2b–7)

Solomon: 2b. *'The joinings of thy thighs are like neck chains wrought by the hands of a master craftsman.*

3. *Thy navel is a finely tuned bowl, that never lacks mixed wine.*
The front of thy body as a heap of wheat set about with lilies.

4. *Thy two breasts like two young fawns that are twins of a gazelle.*

5. *Thy neck as a tower of ivory. Thy eyes like the fish-pools in Heshbon, which are in the gate of the daughter of a multitude. Thy nose is like a tower of Lebanon that looks over towards Damascus.*

6. *Thy head like Carmel: and the hairs of thy head like kingly purple, gathered and bound in many channels.*

7. *How beautiful thou art, and how seemly, my dearest, in thy charm!'*

7:2 of the Septuagint and Masoretic is in the Vulgate part of verse 1. Here both arrangements are followed by splitting the verse: 2a shows the maiden's physical act of stepping away so he can see her, whereas 2b makes clear she has withdrawn to the needed distance that he might see the whole of her – one cannot see someone's legs when one is in their arms. But something else has happened between 2a and 2b: made clear by the reference to the joining of her thighs, it is no longer only her feet he sees. As in her steps she had held her robe, bowing a little, now she draws the robe up, right up and over her head, and with lifted arms above her lets the robe fall behind her to the floor. Now he can truly behold her, and 2b shows that she is quite naked before him.

In Scripture 'thighs' is a formal way of expressing the loins or procreative power. Oaths were made on the sexual organs (indispensible as they are for continuity) by placing 'a hand under the thigh'

(Genesis 24:2, 9; 47:29). The Vulgate expression of 'the joinings of the thighs' implies, specifically, the rounded bit above the leg, which links the outer and inner thigh. The Septuagint speaks of ῥυθμοὶ, the *form* or shape of the thighs. One can assume that the harem regimen (as is still the case for the manicuring of women in the Middle East and Orient and now increasingly in the West) imposed complete bodily depilation, which would have made the inner curves of the thighs as visible as the outer. This creates the image of two circular bracelets or collars at the base of her abdomen. The double image here echoes the two shoes he had just seen – both replace and yet continue the image of 'two camps', and yet they are now about her as a real bodily being, not an abstraction.

The maiden at this point is fully naked and *not* ashamed. Though fully exposed to the view of another she has reversed the self-conscious state depicted in Genesis 3. She has been enabled to this because she knows she is beheld with a look of love and wonder. The lover's words pre-date by centuries those of William Blake's 'Proverbs of Hell': 'The nakedness of woman is the work of God' (Blake 2008: 36). Specifically, the Song says, 'the work of a master craftsman.' Who this master craftsman actually is is answered in Proverbs 8:30: 'I [Wisdom] was beside him as a master craftsman, and I was his delight, rejoicing always before him.' As then, in the day of creation, so now the Shulamite. In the Septuagint, the Greek *harmonousa* (fem.) literally means 'one who holds together', implied in the English expression of a craftsman as a 'joiner'. The Shulamite's thighs are *joined* in the most intimate part of her body.

His regard slowly passes upward and is held for a moment on the centre of the figure before him, the nodal point, on which the legs and in fact the whole harmony of the body converge. Again with the sense of an artisan's work he says, 'Thy navel is a finely tuned bowl, that never lacks mixed wine.'

The Hebrew for bowl in the Masoretic is *'aggān* which occurs only twice elsewhere in the Bible, both in the plural: in Exodus 24:6-8 'aggān are the ceremonial vessels that contain the blood of the sacrifice symbolising 'the blood of the covenant' when it is thrown upon the people; in Isaiah 22:24 'aggān symbolise the clothing of the High Priest as 'the offspring and the issue' of the Davidic line. The navel is, indeed, both the place where blood is stored, and for gestation of offspring. Combining both, the image of wine here symbolises the fulfilment of the covenant through the messiah in David's line. In medieval chivalric literature this vessel was the Holy Grail. Both earlier and later symbolism converge in the Song which speaks from the depths of human experience. For Solomon the navel of the maiden is the very centre of the garden, the root of all religious symbolism and yet has 'no form or majesty that we should look upon it, and no beauty that we should desire it' (cf. Isaiah 53:2). The poet Coventry Patmore (1823–1896), in an essay on *The Point of Rest in Art*, speaks of the navel as 'the only point in the human body which is wholly without beauty, significance and purpose in itself, which is merely the scar of its severance from the mother, [and yet] is the eye of its entire loveliness, the point to which everything is referred for the key of its harmony' (Patmore 1913: 14).

At this point, psychologically, the lover leaves behind 'the multitude' of the archetypes, passing beyond the collective unconscious into the formless unknowing that grasps truth intuitively. The Spiritual Canticle of John of the Cross contains this imageless awareness:

> In the inner wine cellar
> I drank of my beloved, and when I went abroad
> Through all this valley
> I no longer knew anything,
> And lost the herd that I was following.
> (John of the Cross 1987: 225)

However, the eyes of the lover do continue to move, and do not rest there (the Song being part of the mysticism of the image rather than of the imageless). His gaze moves upward, taking in the smooth yet subtly modelled area between the waistline and the breasts: 'The front of thy body as a heap of wheat set about with lilies'.

The Hebrew *'arêmâ* (heap) is used in 2 Chronicles 31:6 to describe the generosity of the first fruits given by the people to the Levites. The image evokes generous, warm self-giving for the sake of others. Like a suddenly poured heap of newly husked grain it is an appropriate image – with that of the navel – for the fertile zone of the woman's body. The giving of wine and bread – both expressed in 7:3 – becomes the new sacrifice of the Eucharist in Christian practice. 7:3 is therefore particularly apposite to the figure of Mary the mother of the Eucharist, who held the quintessential bread and wine in her womb for nine months. Even more is Mary prefigured when we consider the juxtaposed image of being 'set about with lilies' (or rather – as the Greek, Latin and the Hebrew have it – fenced in or walled about with them). Mary's body was open to a generous and warm fertility, her heart is 'a garden enclosed' with flowers.

The next image, as the lover's gaze rises to the breasts, tempers any too strong association of the maiden's body with nurturing: 'Thy two breasts like two young fawns that are twins of a gazelle.' The line repeats an identical line at 4:5, which *continues* 'feeding among the lilies', while here it *follows* 'fenced around with lilies'. Here the youthfulness of the fawns – though associated with the mother gazelle – imply femininity more than a maternal state.

The gaze then turns to her neck, less now a tower of strength than as fair and white as 'ivory' (her strength being her purity). It may be at this point that the maiden, aware now through the quality of his gaze upon her body that he is in complete command of himself, turns her head and lets her own eyes come to rest on him; for it is of these that he now speaks: no longer of the power within them, or with praying her to avert them. He finds them now as liquid depths, dark with her unfathomable love and tenderness: 'Thy eyes like the fish-pools in Heshbon, which are in the gate of the daughter of a multitude.' The Indian Sufi Manjhan when describing the princess Madhumālatī's eyes says of the very shape of the eye, 'They were like fish playing face to face' (Manjhan 2000: 36). One can still see the archaeological remains of the deep fish pools at the old city of Heshbon by the Jordan river – so deep the surface water would not have been disturbed by the fish within. So, her eyes, reflective like still water, are yet full of life and movement. Etymologically *hesh'bon* means the power of thinking, understanding and reckoning *things*. Her eyes are also full of vital and wakeful intelligence.

'Daughter of a multitude (*bat-rabbîm*) contrasts with his reference to her as 'daughter of a Prince' (*bat-nādib*) some lines earlier. From what we have learnt from her background 'working the vineyards' the latter is honorific whereas the former expresses her real social background – she is 'of the masses', a working woman. She was brought up on the land, darkened by the sun, without the education and refinements of the royal court, *and yet she is so full of intelligence.* That is the point of the contrast here – and like a woman brought up in nature she is full of life, a vitality that the court life could never instil.

'Thy nose is like a tower of Lebanon that looks over towards Damascus.' In Jewish and Christian exegesis on the Song the emphasis here is put on the gift of *discernment* vis-à-vis spiritual things (*hesh'bon* being the ability to account for physical things). It was said that good and evil could be actually smelt and you needed a 'good nose' to tell the difference. On the one side the 'odour of sanctity', on the other the 'reek of the devil' who, though he could appear as an angel of light, was unable to counterfeit any good *smell!* The Bride's nose is elevated and lofty, taking in the smell of the sweet cedars of Lebanon, but also, of necessity, it must 'keep awake and sober' (1 Thessalonians 5:6) and look out on Damascus, the capital of the Gentile power of Assyria.[40]

---

40 See, for example, Theodoret of Cyrus's fifth-century *Interpretatio in Canticum Canti-corum* (Norris 2003: 258–9).

Finally, he speaks of her hair – luxuriant and dark – full of deep and mysterious shadows: 'Thy head like Carmel: and the hairs of thy head like kingly purple, gathered and bound in many channels.' As we have seen, Mount Carmel, being richly wooded, is a ready image for a certain stately luxuriance, at the same time conveying the sense of darkness and the mysterious. Also precious: purple dye was the main colour Solomon used for the curtain-veil that surrounded the Holy of Holies in the Temple (Chronicles 3:14).[41] The Hebrew word for hair used in the Masoretic text, *dallâ*, means 'to hand down'. Her hair – having received the careful and elaborate coiffure of the royal harem – is arranged in tresses plaited so as to give to him the sense of falling undulation so similar to a thickly woven curtain.[42]

The lover pauses now, in his enumeration of the maiden's separate beauties, and remains for some moments in silence, with his gaze resting upon her face, yet at the same time holding in loving awareness the white splendour of her form. At last he says: 'How beautiful thou art, and how seemly, my dearest, in thy charm!'

He has now left behind all detailed 'analysis': his eyes and mind have learnt their lesson in completeness, he speaks here from a full heart, in adoration of the flawless loveliness before him but also with deep emotional warmth. This line shows that he is now able to refer all that loveliness – a 'splendour of form' so perfect as to be almost terrible in its impersonal and abstract beauty – to the beloved *herself.* She is *charming.* He is charmed by her, no longer in awe at a beauty that is in a way too formidable. It is also a comment on the modesty with which she has revealed herself, so as not to dazzle or blind his judgement or overpower his will. Her beauty is not 'displayed' or

---

41 Purple dye was extracted from the shells of mussels found only on the Phoenician coastline. It took 8,000 of these shells to produce one gram of dye (Davis 1989: 292).
42 It is along one of these tresses that the Temple veil was 'torn in two from top to bottom' at the death of Jesus (Matthew 27:51ff.) The symbolism of 'hair' for secret knowledge is taken up a thousand years later in Sufi writing (e.g. Ibn Al Arabi 1911): the sciences are 'plaited' so that invisible mysteries may lie hidden in the darkness between what we know.

'exhibited' as something separate from who she is, but is rather mediated (and humanised to him and for him, personally) by her delicate charm. Her action came from and expressed her intimate personal regard, her love for him. She has interpreted and fulfilled his need to 'behold' her (6:12), filling his entire vision and consciousness with the indelible and all-excluding image of her.

This maiden's beauty is something 'given' to her – with which she is endowed, and it is in that sense and to that extent impersonal. *But the way she uses that gift*, her modesty, charm, *are hers alone*. It is by these *personal qualities*, and by a series of actions qualified, characterised and transfigured by her own gracefulness, that she has personally given and conveyed to him *the gift of her image*. Though hers indeed to give or withhold, this gift could only be received in the mode it was given – in love. The 'seemliness' of her actions is, to him, the very perfume of her personality. This is why she appears to him as his 'dearest,' received in all the warmth and tenderness of her own unselfconscious self-gift. For there is one final and all-inclusive sense in which the word 'seemliness' applies: that is, in the total absence from these actions of hers of any hesitation or timidity, of all doubt due to any kind of shame.[43] The self-giving of a woman (as the Song 8:7 stresses yet more) is an entirely natural and spontaneous expression – it can never be 'earned' for it is made with the most perfect freedom, and is therefore completely effortless in its ease, grace and natural warmth.

---

43 The only possible source of shame here is external to herself, from her consciousness of what may be going on in the mind of her beholder: as an artist model need feel no shame until she is looked at in an exploitive way. Here, however, she is not met with the cool objectivity of the artist, nor with a lustful look of one who 'hath committed adultery with her already in his heart', but with a look of love.

The garden of delights

EIGHTH EPISODE
Part 4 – 'The garden of delights' (chapter 7, verses 8–11)

Solomon: 8. *'Thy stature is like a palm tree, and thy breasts to its*
                 clusters …

                 9. *I said: I will go up to the palm tree and will take hold of the*
                 branches thereof: and thy breasts shall be as clusters of
                 the vine … and the scent of thy mouth as of apples …

                 10. *Thy throat like the best wine.'*

Shulamite: *'Worthy for my beloved to his drinking, and for the ruminating of*
                 his lips and his teeth.

                 11. *I to my beloved, and his turning is (ever) towards me.'*

Though the setting remains that of their meeting in the valley at the
foot of the garden, the next section of the Song shows a return to
the image of the garden: the maiden as a garden and the regaining of
paradise in the relationship of the lovers. This part of the poem is not
so much a description of the maiden as an expression of Solomon's
passionate response to her. St Basil the Great (330–379 CE) may give
us the key to that response and its effect on Solomon:

> The soul follows its instinct when it comes to meet Wisdom
> and embraces her like an ardent lover. As Solomon said: love
> her so she may caress you. The body may be sullied by impure
> endearments but in the embrace of Wisdom, when the whole
> soul is united utterly and blended with her, then it will be
> filled and made pregnant with holiness and purity.
>
>   (Quoted in Arnold 1963: 119; my translation)

Up to now the lover's gaze has moved gradually upward from the
feet to the hair, and it is her 'stature', the perfect linear grace of her
form, that evokes for him the image of slender trunked trees. So she

is seen standing with uplifted arms like the branches of a palm: 'Thy stature is like a palm tree, and thy breasts to its clusters.'

It may now be that the maiden, on her part, has become aware that the gift of herself to her lover's visual sense has done its work in him. He had perceived earlier by the transfigured sense of scent, that her body was indeed the paradisal 'garden', then, by the sense of touch not yet sufficiently transfigured he had not been free to enter that garden, but now he has been permitted to *behold* it, visually and intellectually.[44] Having sensed before by sweet odours the presence of the paradisal body, it has now been given him to perceive it with his eyes. And because *this that he now beholds* is no abstract, figurative or symbolic beauty but indeed and most truly *hers* – made personal by her own modesty and grace – he is able to comprehend that what stands before him is completely human, Eden being 'heaven *on earth*'.[45] The image, specifically, is of *the tree of life* in Eden, the investing presence and source of all creation's sweetness, flowing out from her. She no longer fears now that when he draws close to her the sense of touch will once more play him false. 'Purity delights the spiritual senses in innocence' (Gregory of Nyssa in his commentary on the Song of Songs, quoted by Danielou 1951: 104). So it is perhaps at this point that she may be seen to extend her arms towards him, with a little summoning gesture like the waving branches of a tree, for his next words are these:

> I said: I will go up to the palm tree and will take hold of the branches thereof: and thy breasts shall be as clusters of the vine.

---

44 'To see' is the only sense verb that has distinct cognitive and perceptual meanings.
45 The parallel here is with Peter, James and John on mount Tabor who see a revelation of the risen and glorious body and yet in the end 'see only Jesus'. Matthew 17:1–8, Mark 9:2–8, Luke 9:28–36.

With these words – conscious on his own part of a new and deep tranquillity in heart and mind – he goes towards her, and they enfold each other in their arms.

Coming close he whispers: '… and the scent of thy mouth as of apples'.[46] But before his lips can touch hers, she puts her arms around his neck, at the same time throwing back her head so that it is upon her *throat* that his lips are pressed. So it is, then, that he continues: 'Thy throat like the best wine'[47] – but she breaks in upon his speech, taking up his word, and for the first time since the opening line of this chapter she speaks, in low tones full of concentrated joy: '… worthy for my beloved to his drinking, and for the ruminating of his lips and his teeth.'

These are strange, almost fierce, words: as if she would now breathe out, from her throat and mouth, her inmost soul and give it to him, willing herself to him as a draught for his thirst, as an aliment for his hunger. The echo here is with the opening line of the Song – 'Let him kiss me with the kisses of his mouth' – as if she would be absorbed by him through this simple bodily contact. So, it may be they do stand for a long space, motionless and silent, in close contact of body with body, of soul with soul, coming back to their original intention and yet now maybe the closest and most complete of the contacts which, in this Song, we have been witness to.

Then, as may be, after some while in this intense stillness, she murmurs like a happy child: 'I to my beloved, and his turning is (ever) towards me.'[48] The sense of her words is simply: I am his, and he is mine, now, and forever. Her joy is full. There is great significance in

---

46 Septuagint has 'the scent of your skin', the Masoretic, 'the scent of your nose', the Vulgate (taken here) fits better with the evocation of apples, which were used to sweeten the breath.

47 Here Septuagint, Vulgate and Masoretic all agree. Again, in terms of literal implication, the maiden is tall (as a palm), for only if her height were at least equal to his own would it be possible for her to receive, thus, her lover's kiss on her throat.

48 The addition of the bracketed word is necessary here as the Latin, translated by Douay-Rheims as 'turning', is *conversio*, which (as in the vow of St Benedict's Rule) implies a sense of *continuous* orientation.

these words, for the fact that the turning of *his* desire is towards *her*, vis-à-vis gender, reverses the consequences of the Fall in Genesis 3:16 where God says to the woman, 'your desire will be for your husband, yet he will rule over you.' The Hebrew for 'desire' here in the Masoretic text is *tesuquat*, only used twice more in the Bible: one chapter later in Genesis 4:7, where God warns Cain that 'the *tesuquat* of sin is turned upon him', that he may not act on its prompting (which he does), and also here in Song 7:11. The implication is that due to the Fall, desire has become destructive, and as the woman tries to *possess* her husband he will try to hold her back and *control* her. However, here in the Song the man and woman – as in a paradise regained – are turned towards each other. In these words we see that the maiden realises that she can now give freely and without a shadow of reserve that which he has now become capable and worthy of receiving. Hence the great relief in these lines: the old war between man and woman (ever since the exile of Adam and Eve) is over. She can express her love – free, as it has always been, of any manipulation.[49] She can deliver herself, wholly and completely, into the hands, heart and soul of the one she loves *because there is a complete equilibrium between them.*[50]

Standing together, the chemistry or magnetism between this couple is more than a sexual harmony, it is a reconciliation of two distinct organisms in a state of perfect equilibrium and peace. From now on they are no longer looking at each other but at the world, as Adam and Eve gazed in wonder at the beauty of paradise. D. H. Lawrence comes close to this *transcendence of ego*, only once, in *Women in Love*:

---

49 This is why the maiden in the Song so resembles the Immaculate Heart of the 'New Eve' – able to love without any possessiveness like the original 'mother of all the living' before the Fall.

50 It is for this reason that such modern clichés of 'abandonment' or 'surrender' in love miss the point that love is a mutual and completely equal, free, active, conscious, intention and choice *for* the other.

In the new, superfine bliss, a peace superseding knowledge, there was no I and you, there was only the third, unrealized wonder, the wonder of existing not as oneself, but in a consummation of my being and of her being in a new one, a new paradisal unity regained from the duality. How can I say 'I love you' when I have ceased to exist, and you have ceased to be: we are both caught up and transcended into a new oneness where everything is silent, because there is nothing to answer, all is perfect and at one. Speech travels between the separate parts. But in the perfect One there is perfect silence of bliss.

(Lawrence 2007: 369)

And yet, in the Song here, according to the modes of paradise, the woman who was first drawn forth from the side of man has returned to his touch (the salute of his hands and lips), to his scent, and most of all, to his vision, *as beauty*. Only three things survive beyond the ego: truth, goodness and beauty. A trinity that speaks of the unity of love.

Up and away: nature and grace

EIGHTH EPISODE
Part 5 – 'Up and away: nature and grace' (chapter 7, verses 12–14)

Shulamite: 12. '*Come my beloved let us go forth into the country, let us abide in the villages.*

13. *Let us go up early to the vineyards, let us see if the vineyards flourish, if the flowers be about to bring forth fruit, if the pomegranates blossom: there will I give thee my breasts.*

14. *The mandrakes yield up their odour.*

Within our gates are all fruits: the new and the old, my beloved, I have reserved for thee.'

These three verses, the last in chapter 7, are marked off by a paragraph break in the Masoretic. Here we have the *sera*-song, the evening raga, which mirrors the *alba*-song of episode 2, both in the form of an eclogue. The turn is outward, an invitation to celebrate love in nature. Both are sung by the maiden: in the morning she portrays the invitation as coming from 'the voice of my beloved', here she speaks as from herself.

The sun is now beginning to set over the valley, the maiden loosens herself from her lover's embrace and takes up once more her discarded robe, he helps her to put it on as she draws close to him again and, smiling, calls him away into the hills – away from even so much kingly luxury as this royal garden with its small hunting lodges. Away from all containing walls, 'into the country' (in Latin and Greek literally, 'in the field'), into the ambience where she was brought up, 'in the villages' surrounded by the vineyards and fruit trees that were cultivated around Jerusalem to supply the city. One glimpses her joy as a child, free in open contact with the sweetness and simplicities of nature.

The lovers can now be seen walking in the evening light towards the foot of one of the wooded hills, which rises at a short distance out of the valley (into which he had *descended* in his anguish). They *ascend*. The close woodland thins a bit as they reach a certain height on the flank of the hill, and the upper portions of the slope are terraced here and there for the cultivation of wine – the 'vineyards.' 'Let us stay [the night] in the villages,' she says, let us start a new life away from handmaids and court. Let us be free. All things are possible.

In horticultural terms the unexpected allusion is to mandrakes – they do flower in the springtime and are indigenous to Palestine, but are no cultivated fruit. Only small doses of the root provide a narcotic and emetic stimulus (to eat a whole root would be poisonous). Seeing the significance popularly attached to the plant as a 'love-charm' its introduction here is not accidental. Yet also, the peculiar shape of the root corresponds roughly to that of the human body. When pulled out of the earth it gives forth a sound somewhat like the cry of a child. The immediate context of the 'mandrake' image succeeding to that of 'fruits, new and old' suggests that the maiden makes a brief allusion to a hidden root – the possibility between herself and her lover of having children.[51]

Through the 'breaking open' of the suffering they have been through all the possibilities of love are there. At this point she is totally open *to what may be* 'within our gates' – within the prospects of their relationship 'are all fruits: the new and the old.' All 'reserved', or 'treasured up' (as the Hebrew has it) for him. So, as they step out into nature the old intention of their love – expressed as friendship and soul-love – is kept and saved while, at the same time, she is ready for 'all things new' (Revelations 21:5), even natural fecundity:

> Behold, I am doing a new thing;
> now it springs forth, do you not perceive it?
> I will make a way in the wilderness
> and springs in the desert.
>
> (Isaiah 43:19)

What was closed is now open, what was sealed is now loosed. The generative impulse is integrated with personal love. She says that 'There [in that place where love is complete and all inclusive] I will give thee my breasts.' Through her suffering a new maternal aspect has been born in her, no longer exclusive to Solomon but open to all, as Isaiah 66:10-11 says:

> Be glad with her, all you who love her:
> rejoice for joy with her, all you who mourned over her:
> that you may suck, and be satisfied
> with the breasts of her consolations,
> that you may savour with delight her glorious breasts.

---

51 Yet, as with the mandrake, *too much* childbearing in the pre-modern era was likely to kill.

And yet the personal bond with her lover remains; she summons Solomon on a journey away from the court, from his kingship, from his role in the world. A hard journey of letting go – no wonder she *had* appeared to him as one arrayed against him like an army! For through her he could lose all that *his* armies were to defend. He could lose his kingdom. No doubt, on this journey of letting-go she would strengthen, cherish and nurture him. She summons him upwards, grace building on nature, beyond all that he has been, to the heights. The valley is already dark, the light of the setting sun still illumines the uplands, however, in which they walk. The Song gives no more words in this episode, but we could hear her speaking to her beloved the words John of the Cross gives her:

> Hide yourself, my love;
> Turn your face towards the mountains,
> And do not speak.
> > (John of the Cross 1987:225)

And maybe the lover replies, as if initiated into the fullness and wildness of nature as night falls upon them, iterating the spirits of creation:

> Swift-winged birds,
> Lions, stags, and leaping roes,
> Mountains, lowlands, and river banks,
> Waters, winds, and ardours,
> Watching fears of the night.
> > (Ibid.)

And, as they lie down together in each other's arms in some protecting recess of the highlands, he prays that the fierce aspect of nature may be kept at bay:

By the pleasant lyres
And the siren's song, I conjure you
To cease your anger
And not touch the wall,
That the bride may sleep in deeper peace.
The bride has entered
The sweet garden of her desire,
And she rests in delight,
Laying her neck
On the gentle arms of her beloved.

(Ibid.)

The garden of the maiden's desire is in the heights; from which there are views, possibilities as to descent. The lovers may not have actually climbed very far but psychologically her intention was to *see further*, so as to discern *where* they are to go from here. She has made passing reference to the physical fertility that had been potential between them: whether it is to be left latent or as part of their love's fruition, she does not know. All she knows is that the 'new fruits' she discovers in the heights will also be *for him*. In these lines the maiden seems to offer up everything, including her natural instincts (symbolised by the mandrake) as sweet-smelling sacrifices that 'yield up their odour' *for him*. The text, however, offers us no indication as to whether a like and absolute *self-giving* has been taking place in the lover, for it is with *her words* alone that we reach the end of the longest and most complex episode of the Song, and are left in suspense as to *his* response.

The dilemma

NINTH EPISODE
Part 1 – 'The dilemma' (chapter 8, verses 1–4)

Shulamite: 1. *'Who shall give me to thee for my brother, sucking the breasts of my mother, that I may find thee outside and kiss, and kiss thee, and then may no one despise me? ...*

2. *I would then take hold of thee, and lead thee into the house of my mother, and into the bedroom of her who taught me ...*

and I will give thee a drink of perfumed wine, and new (or unfermented) wine of my pomegranates ...

3. *His left hand under my head, and his right hand shall embrace me.'*

Solomon: 4. *'I adjure you, daughters of Jerusalem, neither arouse nor cause to awaken the beloved until she pleases.'*

With the opening of chapter eight we are again brought suddenly upon a scene and a dialogue which have already been for some time in progress, though, according to custom, the text offers no indication as to the time that has elapsed since we saw the lovers walking 'into the country' at the close of eve. However, the continuity of the imagery from the closing words of the previous scene suggests that we are witnesses here, at the coming of night, of the ending of their walk. We are now facing – as are the two protagonists themselves – certain ineluctable conclusions, and are about to witness the last and inevitable parting.

The words which we first hear are, once more, those of the maiden; and they are charged with a sense of urgency – almost of wildness – which sets the key of strong emotional intensity in which the Song at last burns itself out. It is evident we have reached the scene just too late to have heard the words which have preceded these: words which, in view of all that is now opening before us, can only have been of anxious and agonised entreaty.

The key implication as to what has been happening is that her whole question turns upon their ability to stay with each other 'outside' of the harem. The Masoretic has 'in the street'; another example of the value of reading these ancient texts together, for *together* they make a clear allusion to the description of the 'loose woman' in Proverbs 7:12-18 (called 'Folly') who is 'outside, in the street.' Folly seizes the man she loves, and kisses him. This woman is 'outside' of her home – by which Proverbs means 'acting as an adulteress'. More pertinent to the Song the maiden chooses to be 'outside' of the harem and thus will be considered by others simply as a prostitute, even if her 'client' is the king.

One has to remember that the royal harem is a respected convention in ancient kingdoms. For the king, however, to relate to a woman simply 'on the street' would be a dishonour to him and to the harem – the king would probably just receive hidden disapproval, but the maiden would be considered a disgrace and a threat, she would be 'despised.' Earlier that night (verse 3:4) she had indeed been able to 'find him without' and 'take hold of him, and lead him' back from the city to be with her. But they both know that such a spontaneous, open and anonymous rendezvous cannot be repeated, as her experience at midday amply proved.

In these first words of the maiden we are propelled into the very centre of the dilemma – she will not take a place in the harem. Her hope had been that he would leave everything, sacrifice the proscribed roles of his kingship, or even his kingship itself if need be, so as to journey with her *away from all that*. The memory of the harem still wounded her. But he cannot, he will not. Though his father David had been brought up as a shepherd, Solomon was brought up in the context of the court. By challenging that she challenges all his conditioned identity. Moreover, he knows he *should not*; he has been anointed king and he cannot abandon a calling and responsibility committed to him by his illustrious father. Whether one likes it or not, kingship comes with all its privileges, observances and customs.

They cannot run away. The question turns as to how they can continue to relate *in* that world? Is their relationship possible at a social level? Personally and sexually they may be supremely suited but the vast difference of their backgrounds would mean a marriage would be considered by his other wives – and the powerful tribes they came from – as a debasement of the social level of 'queens' in the court. And anyway, what would marriage mean *in this case*? At this point he had already 'sixty queens' (as the Song tells us) and ended up (according to 1 Kings) with seven hundred! Marriage was merely a symbol of political alliance. Wives, anyway, were still part of the harem – only, because of their high birth, at a higher level – only the daughter of Pharaoh had a palace built for herself independent of the harem. If he 'were her brother' then she would indeed be of such a high state that, as part of the royal family, she may be able to meet him 'outside', but she isn't. In the views of the world their relationship could *only be* within the structure of the harem.

Could he not, as king, meet her at intervals 'outside' all of that … arrange things? But no, she would be despised by the harem as someone who thought herself 'above' the institution, as someone with 'pretentions beyond her class', in the end as a 'loose woman' – all the jealousy of a group of women for one who had flouted conventions. Her life itself would be in danger as someone who had 'led astray the king' and refused to take all the 'social benefits' of the harem.

In fact so inconceivable is it that she should again descend with him to court and city, that it has never so much as entered into the mind of either to have seriously suggested it. Instead, in these lines we hear her cry out (the Authorised Version gives an even stronger sense of the agony of mind that here finds expression): 'O that thou wert my brother …' If they *were* brother and sister they *could* meet, and no one would think ill of it. And such is the irony and tragedy that, in respect of the insinuations of the world, their relationship *was* brotherly and sisterly! But people would not believe that – who would – unless they *were* brother and sister. Hence her cry. And the heartbreak is that she is only asking for what is actually spiritually the case – it would only be possible for others to believe that, however, if they were *biologically* so.

These words, in whatever version – with their note of utter desperation – are those of one standing at last face to face with the stark realisation that all – the best, the most, the only thing to be desired in her life – is about to disappear from it forever. They are spoken with a full and perfect realisation of *what* is now about to pass away: that incredible quality of their relationship that made them like children of the same mother, Wisdom. Her words express a desperate and exasperated yearning for some impossible degree of closeness in constant and unbreakable communion. In the phrase 'sucking the breasts of my mother' we see the maiden's hope, and her despair, that they might have both been *children of Wisdom* living together even in the conditions of this world.

She pursues her fond and hopeless dream still further when she adds, 'I would then take hold of thee, and lead thee into the house of my mother, and into the bedroom of her who taught me.' Again it is *she* who will 'take hold of' him. And, as in the former case at 3:4 (the details of which are here deliberately echoed), it is of no earthly mother that she speaks but of divine wisdom, 'justified in all her children' (Luke 7:35).

The Septuagint ends 'her that conceived me', which implies that the last reference is to a feminine figure. The Vulgate and Masoretic have this figure as *teacher*. The Vulgate has *docebis* (second person sing.) '*you* will teach me', which, in this sentence, means that the one she is speaking to, Solomon, will teach her. The Hebrew, however, can be equally rendered in the third person feminine, and covering all tenses – 'she who teaches, taught, will teach me'. This fits the earlier part of the line much better (which refers to the mother). It seems more likely that Wisdom as mother is the one who does, did and will do the teaching. The maiden is sharply aware of *who* it is who guides and governs her, and *through whom* she in turn is a guide to him. At this point she needs divine wisdom to see *how*, in any way, they may be able to *stay together* (Jerome's use of the future tense in *docebis* fits this sense that the maiden is expressing a last hope that she *will be* taught in this difficult matter).

The maiden's close filiation to Wisdom means that she cannot countenance the 'way of folly' of Proverbs 7. The mother's bed-chamber is the *opposite* of the woman who seeks her lover 'outside' in the highways and street corners. As a child of Wisdom she would not corrupt him (as Folly does) but rather would *make him wise*. And it is with this promise that the maiden's next words can be understood: '… and I will give thee a drink of perfumed wine, and new (or unfermented) wine of my pomegranates'.

We have seen that pomegranates in the conventions of Eastern erotic poetry are a synonym for breasts, and indeed this line relates directly to Song 7:13 except here she has *become* the symbol – saying 'my pomegranates.' The merging of symbol and person at the end of the Song is highly significant (as we will see in Part Three). At this point in the poem the merger maps her feminine body onto the temple that Solomon built: which, as we have seen, was replete with pomegranate imagery. Her body thus becomes theophany (or in Christian terminology, sacrament); bringing about that which it signifies. Her breasts, which he had perceived at the beginning of the Song as '*better* than wine and fragrant with the best perfumes' (1:1-2), now actually *give that better wine* – the new, pure and perfumed wine of *wisdom*. In a hieratic way she makes something present, through her body, which wasn't there before.

A later close parallel exists with the 'draft of Enoë' given by Matilda which makes Dante ready to enter into and see the things of heaven (*Purgatorio* 33:127). But the greatest expression of 'woman as the source of the new wine' is Mary of Nazareth who produced a drink that was heaven itself. This is the 'new fruit' which the Shulamite has 'reserved' for Solomon. 1 Kings 7:13-22 describes the capitals of the two pillars that stood at the entrance of Solomon's

Temple as engraved with pomegranates – two halves of the pomegranate that led to the inner mystery 'hidden within'. As Solomon in the Song is still a young man, these words of the maiden hint that the temple he *later* built was imagined and configured as an expression of, and home for, the Shekhinah of divine wisdom.[52]

The maiden, despairingly and almost wildly, offers to Solomon the very wisdom that he had made his life's search and aim. And yet it is even with these words themselves that the full realisation of failure takes possession of her; for the following lines show her distraught, worn out with the force of her pleading, once more lying down in her lover's arms: 'His left hand under my head, and his right hand shall embrace me.'

There is indeed the deepest pathos in her repetition *here*, and at *this* juncture, of those childlike words – echoes as they are of the first hours in the dawn of their love. It is as though her mind, worn out and weary with its present anguish, were seeking to escape by a return into its memories. A last attempt to regain that bliss of togetherness once more, where she knows it is soon to be impossible – in his arms. And her lover, yielding – as it would seem – to this simple impulse in her, and also to escape from his own agony, with soothing and caressing touches composes her to rest against him. He murmurs one last time his old solemn adjuration, though, in the country now, even those 'daughters of Jerusalem' of the garden are far absent.

'I adjure you, O ye daughters of Jerusalem … that you stir not up, nor awake my loved one till she herself please' (3:5). But it is now in a significantly shortened form – no longer 'by the roes and harts of the fields', as if he himself can manage no more.

---

52 Shekhinah meaning 'dwelling' or 'settling' of the Spirit of God in its feminine form, has associations with wine in the Jewish Kabbalah. Our Lady as 'the holy place' where the Spirit of God came to dwell, and as the New Ark of the Covenant, which was hidden behind the veil at the centre of Solomon's Temple, carries a similar (but fully personalised) significance.

Before we end this section let us take a look at the lover who has been, as it were, hidden behind words that have all come from the maiden. He is faced with a choice that is nearly impossible for him. Had he not prayed for wisdom? Here he has her. But did he not pray *so that he could rule well* (1 Kings 3:9)? And here was a relationship that challenged all the prerogatives of his royal estate: a complete marriage that was quite incompatible with the physical and social relations with women that were expected of him as king. He recognises this dear woman has a special meaning for him, but thought this 'new wine' could somehow fit with the old. But this is an unfermented wine: it could not be contained within the old wineskins. If they tried to live back in those wineskins what would happen? 'The wine will burst the skins – and the wine will be destroyed' (Mark 2:22).

He could foresee it all; the very notion of the harem would be quite unbearable to them both. He and *it* (impersonal as the institution is) would break apart. One of the main symbols of his kingship would turn against him. And worse: in the midst of all this the new wine would itself be spilled and lost, this incomparable maiden would fall into the mud of their slander and malice. No, it would not work.

Nor could he give up that statecraft he had mastered through upholding the traditions of his father, establishing them in the elaborate ceremony that made clear *that he was the king!* He could not let rumours spread that 'he has been led astray by a woman' – with his many enemies, even in the family of his father! He could not risk the peace that had been the hallmark of his rule. The harem was a political symbol that emphasised that *he* was the anointed King in Israel. One committed to the customs of his father, to whom it was the privilege – nay, the prerogative – to have the love of not just *one* woman, least of all one 'outside' of the harem. Were not the political implications of the harem made clear when my half-brother Adonijah tried to get some foothold there in asking for one of the most beautiful maidens (1 Kings 2:10-25)? Once the harem is challenged the next thing is the throne!

The fabric of the state was indeed like a garment – it may be imperfect but if you tried to incorporate some totally new piece of material into it, then that new piece would only pull away in aversion to the old structures, and an irreparable tear in those structures would result. *He* held the state together as a symbol of continuity and of stability. This new wine this new piece of cloth – oh the agony of the realisation! – would tear *him* apart! This new and beautiful garment – the body of this incomparable maiden – *could not be for him*! Insofar as he is tied into, and part of, the old fabric of society, insofar as the wine of women's love had to be contained in the harem, he could not, and *would not*, risk it. Then, looking at the soft maiden in his arms, he adds in his mind – 'for her sake as much as for my kingdom'.

He knows he is bound, committed to re-descend into the knotted labyrinth of the royal estate. He realises in all its bitterness – like many another kingly lover before and after him – the full extent of his own helplessness in the face of his destiny. Oh, far more agonising tension of having to lose not only her, but his *vision* of the earthly paradise that was lost to Adam and Eve and seems now to be lost again! He, who has been allowed for a brief moment to stand with *her*, within the frontiers of the risen life, first perhaps among all men since the world began, to see again (having not yet seen death) 'the world of happy eternity', must turn back from that vision. He must descend into the passing of slow time, creeping on in its petty pace, in this fallen world. He has looked into eternity; but God, and his earthly father, having set him inescapably within the kingly state, have told him to turn away! The function of a king is exercised in *time* – the king is a creature of time. Where another, humbler man might indeed 'give all the substance of his house' for such love as this, and 'despise it (as well he might!) as nothing', a like freedom may never be the lot of a king: the 'house' of a king is not his own that he should do with it as he will.

And so we see here the royal lover, having been offered a cup of new and unfermented wine, is left draining the last bitter lees of his old existence. All he can do is embrace with what strength he has this maiden whom he loves so much, cradle her own wearied head in his hands, and state to himself his determination that, whatever happens, *she* will not be disturbed or contaminated by the intrigues, the 'advice', the 'stirring up', of the daughters of Jerusalem. In his last adjuration into the night air he affirms that *they* will hear nothing of this, they will leave her in peace. She will not go back there. She has her own guide, who is quite other than them.

Love is as strong as death

NINTH EPISODE
Part 2 – 'Love is as strong as death' (chapter 8, verses 5–7)

Shulamite: 5. '*Who is this that cometh up from the desert abounding in delights, leaning upon her beloved?*'

Solomon: '*Under the apple tree I awakened thee: there was thy mother corrupted, there was violated she that bare thee.*'

Shulamite: 6. '*Set me as a seal over thy heart, as a token upon thy arm: because love is as strong as death, jealousy is hard (relentless) as the grave: the lights of love are lights of fire and of flames …*

7. *Many waters cannot quench (the fire of my) love, nor floods overwhelm it: if a man should give all the substance of his house for (my) love, people would despise him as nothing.*'

It is indeed as though she were not sleeping, but inhabiting, for a few moments, some still and magical borderland of half-dream, peopled with fragile and fleeting memories of the vanished days. For her next words are spoken as if from behind a veil, divided by an intangible barrier from the world of present realities; words of peculiar and haunting significance that point back to and echo the words she had heard, as if in a blissful dream, on the previous night (now seeming so long ago!). Then, she had heard him formulate his own inner vision of *who she is*, as one 'that goeth up by the desert' full of perfumes (3:6).

Solomon, however, is now aware of a more immediate actuality, that they cannot spend the night in the open country. Night is indeed coming on and they must make their way to the villages, as she had proposed (7:12). In this perfectly practical step he must lead her. He helps her up and with her leaning on him (after the exhaustion of this extraordinary day) they continue walking until they see the lights of a village, where they can find somewhere to stay. As they approach she smiles to him – that smile so touchingly *hers* – and sets forth what she imagines the villagers will say when they come, not by the road, but over the fields 'from nowhere': 'Who is this that cometh up from the desert abounding in delights, leaning upon her beloved?'

He gets her humour! How they, the villagers, will immediately notice *her attractiveness*, saturated as she is with the perfumes of the harem, and wonder who *she is*! All *he* will be is 'her beloved', the one this delightful girl is 'leaning upon', of no particular interest in himself. And all the time he is their king!! But in his country clothes they won't think of that – none of them would have ever got near enough to him in Jerusalem to recognise the countryman coming up out of a field now. If he approached with his guards and entourage, carried in his travelling palanquin, then maybe. Not this man with mud on his shoes who they can only think of as lucky to be beloved by such a girl!

Deep down in the maiden's inner world, however, there is a profound realisation going on. Her lover had already discerned it in her the previous night when he spoke of her 'going up by the way of the desert'. Like the figures of Judith and Susanna and many others she is 'a true daughter of Israel', having a heart that is formed, as the Israelites were, in the desert (for forty years) leaning on God as their support.[53] Wilderness is not the setting of the poem: his, and now her evocation of it expresses the inner experience of *the people* at their most formative moment. And it is 'to the people' in the villages that she now 'comes up'. Kings come and go, but the people remain. Where he had seen her 'going up *by* [*way* of] the desert' she now 'comes up *from* the desert.' Such had the trials and tests of her life been, that now she is as one who enters the promised land. The *very phrase* is in the Book of Numbers when the twelve scouts sent by Moses '*went up* and explored the land [of Canaan] *from* the wilderness of Zin' (13:21). The scouts brought back grapes, pomegranates and figs to show it was 'a bountiful country – a land flowing with milk and honey' (27). The Shulamite *is* the promised land, 'abounding in delights', as the villagers would say.

The village is the true heir of the tents of Israel in the desert: despite the waging of wars, the making of kings, the building of palaces and temples, it is the country folk who have the land, and know it. And yet do they? For as she approaches, they ask, 'Who is this?' The promised land of Israel is but the figure of the original 'land' given to all humanity, the garden that 'the Lord God had planted in eastward in Eden' (Genesis 2:8). Her 'coming *up from* the desert' is the return of humanity as a whole (*Adam* meaning 'Mankind'), and not just Israel, from its exile *up to* paradise.

Throughout the final episode of the Song it is as if things are beheld in an intensified light; nature has passed into grace, pointing to the spiritual garden that the mystics have seen symbolised in the Song. *But the human story is still the substrate of that vision* as the human journey was the very matter of the Covenant in the desert. So often the human pathos of the Song, especially at its end, has been lost in immediately moving on to spiritual meanings, which *may indeed* be in the Song but become unrealistic and abstract when loosed from the human story. Grace builds on nature. Without the literal

---

53 The people of Israel (as a 'who' fem. pronoun, not a 'what') are expressed in her (as Rabbinic commentators on the Song have always seen).

narrative meaning we lose the fact that the Word was made flesh if not in a historical then in a literary form in the Song. And that is why the meaning of the Song remains within the *personalities* of the lovers, in particular of the maiden who is the leading character (up to this very point): the question is not *what does she represent*, but '*who is she?*'

We can imagine that the lovers do find accommodation, a simple room in a farmer's house. Their hosts, a farming couple, have no idea who this couple may be, but had not Moses taught them to give hospitality to sojourners (Exodus 22:21)? They do notice that the maiden has an uncommon beauty about her ('abounding in delights') and that the man is clearly 'her beloved.' After being given a drink of village wine and some bread they are shown a simple loft room where they can stay, and they lie down exhausted in each other's arms under the beams of the wooden house. It is this which makes Solomon think of something she had said to him on their first evening together (only a day ago): she compared him to a tree, an apple tree, under whose shadow she rested (2:3). This low roof – low compared to 'the trees of the forest' or the rooms of the palace – reminds him of it.

Strange words. It is through the sharpness of the lovers' shared anguish at the prospect of imminent parting that their inner world is enhanced and quickened. It is out of the strange trance like condition that enfolds them that the slow, almost dream like sentences are uttered, carrying with them a weight of significance far exceeding their conscious awareness.[54] 'Under the apple tree I awakened thee: there was thy mother corrupted, there was violated she that bare thee.' She has indeed, through this relationship, been 'awakened', and

---

54 If the last episode of the Song seems 'fragmentary' this is not because it is 'unconnected fragments collected at the end' as a number of modern commentators believe, but because the words are spoken as if from deeper stratum of consciousness having at times the disconnected quality of dreams – but dreams that express more than the 'logic' and 'coherence' of outer events.

that transformation, her lover realises, started back then. It was then, when they first came to stand to each other as lover and beloved, under the branches of the little fruit tree to which she had likened him.

> Beneath the apple tree:
> There I took you for my own,
> There I offered you my hand.
> (John of the Cross 1987: 225)[55]

But what of the mournful reverie which follows, the enigmatic and deeply melancholy qualification of this tree? It is as if he has seen into Eden, the forgotten garden closed to waking consciousness, and has seen there *the tree* that was the cause of humanity's fall. The tree under which they had met was none other than *that* through which Eve – 'the mother of all the living' – was violated by the serpent's guile, and corrupted. It is as though (while watching over her in those moments of her still forgetfulness) the burden of his meditations may have been somewhat thus: 'It was indeed under an apple tree that I awakened you to love – to a love such as you and I have known it, and few others; but it was also under an apple tree that your and my mother were awakened to the knowledge of good and evil. As we, in our love, have known great good, we also know much evil: this fallen world will always corrupt and violate the good.'

The lover's words proceed from him as from a mind overburdened and tried beyond endurance. Even as king he can do nothing – or even more *because he is king* he can do nothing. He rules in a fallen world, he must rule with the Prince of this world, by the sort of statecraft that is *only* 'wise as a serpent' (Matthew 10:16). Only one whose kingdom was not of this world could be 'as innocent as a dove.' That option was not open to him. Had he been of a humbler state, he may have been able to leave it all behind, but still – and this

---

55 However, the Song implies the latent love was awakened in her not by touch but by a kiss, for *then* she said, 'his fruit was sweet to my *taste*'.

is the crux of his new reverie – *they* would still have to live in a world that was fallen, that was always a mixture of good and evil. He seems to say to her, 'How can the absolute goodness and innocence of your love, of *our* love, continue *here*? From these heights any way forward would be down.' Such may be the melancholy but realistic substance of his thoughts.

In response the maiden says the lines which are the most famous in the Song, and rightly so, for they show the *incredible depth* of her character – that at this point of despair she shows him the way. There is a way to keep their love, pure and inviolate, and yet not within the terms of this world: 'Set me as a seal over thy heart, as a token upon thy arm: because love is as strong as death, jealousy is hard as hell: the lights of love are lights of fire and of flames.'

These words are full of the acceptance of their inevitable separation and yet they are also the great injunction she gives to her lover. If he, Solomon, sought and prayed for wisdom above all else, well here he is given it. She is wisdom, and he is to set *her* as a seal over his heart so that, from now on, in her absence, he will always *love wisely*. Also as a token on his arm, so that from now on, in her absence, he may *rule wisely*: his actions must do what his heart knows is right. As she is 'a fountain sealed' he is to be a 'heart sealed' *by her*.

The first line finds its counterpart in the Proverbs attributed to Solomon: 'Let love and faithfulness never leave you; bind them around your neck, write them on the tablet of your heart' (3:3). It also raises her words to the level of a divine command, and herself to the figure of Moses through whom God spoke:

> These words that I am commanding you today shall be on your heart … Bind them for a sign upon your hand, and they shall be as frontlets between thine eyes.
>
> (Deuteronomy 6:4, 8)[56]

---

56 The place 'between the eyes' being the third eye of unitive vision, the eye of *wisdom*.

In these lines, the maiden, who a little while ago had been 'leaning upon her beloved' (as the people of Israel lent on God in the desert), now reaches her *full stature*; a woman of power, a new Moses, truly (and not just in his projection) almost divine – a prefiguration of one whose heart was sealed immaculately from the melancholy tree, a seal set on her eternally by the heart of her Son. Prefiguring one who worked in her life as a 'handmaid', her arms always set to helping others – for they carried the token of the outstretched arms of her Son. The token the Shulamite urges Solomon to place upon his arm is, proleptically, the cross.

'Greater love hath no one than this, that they lay down their life for their friends' (John 15:13). In saying that 'love is as strong as death' the maiden is saying that love is *like death* – dying that the other may live. She must disappear, so that he, Solomon, may go back and rule his kingdom and live out his calling. Love must go to the point of dying, that is, disappearing, so that the other may be free.

The reference to hell in the next line is, for the Jews, less a place than a *non-place*; it is *sheol* – the land of shadows. Love must go so far as to willingly enter that land for the sake of another. The Hebrew *quin'ah*, sometimes translated 'passion', is accurately translated by Jerome as 'jealousy'. *Quin'ah* can express a positive ardour; 'Jealousy for [God's] house has consumed me' the Psalmist said (Psalm 69:9). Or it can be a negative state of mind, as one of 'Solomon's proverbs' says: 'A sound heart is the life of the flesh: but jealousy the rottenness of the bones' (Proverbs 14:30). The adjective 'hard' or, as some translations have it, 'relentless', could apply to both. Certainly, the thought that he whom she loves with all her heart would be departed from her bodily is hard enough, *but that he might lose faith with her and give his heart to others*, that would be too much for her, as hard to endure as hell. And yet she understands that, because of the harem, even this last consolation 'of faithfulness' is to be denied her.

The comparison with *sheol* and death inclines one to think she is also referring to a jealousy in which there is no ardour and no

passion, but the corruption of a convention, of an institution whereby sex had become merely political, part of the pecking order of
society – 'the rottenness of bones.' She hints at *what she would have
had to face* from the harem, from her brothers, and from the political
status quo if she did not disappear, if she did demand from her royal
a complete and exclusive monogamous relationship. *Their* jealousy
would '*give her hell*'; she would in fact probably be killed (cf. Luke
11:49: those sent by 'the wisdom of God' will be either killed or
persecuted).

The world is never prepared for what is really *exceptional* – that is
different from all else – therefore, she realises, her fate must be that
of the exception (i.e. concealment, hiddenness from the world), or
else the world would violently repudiate her. Hers will henceforth
be the spiritual isolation – the piercing loneliness of the inward
'heights' – where her soul must abide till death. And yet 'the lights
there,' she says, 'are the lights of fire and of flames.' There is no
commentary here on the state of mind of the maiden that matches
the incomparable words of John of the Cross. We can imagine the
maiden speaking of those 'lights of fire':

> O living flame of love
> That tenderly wounds my soul
> In its deepest centre! Since
> Now you are not oppressive,
> Now consummate! If it be your will:
> Tear through the veil of this sweet encounter.
> O sweet cautery,
> O delightful wound!
> O gentle hand! O delicate touch
> That tastes of eternal life
> And pays every debt!
> In killing you changed death to life.
> O lamps of fire!

In whose splendours
The deep caverns of feeling,
Once obscure and blind,
Now give forth, so rarely, so exquisitely,
Both warmth and light to their beloved.
(John of the Cross 1987: 293)

It is of this love burning within her that the maiden speaks the last lines of her prophetic and incandescent discourse: 'Many waters cannot quench (the fire of my) love, nor floods overwhelm it: if a man should give all the substance of his house for (my) love, people would despise him as nothing.' She, secure in the knowledge of her own love's strength, assures him also of its perpetual endurance, and of her own never-to-be-broken commitment to him, whatever comes. In the face of the flood of this world, which has swept away the possibility of their remaining together 'the small white dove *has* returned to the ark with an olive branch' (John of the Cross 1987: 226). An olive branch but also a challenge to him: *for the sake of that unbreakable love* should you not consider everything – 'all the substance of your house' – that is, your kingdom – 'as *nothing*'! Is there not a higher calling than king, a calling she gives, as Wisdom, to stay with her, maybe assuming another and unknown identity, to create with her a high and hidden solitude for two? The choice lies wholly with *him*; for she on her part – in view of what she is, and of what she has to give – can demand, with perfect justice, *all*. In view of that the rest *is* nothing (or simply 'rubbish', as St Paul knew; Philippians 3:8).

And yet she recognises that if he were to give it all up, paradoxically the 'world' would despise *him* as a nobody. As Shakespeare's Richard II makes so clear, a king without a kingdom is nothing. Such was the politicisation of marriage around the royal person of Solomon – a king without a harem would be despised as nothing! Her last words are a resignation to what is inevitable – for him as he will not change *it*, and for her as she cannot be part of it. But also a final, desperate, and near-sarcastic challenge from the heights of her wisdom to the pettiness of his 'worldly wisdom' that is really folly.[57]

With these words in many ways we reach the end of the Song – full as they are of tragic human pathos as well as the sublime heights of wisdom. It is the end of *the great day*, which, in Jewish understanding, started with the evening before. The day ends with the lovers in each other's arms, still in love. 'Many waters', that is the trials of life, 'cannot quench love, nor floods' that is the tears of separation, 'overwhelm it.' Here, in the context of *the people of God*, the two lovers gaze into each other's eyes:

> Deep is calling to deep, in the roar of waters,
> Your torrents and all your waves have swept over me.
> Yet, by day the Lord will send his loving kindness,
> And by night I will sing to him, praise the God of our life.
>
> (Psalm 42:7-8)

The little sister

TENTH EPISODE
Part 1 – 'The little sister' (chapter 8, verses 8–10)

Shulamite: 8. *'Our sister is little and hath no breasts.*
What shall we do for our sister in the day when she shall be
spoken to? …
9. *If she be a wall, let us build thereon defences of silver: if she be a*
door, let us make it fast with boards of cedar …
10. *I am a wall: and my breasts as a tower, since I am become in the*
face of him (whom I love) as one finding peace.'

---

57 Cf. 1 Corinthians 3:19: 'For the wisdom of this world is foolishness with God. For it is written: 'He traps the wise in their craftiness.' Ecclesiastes shows Solomon as an older king, trapped.

There are two 'Appendices' to the Song, which are not just fragmentary additions (as nearly all commentaries mistakenly suggest), but give yet deeper insight into the character of the maiden who, by now, is quite clearly *the* character of the poem. These two appendices offer us vignettes onto her life in the world. Her soul from henceforth may dwell in the heights, but she too must 'descend' and live in this world as it is. As the psychologist James Hillman once wrote, 'Wisdom is that union of love with necessity where feeling finally flows freely into one's fate, reconciling us with an event' (Hillman 1989: 280).

The final conversation in the Song is in a different tone, so much so that commentators have seen this as the work of another poet. And yet, the imagery is of a piece with the earlier episodes. The difference lies rather in that these lines are, as it were, post-romance – they take place outside of 'the great day', in the cold light of passing time.[58] The maiden is speaking of what concerns her now, as she must make a decision as to her future.

We can imagine the lovers waking with the dawn, having slept wrapped in each other's arms. Again we are introduced, as it were, some time into the conversation. During the night she has accepted with grief the situation between them, has given up on any more fruitless pleading, and turns her mind towards where *she* must return, her family home. Having rejected the harem completely this is her only choice. Her mind turns to all that now remains to her, and particularly to the thought of her 'little sister' whom she is to see once more. We are reintroduced here at the end of the Song to the difficult family situation that was her 'home' (put before us briefly but cogently at 1:5). If Solomon's task was the ruling of a kingdom, she also had her task in this world; to care for and protect her little sister. If Solomon's kingdom – symbolised for many by the harem – was under threat from his own family who make claims upon it (the story of Adonijah), then *she too* has something she must protect from

---

58 As with the introductory verses 1-6, the last seven verses are outside of the *great day* and between these two the *great day* is framed.

her family: a sister who (like Abishag the Shunnamite and herself) is in danger of being 'married off against her will'. 'The day when she shall be spoken *to*' is, namely, when her brothers *tell her* she must get married. The Hebrew here has *ledabber be* – which in the Bible denotes some form of disapproval or hostility: speaking *against* someone.[59]

Musing on her own task of being 'a mother to her little sister' she regains a sense of calling in her life even without 'her beloved'. Her experience of their time together has indeed *strengthened* her and it is in these images that she shows that she will be a *formidable opponent* to her brother's attempts to 'sell' their little sister as merchandise. The time she has spent with her lover has also showed her own vocation as a 'garden closed' as a 'fountain sealed', as one inviolate and incorruptible, and as one *who can stand alone*. If she discerns that same nature in her little sister then she will reveal it to her, so she will also 'hold out' against 'them'. 'If she be a wall, let us build thereon defences of silver: if she be a door, let us make it fast with boards of cedar.' In other words, when the time comes that they try to marry her off, if she feels it is not right, then I will fortify her yet more: I will build and establish her – even now, before that time – that she will hold her neck high, that she may be stiff-necked in her resistance, that she may be like me whose neck is 'a tower of David, which is built with bulwarks, a thousand shields hanging from it, all the armour of strong men' (Song 4:4). If it seems she be weak, and unsure, like a door that can be opened or closed, then I will teach her never to give herself except when she is certain, I will board up any vacillation towards the opinions of others with wood that cannot corrupt, until *she pleases*, as you, she adds, my dear lover, made sure that my love was not awakened against my will.

Her ensuing words, spoken with her new-gathered strength, do bear out and confirm that this is indeed her meaning: 'I am a wall: and my breasts as a tower, since I am become in the face of him

---

59 e.g. Numbers 12:1 'Miriam and Aaron *ledabber be* (*spoke against*) Moses', and Numbers 21:5 'the people *ledabber be* (*spoke against*) God.'

(whom I love) as one finding peace.' She herself has passed through the testing: her will is her own: in the anguish she has just passed through she has retained her old strength and found a new peace. It is to this that she will build up her little sister – to one no longer at the mercy of others' bullying or of her own mental vacillation and indecisiveness.

Peace – the word seems to echo in her mind – that is the name of the one she loves, Solomon – 'the peaceable'.[60] If she had taught him wisdom and strength, she had also learnt from his tenderness and gentleness towards her: she had found peace. A peace that she will carry with her even in her struggles – 'a peace the world cannot give' but which he has shared with her, and has left with her.[61] Is it not through him that she has come to know herself? Is it not owing to him that she realises herself as 'the elect of her mother' – the chosen one of heavenly wisdom? Even the agony of their parting has strengthened her, and now she looks again at her lover with an intent and steady gaze. As her parting gift to him she speaks to him one last parable taking up her own last word – peace – to make a play upon his name.

The vineyard

TENTH EPISODE
Part 2 – 'The vineyard' (chapter 8, verses 11–12)

Shulamite: 11. 'There was a vineyard of Solomon ('the peaceable') in Baal-hamon (the populous place): he gave it over to keepers; a man will bring a thousand pieces of silver for its fruit …

---

60 It is no coincidence that the forty years of King Solomon's reign (970–931 BCE) was distinguished from those before and after for its peaceableness (1 Chronicles 22:9).
61 Future words of one descended from Solomon (John 14:27). Her lover will indeed go on to have children with another, and yet she can think of it now with renewed strength and calmness, even of gratitude.

12. *My vineyard is in my own person.*
A thousand are for thee, Solomon ('the peace-giver'), and two
hundred to those who keep its fruit.'

The presence of this parable in the poem has constituted a major problem for a large number of the commentators, and the conflict and diversity of opinion as to its significance (and even for its *raison d'être* in this context – is it, for example, 'a copyist's error'?) is just as great. But if the *story of the Song* is made clear, as it has now been, this passage also becomes quite clear. In the very moment of parting with her lover the maiden gives him a final and solemn declaration – an asseveration of her troth. We can picture that the lovers have said their farewells to their still-rather-astonished hosts in the village – they have walked a little distance down the road until they come to a junction: one road turning back to Jerusalem, the other to the hill country from where *she* came. There they hold each other once more. The maiden feels the anxiety of her lover for her, and, in the role of Wisdom, tells him a parable.

Firstly, it is to be noted that in the Septuagint and Vulgate the 'keepers' are distinguished from 'a man' – the former being plural, the latter clearly singular (*vir* rather than *homo*; ἀνὴρ rather than ἄνθρωπος). The 'keepers' are the 'brothers'; the man is the one to whom, through their arrangement, she is to marry. The Masoretic has a curious singular referring back to the keepers, usually translated as 'each one [of them]' it is better translated as 'one among them'. The implication is that this singular man is either simply a farmer like them, or she is actually being made to marry one of her half-brothers.[62] All considered, the full poignancy of verse 12 comes out: *the vineyard is her*; she belongs to Solomon; and yet 'her keepers' will sell her to 'a man'. When she returns, her brothers, in the society of her time, will have authority over her. Most likely they

---

62 Ancient Israel seems to have been ambivalent on half-sibling marriage, practised by the patriarch Abraham (Genesis 20:12) and yet prohibited by Moses (Deuteronomy 27:22).

sell her to 'one among' the local farmers for marriage, for *fruitfulness*, as a worker and child-bearer. Or, more ominously hinted at in the Masoretic, they marry her legally to one of themselves so that she has no right to her own land.

She had been given into the care of the harem, and so her house, her small vineyards, had accrued to her brothers – as legally she had departed and had 'no more need of it'. They had inherited them. Now, on her return, she has nothing, is merely a reject from the harem; she has no dowry. But she is beautiful, she is extraordinarily beautiful, and she would be very attractive to someone who does not need money, to a rich man, maybe a much older man looking for a new wife and new issue. Such is her beauty that she is 'marketable'. Her brothers (venial as ever) will sell her for a thousand pieces of silver.

This last prophesy she makes as to what her life *in the world* will be links back to and explains the opening lines of the Song 1:5: that is what her brothers *had* tried to do – she had been able to resist, for *then* she had her own means, she had her mother's old house and small vineyards, in which she could earn her own income. After she refused to marry this 'man', they had destroyed her vineyards; still refusing, they packed her off to the harem. What she had, modest as it was, would be theirs and they'd get their commission from the harem officials. On her return, to the only place which she could call home, she would have to make what explanations she could to her family, to endure the utter incomprehension of the 'sons of her mother' – certainly their sneers, probably their taunts. Their sole motivations, in the end, however, will still be venial. She foresees their next plan. It is to such 'keepers' that Solomon is now giving over 'his vineyard'. In no way is Solomon the vendor, or is the sum payable to him (as some commentators have depicted it); he is, as he knows, losing her, not buying her.

In this parable we see that the maiden, from the height of her prescience, realises fully all that is now before her – all, in fact, that now remains to her. The name she gives to the place where she will be is Baal-hamon – places of that name did exist in Judea, however the poignancy of the name is that *she* who is distinctly 'one', 'unique', exceptional, alone and separate, will be living in what is translated as 'the populous place.' Moreover, the place is named after the old Canaanite god Baal, and even more specifically Baal hamon – a fertility god whose cult spread from Tyre and Carthage in the fifth century BCE (that is, some time prior to the writing of the Song). Unlike the Canaanite bull symbol, its symbol was the ram with horns. The archaeological record seems to bear out accusations in Roman sources that the Carthaginians burned their children as human sacrifices to him (Lancel 1995: 194). Israel's prophets considered Baal to be a demon. She herself is a prophet and she knows. The whole meaning of verse 11 here is that *the vineyard of the peaceable one will be in a most unpeaceful place!*

The one person among them all to whom she may turn with any expectation of a wholehearted welcome will be the one who has missed her, the person of least account in the household, the 'little sister', not yet of marriageable age. And it is towards this child that her thoughts and solicitations have already centred, and whose loving – if also uncomprehending – sympathy she will requite by guiding and protecting her, as she, with all the wisdom of a spiritual motherhood, *knows she can.*

One might ask: why would Solomon allow her to return un-provided-for to her former harsh conditions? Yet any such 'provision' could only serve to one end – as a 'marriage portion' – and it is precisely against any such marriage – as one among the many, ratified by a financial transaction – that her soul is in revolt. And for her – having come from the harem – to remain unwedded would brand her in the rough world of the country always as a harlot. She sees no other prospect before her – since she is of a marriageable age, and now is dowerless – than to be sold into matrimony by her brothers and, as soon as possible, to remove from the household a lively source of disesteem.

Yet even now, within herself, she knows that neither 'the sons of her mother' as the vendor, nor the prospective bridegroom as the buyer, can exercise any power over *who she really is*. This makes sense of the change in verse 12: in *property terms* (which is the imagery of this parable) she makes it clear that the rights of the 'buyer' are only *usufruct* – that is, they enjoy the use and advantages of another's property but not ownership. Their right over her is a *leasehold*, and Solomon, she seems to say, *has full and permanent possession of her*. 'My vineyard,' she says, 'the vineyard which is *mine*, is in my own person – it is myself; and it is therefore, in the last resort in my own disposition, and cannot be traded away by others. If, now, it is to be 'given over to keepers', I will see to it that its full value – that is the 'ownership price' of a thousand pieces – shall be kept for you, O Solomon! Have I not already vowed 'the new fruits and the old' wholly to you? And those who would trade in me for the 'produce' – that is my body's fruit – shall have but two hundred, that is *rental value*. They can make what they can out of my body, but *me* … I will always be yours!

And now, as if willing her whole soul to stay with him, she turns, and moves away slowly, with bowed head, towards the homestead of her childhood.

Last words

TENTH EPISODE
Part 3 – 'Last words' (chapter 8, verses 13–14)

Solomon: 13. '*O thou who abidest in the gardens, the children/angels/friendly ones hear and obey thee: make me also to hear thy voice!*'

Shulamite: 14. '*Escape (flee to the country) O my beloved, and make thyself even as a roe and a young hart (free) upon the mountains of spices.*'

Simeon Solomon, *The Blessing on the Lovers*, from *Eight Designs on the Song of Songs* (1878)

Her lover stands motionless – and then, as the distance increases between them, he realises in one last agonising moment what it is that is passing away from him, never to return. He cries out, with a heart charged with memories of her 'in the gardens'. As that memory of her is imprinted forever in his mind, he will always see her dwelling (present tense) in the gardens. In 8:13 the ancient versions of the Song are somewhat contradictory about the gender of who is spoken to, who the 'thou' is: the Vulgate gives *quae*, which is feminine, the Septuagint has καθήμενος (masculine) – 'he who is seated in the gardens'. The Hebrew pronoun could be either. However, the rest of the sentence gives strong hints that it is the maiden who is spoken of.

The 'thou' is in the garden with others. All versions agree these are 'companions' or 'friends'. However, in the late Classical period Jerome's use of *amici* has more formal associations of a 'courtier' or 'minister of a prince' (Lewis and Short 1996: 2 Amicus C, p. 106). And notably the verb for 'to hear' that Jerome uses is *auscultare* which means 'to hear obediently, or attentively' as it were to one above you (it is the verb used by St Benedict at the beginning of his *Rule* – composed like the Vulgate in the late Classical era – to express listening 'to the words of a loving *master*'). If Jerome's *amici* were friends or companions the verb for hearing (between equals) would be simply *audire*. The Septuagint has προσέχοντες, which, as a present participle, means 'paying attention', not just hearing but 'giving attention to', or 'listening out for instructions'.

We are left to imagine *who* these might be: medieval commentators (familiar with late Classical Latin) have read these as angels (the ministers of God).[63] The closest biblical text, however, is Wisdom speaking in Proverbs 8:32-4, which in the Authorised Version uses the perfect word, 'hearkening':

---

63 For Bernard, angels were understood to translate spiritual reality into that which could be apprehended by the bodily senses and the imagination (Bernard of Clairvaux 1979: 207).

Now, O children, hearken to me:
Blessed are those who keep my ways.
Hear instruction and be wise,
 and do not neglect it.
Blessed is the one who listens to me.

One is free to imagine that in this line, Solomon is imagining her, in a garden – that of the wealthy man who has 'bought her' – surrounded by the children she will have. She will teach them to be wise. And he says to her 'make me also hear thy voice!' In her absence, in other words, Solomon still wants to learn from her *as Wisdom*. Or it could be, literally that she is able to teach him though sending angels: the Song is from an era when the spirit world was taken as fact. The Book of Enoch, part 1, which is roughly contemporary with the Song, has an interesting passage at 42:2-3:

Wisdom went forth to make her dwelling among the
   children of men,
And found no dwelling place:
Wisdom returned to her place
And took her seat among the angels.
And uprightness went forth from her chambers.

(Enoch 1921: 61)

That Solomon himself came to be able to command angels and spirits (as well as his own people, and the animals) is witnessed in the Qu'ran; for example, 'And before Sulaiman were marshalled his hosts – of Jinns, and men and birds, and they all obeyed' (21:17). Or, the companions could be the 'schools of instruction' that Solomon was supposed to have founded with the Temple, that *they* will listen to Wisdom and *he* will hear it from them.[64]

---

64 On these 'centres and transmitters of didactic wisdom' see Von Rad (1972: 15–23). However, evidence for these 'schools' in Solomon's time is not substantial. The

Anyway, at these words of his, she pauses in her slow retreating steps; and once again turns, reaches out towards him both her hands, and says her final words, giving a last counsel as to *how* in future he may indeed continue to hear her voice: 'Escape (flee to the country) O my beloved, and make thyself even as a roe and a young hart (free) upon the mountains of spices.'

This verse combines the maiden's association of her lover with a roe and young hart (at 2:9 and 2:17) with the lover's association of the maiden with 'a mountain of myrrh and hill of frankincense' (at 4:6). The combined association implies simply *that they can be together*. And yet ... and yet ... we must remember that the last time she uses the image of a mountain (at 2:17) it is 'the mountains of *Beter*' – that is, of cutting, of separation. What she says here is '*make yourself even as ...*' or simply '*be like ...*' She is doing exactly what he imagined her to be doing in his words just past: she is teaching him *what to be like* – as one teaches a child how they are to grow up. And what does she teach? 'Make yourself *as if* we were together even if *we have to be separated*. As I will always be with you, come what may, so you can always be with me. Make yourself free. Even if you can't come to see me in the country – such would be scandalous to the etiquette of the harem as it would be to the new family life I will have to lead – still you can be free in your heart *to be with me*.' The key word is at the opening: *fuge* in Latin, in the Masoretic text בְּרַח, which despite attempts to translate it as 'make haste' or 'come away' is, as the Latin, a movement *from something*, rather than a movement *towards* (see Kingsmill 2009: 283, n. 101). The maiden is not saying, 'As soon as you can get away come *to* me!' she is saying, 'Escape! Flee *from* what binds you! Flee *from* your attachment to honour, wealth, pleasure and power and the

---

Qu'ran and Chronicles speak of Solomon as becoming increasingly wise as he got older: that no wiser king ever ruled. Yet 1 Kings 11:4-5 portrays him as having lost his way at the end. One of Rumi's poems on 'Solomon's Crooked Crown' has this verse: 'Even the wisdom of Plato or Solomon can wobble or go blind. / Listen when your crown reminds you of what makes you cold towards others' (Rumi 2011: 191).

ceremonial glories of your role and become free, light-footed as a roe and a young hart, and then you will find that *you are with me*, always.'

The important thing is – when he can, even if it be only in the hours of the night when no more demands are made on him – to divest himself of his official *persona* as king and the ceremony of his 'house' and become his natural self again, as he had been, with her in the country. After the 'way of images' that is the Song, the maiden points him towards the way of 'letting go' which, from henceforth, will be the way he will find her, and the way he will be united to her. A last commentary on the king's 'flight' we could read the words again of John of the Cross:

> Upon a gloomy night,
> With all my cares to loving ardours flushed,
> (O venture of delight!)
> With nobody in sight
> I went abroad when all my house was hushed.

> In safety, in disguise,
> In darkness up the secret stair I crept,
> (O happy enterprise!)
> Concealed from other's eyes
> When all my house at length in silence slept.

> Upon that lucky night
> In secrecy, inscrutable to sight,
> I went without discerning
> And with no other light
> Except for that which in my heart was burning.

> It lit and led me through
> More certain than the light of noonday clear
> To the place where one waited near
> Whose presence well I knew,
> There where no others might appear.

Oh, night that was my guide!
O darkness dearer than the morning's pride,
O night that joined the lover
To the beloved bride
Transfiguring them each into the other.

(John of the Cross 1960: 27–29)

With this last bit of advice to him she turns slowly away once more, as he on his own part also slowly turns: and the two lovers walk away, separated forever in body and yet united in a love that is *as strong* as the 'death' they are now going through.

They go back to the world. And yet when, in all the demands and difficulties of life they can come to a place of rest and solitude, they will find in their hearts that light that no torrents and floods can put out. Then they will leave everything and everyone behind, as if dead to the world, and turn to the one they love as in the noonday. And yet this must be by night, not within the light of this world. Purified by tragedy, in the agony of this world's separation, they can hurry into each other's arms and become one. The Song is the template for all romantic love that points to something not of this world, that is so intense that it cannot be realised in the light of this passing age: Tristan and Isolde, Dante and Beatrice, Romeo and Juliet, Baile and Aillinn, Novalis and Sophie, they point to a union more enduring than the grave – an eternal love.

So we come to the end of the Song of Songs which is Solomon's. We have been guided by the fact that it is about Solomon and in that light much of the story and the symbolic meaning fits into place. Whether the Song is in some way an oral tradition that does go back to him cannot be proved. However, the writer of the Song on which the surviving versions we have are based certainly knew of Solomon and entered into the spirit of the character of the king who was known for his love of Wisdom. Dante puts Solomon high in heaven among those who contemplate the beauty of God, and yet the words

Solomon speaks 'in a modest voice' in *Paradiso* 14:43-5 speak of the resurrection of the flesh beyond this life: 'When, glorified and sanctified, the flesh is once again our dress, our persons shall, in being all complete, please all the more.' As if he had met someone in heaven who had pleased him already so much on earth.

When Solomon and his Shulamite separated in the Song, the love between them continued to burn in their hearts; one can hope that in heaven they will be bodily together again – maybe not in the way of marriage, for there the body will be of the way of angels, but in a union of love that is complete, as Dante said, 'from the head right down to the feet.' Solomon's love of his Shulamite is, indeed, echoed in the wonder Dante shows for Beatrice even after she has died. As death transfigures Beatrice into a vehicle of grace for him, so Solomon's separation from his love transforms his Shulamite into an *inner guide*. She becomes his teacher in wisdom. We leave the last words to Dante, as he sings of Beatrice in *La Vita Nuova* in a way that could be a *précis* of the Song:

> My lady is desired in the height of heaven;
> Let all her virtues be known through me.
> I say: whoever wishes to be a noble lady
> Should walk with her; for as she goes
> Love ices the hearts of wicked men,
> So all their thoughts are frozen and wither.
> Whoever is able to stand and regard her
> Becomes transfigured or else he dies.
> When she chances to find a man worthy
> Of seeing her, her power is displayed,
> For she gives a greeting and he is made
> So humble, all sins leave his memory.
> For God has granted such grace to her will
> That he who speaks to her meets no ill.
> Love says of her, 'How can a mortal thing

Have beauty and purity in such wealth?'
He looks at her, swearing to himself:
'God meant her as a new creation.
Her form is just that pearl colouring
Which suits a woman, without excess
She is nature's summit of goodness
And beauty is judged by her perfection.'
As she directs them, her eyes dart
Flaming spirits of Love around,
Who, through the eyes of those who see,
Pierce the heart's deep mystery.

(Dante 1964: 65–6, with last lines my translation)

The Symbolic Sense

The story of the Song at the human level shows how the literal and the spiritual meaning are in fact interwoven. The Song, we have seen, can be read on several levels at once and the reading of the text on one level doesn't prohibit its meaning at any other level. The greatest biblical exegete from the Christian tradition wrote, 'Just as a human person consists of body, soul and spirit, so in the same way does scripture' (Origen 1979: 182). The journey is towards an integral reading that is fully human, and fully divine. As grace builds on nature, the symbol comes out of the story. The last part of this book is concerned with unpacking how the numinous and the natural relate in the Song.

The secular and religious divide

There was much debate in the early days of Rabbinic Judaism as to whether the Song was fit to be included as a biblical text. The debate revolved around whether the text was seen as 'clean' or 'unclean' in the eyes of the Rabbi. At the Council of Jamnia in 90 CE a vociferous camp, led by Rabbi Judah and Rabbi Simeon, thought the Song 'renders the hands unclean' (Alexander 2003: 34). The champion in favour of the Song's inclusion was Rabbi Akiva, whose praise we have heard, but the debate continued for some decades further. The concern, for these early Rabbinic fathers, was that the poem might be read simply as a love story – about a man and woman's erotic desire for one another. To overcome this problem, an allegorical exegesis was demanded: God and the author of the Song, they argued, had designed the poem to present a higher meaning. The problem is there is nothing in the text which overtly points out that it should be read as a sort of parable (as there is in the explanations and keys for interpretation that often came with Jesus' parables). The fathers of Christianity, like the Rabbis, treated the Song, however, as just such a parable. By the end of the Middle Ages quite a set of keys as to its meaning had accumulated. Unlike the Rabbis the Church fathers were also nearly all celibate. As Denys Turner argues, 'together with the more general, theological and literary reasons for reading the Song allegorically, a primary ascetical motive was to denature the text itself, to neutralize its power to arouse forbidden passion' (Turner 1995: 161).

The tension between the use of erotic imagery, on the one hand, and the ideal of virginity, on the other, is a recurring theme in the history of Christian mysticism, but nowhere more noticeable than in readings of the Song. Origen felt that this Song with its abundance of images and sensual emotions expressed the quintessence of the mystical life. No one can accuse Origen of denying desire; for him God was 'Passionate Love', and mysticism based on the divinisation of human *eros*. One could say Origen turned the Song into a means of Christian Tantra. In his prologue to his commentary he writes: 'The power of love is none other than that which leads the soul from earth to the lofty heights of heaven, and the highest beatitude can only be attained under the stimulus of love's desire' (Origen 1956: 24; see also ibid.: 35). Indeed, sexual love was but *one* form of *eros*, which in effect could involve longing for anything, but Origen felt that this was the most all-consuming desire and *thus* was what needed to be transferred onto God. For Origen (as for most of the Church fathers) the transformation had to be so complete that the physical aspect of *eros* was to be left completely left behind. Mysticism was divinised *eros*. The power of yearning desire implanted in the soul by God (who is desire itself) must be led away from its pursuit of material satisfactions and educated by the Word to pursue its true object, the love of Love itself. Origen was one of the very earliest proponents of celibacy as the best way of transforming the sexual energies completely into prayer, and the great textbook for this transformation was the Song.

For Origen the 'spiritual senses' acted as the bridge between the outer and inner person, between carnal and heavenly love. Through these senses the spiritual meaning lying behind the images and language of the Song could be savoured. Origen felt the Song had been transmitted through human and angelic ministration to reveal how God relates to the soul. Through the spiritual senses the mutual longing of God and the soul in the Song could be heard, tasted, touched and inhaled. The soul has 'organs of mystical knowledge … a sensuality which has nothing sensual in it' (Origen 2017: 33) through which the sharpness of sense experience (before the fall from paradise) regains its primordial intensity. And yet, those who read the Song must pass through the words to the very breath of the one who speaks:

> When her mind is filled with divine perception and understanding without the agency of human or angelic ministration then she may believe that she has received the kisses of the Word of God himself … She yearns and longs for him by day and night, can speak of nought but him, can think of nothing else, and is disposed to no desire or longing, except for him alone – that soul then says in truth with the Bride of the Song, 'I have been wounded by love.'
>
> (Origen 1956: 61, 198)

St Bernard took up many of Origen's themes in his *Sermons on the Song* but emphasised that it was not through denial but through the redirecting of carnal love (*cupiditas*) that we come to real affection (*affectus/amor*) (Bernard of Clairvaux 1995: ch. 8–9). And yet, still, in order to transmute sexual energy chastity was required. The 'tender, wise and strong affection' of the Song was, for Bernard, a valuable tool for overcoming 'the sweet enticements of the sensual life':

> Sweetness conquers sweetness as one nail drives out another … Love affectionately, discreetly, intensely. We know that the love of the heart, which we have said is affectionate, is sweet indeed, but liable to be led astray if it lacks the love of the soul. And the love of the soul is wise indeed.
>
> (Bernard of Clairvaux 1971: 150)

Yet, in relation to 'the sensual life' this is arguably still a form of sublimation. The issue of how to interpret the concrete sexuality of the Song has always proven the cutting point, and more or less marks the divide of religious allegory with post-Freudian interpretations today. If the Song is a parable then why choose a concubine annexed to a king's harem as a symbol of chaste virginal purity? Oils, scents, nakedness and breasts, all at the centre of the Bible. Why not choose a dove, a lily, to represent the people of God or the human soul? Why choose (literally) a sex symbol? A portrait of sexual longing to evoke something that is not physically sexual at all?[1]

The history of the interpretation of the Song could be seen as a concerted effort to pin 'fig leaves' (or gossamer veils) on the nude figures of the Sistine Chapel, for fear of misinterpretation. The secular camp could be forgiven for asking: 'Is this not a case of the Emperor's New Clothes?' And yet an intertextual biblical approach to the Song considerably deepens our appreciation of the relationship between the maiden and Solomon, and the genius of the poetry. The Song is a repertoire of the Bible. To treat it as something unrelated to other biblical texts is to deny the very language and history

---

1 As Bernard McGinn says, 'The tension between the use of erotic language, on the one hand, and the ideal of virginity, on the other, has been a recurring theme in the history of Christian mysticism' (McGinn 1992: 209).

of the Song. As a Solomonic text it takes place within a tradition, one inextricably linked to Wisdom. But contextualising the Song should not be done at the cost of the characters depicted in it, and the nature of the love they share. Any interpretation – however rigorous – should not straitjacket the lovers: the human wants, desires and the need for love expressed in the Song. Their love may be 'from the soul', but that does not make the Song any less sensual. Sensuality that expresses *personal* affection is beautiful and fragrant in all relationships, not just the sexual. *Affection* is key. Human love can run all the way to God.

The debate as to whether the Song has a secular frame of reference or a religious one ignores the fact that it is base metal which is transmuted into gold. As the great contemporary scholar of mysticism Bernard McGinn writes: 'It is important to point out that [with the mystics] what is involved is not so much the disguising of erotic language as the full and direct use of certain forms of erotic expression for a different purpose – the transformation of all human desire in terms of what the mystic believe to be the true source' (McGinn 1992: 210). Physical attraction for another human being may excite the passions but it also incites love. Passion can just as well develop into hate but if orientated towards friendship and selflessness then a new higher energy of union develops: no mergence (which would mean a loss of passion), but a discovery of *personal* connection. Those who are truly inseverable are always in relation to each other.

The value of the relationship portrayed by the Song is that it can be read at all levels: spiritual-soul friendship, physical–sexual compatibility. Neither need be divorced from the other. They are brought together in the text of the Song. The transformation of attraction into love described in the Song is key to its importance in the modern world: that the energy of union finds fulfilment in the gift of *companionship*. Sexual attraction may be a root of love, but when love grows and flowers it is found in a new way – as a fruit of love. Wisdom advises keeping the whole plant in view. To start with love, before moving towards sexual intimacy, may be a wise lesson of the Song today.

At its core, the Song treats Solomon and the maiden as ordinary human beings, passionately drawn to each other and falling in love. As the story unfolds they both come to feel that this love goes to the depth of who they are: 'Thou hast wounded my heart, my sister-bride'; 'My soul melted while he spoke … I faint with love.' If the poem is a spiritual journey experienced through a couple's deepening relationship then it shows that spirituality is the deepening of *personhood in relationship* (the Trinitarian definition of God). To bring the Song back to life and make it accessible doesn't necessitate dumbing it down to the level of a racy novel, or soft porn. The Song needs all its dimensions working together at once if it can inspire people to be whole again.

The divide between the secular and religious approach does nothing but impoverish the Song. To excise all the allegorical reading, or to prohibit the human love, are equally narrow. Each way in has its relevance: a religious interpretation opens the possibility of a mystical state of union; a secular reading maps the journey of human relations. In the end, as the Kabbalist Book of Zohar says, 'The impulse from below calls forth that from above' (Scholem 1995a: 233). Selfless human love leads to union. The Song may well help people alienated from religious imagery to come back to it through a story of human love. If one reads the Song simply in a poetic sense – as one might any secular poetry – then its extraordinary wealth of symbolism may prompt further exploration. Every reader, in the end, decides for themselves what layers of meaning bear relevance or validity for their life. The job of the exegete is simply to present the wealth and range of meaning this poem affords. Commentaries only encourage the reader to quietly go back and 'graze among the lilies'.

'Everything above and below comes about through male and female,' says the Zohar (2:15). In psychological terms, accessing the *anima* or *animus* may offer the space for an 'ideal love', opening up a dream of wholeness. However, when faced with real human relations such ideals can lead to expectations and projections onto others that are necessarily disappointed. Dreams are, in the end, about the one who dreams. A spiritual idealisation of the erotic can be a mere mental glorification, removing the one 'in love' from the ordinary realities of desire. Still, love is the arena of longing, which can reach mystical heights. We might agree with McGinn that for the mystics 'desire exists on a higher level than that usually experienced in this life, and hence for them "transformation" in the sense of elevation to this higher level, rather than mere "idealisation" would be a more accurate term for the change involved' (McGinn 1992: 210). Mystical use of the Song was to direct *eros* and *affectus* towards its transcendental source and goal, God. 'He set in order the deep love within me,' says the maiden in the Song (2:4). 'From the transformational point of view,' McGinn continues, 'human sexual desire is always an image of the true (not merely 'idealised) *eros* [and] the most sublime function of human *eros* and the language that represents it is to serve as a privileged symbol, a way of revealing this hidden higher reality.'

The marriage of spirit and the flesh in ordinary human relations is something pointed to but not realised in the Song. That the lovers cannot live together is the pathos and tragedy of the poem. Solomon has to return to his role as king, into which he can integrate the divine Sophia. However, the creaturely Sophia, the *human mode* of wise love, is lost to him. And yet the poem does not end with an eternal gaze towards heaven: the last episodes recognise that the step back into the world is necessary. Within the dispensations of their time true love could not be lived, and the Song looks to a future fulfilment:

When the wine gave out, the mother of Jesus said to him, 'They have no wine.' And Jesus said to her, 'Woman, what concern is that to you and me? My hour has not yet come.' His mother said to the servants, 'Do whatever he tells you.'

(John 2:3-5)

The end of the Song

A parallel to the Song among the Wisdom Books of the Bible is the Book of Job; both have a fictional/historical narrative that carries a sapiential message. If Job represents the archetypal 'male' psyche – as Carl Jung argued – then the Song depicts the eternal feminine.[2] Job is a tragic story that has a happy ending – at a human level he gets back his health, wealth and a new family, in terms of wisdom he is justified as innocent. The Song, however, is a happy story that has a tragic ending. We see the wonder of the lovers' discovery of each other, the joy of their time together, but in the end – due to the conditions of life – they have to part, and it is unlikely they will see each other again. One medieval commentary – in fact the only one written by women for women – sees clearly the change between the exuberance of the opening lines and the fulfilment of love in separation depicted in the closing lines. The Benedictine nuns of Admont in southern Germany, in around 1160 wrote the first vernacular (non-Latin) commentary on the Song, as a love-poem expressing the alternating sense of divine presence and absence. They saw the deepening of love as the soul is weaned from the need for consolations. The 'Epilogue' to their commentary sums up, for them, the purpose of the Song:

> Now understand this:
> This book began with kingly joy.
> It ends with pitiful lamentation.
> It began with a kingly song,

---

2 The Book of Job, like the Song, is hard to date but is generally assumed to be a little earlier, from between 600 and 300 BCE. Carl Jung, in *Answer to Job*, wrote 'Here Yahweh comes up against a man who stands firm against the injustices of life, and clings to his rights as a creature' (Jung 1965: 54). Though God proves 'stronger than man', Jung sees God as 'morally defeated' by Job: that is, God comes to be seen a 'mixture of opposites', *present in* the rights of what he creates, and also *in* that which he does not cause, like injustice, evil and suffering.

Now it closes with inner weeping.
It began with a Divine kiss.
It departs in love fulfilled,
    for it teaches the loving wisdom of God.

(McGinn 1994: 348)[3]

Is the Song simply another of those countless stories of the separation of lovers because of the cruel world? Is the depth of their love unrequited because of Solomon's 'work commitments'? Or is there a sapiential message which gives meaning to their separation? The fact that the Song has always been treated as sacred, as hinting at another world, should make us consider whether these are, in the end, just 'ordinary lovers', or whether as a pair they carry archetypal significance. It seems that, in their love, and if even for a few moments, they found their way back and stood *together* in the primal Eden, and that of the two, it is the woman who has realised the fact the more deeply.

To repeat Sergei Bulgakov's insight, 'the Divine Sophia and the creaturely Sophia are not two but one, although in two modes of being.' In the Song the creaturely Sophia, or wisdom, is depicted in the humanity of the maiden who yet carries the mantle of divine Wisdom. At a human level, the story ends in a separation, but in terms of Solomon's relationship to Wisdom the relationship continues. In fact, for him, the human relationship is the catalyst for learning wisdom: the Song ends with the maiden's hope that he will continue to 'listen to her voice.' In the human 'mode of being' there is a separation; Solomon loses his creaturely Sophia, his Shulamite. In the 'divine mode' there is a union through his 'harkening' to Holy Wisdom.

In a later book Bulgakov expands yet more gnomically (with the rather technical language of Orthodox theology): 'Human nature has the capacity for receiving a hypostasis [personal significance] after the likeness of its prototype, the Divine Sophia' (Bulgakov 1993:

---

3 In the penultimate line *durnahtiger* can also be translated as 'through and through' or 'perfected', where love is not dependant on presence but remains strong in absence.

79). In terms of the Song this means the maiden, becoming who she really is, takes on the likeness of Wisdom for her lover. The caterpillar becomes the butterfly, emerging from the chrysalis of separation, and yet the two modes are of the same being.

The Jewish tradition of Kabbalah in its exegesis of the Song sees the Shulamite as the Jewish people, the human soul and the Shekhinah of God, mapping together the earthly, psychic and heavenly nature of the feminine. Body, soul and spirit are united not only in *her* but in *their relationship*. Gershom Scholem, the great student of Jewish mysticism, suggests that through the use of the Song of Songs in Jewish and Christian mysticism the ancient symbol of *hieros gamos*, the sacred marriage between a god and a human, took on remarkable new life (Scholem 1995b: 106).[4] The medieval Kabbalah interpreted an earlier Jewish tradition of the Shekhinah more specifically as a feminine figure variously known as the Heavenly Mother, Matron, Queen, Bride and Wife of the Godhead, Princess, the divine daughter, etc. Similarly, in Jewish popular devotion and in the celebration of Sabbath liturgy, the Shekhinah becomes the mystical Ecclesia of Israel, identified with the Sabbath, which becomes Queen Sabbath, the symbol of the soul at rest, the bride of the Song of Songs, the Virgin Israel who, at the festival of Shavuot (Pentecost), is married to the Bridegroom, God. This is paralleled chronologically and thematically with the development of devotion to Mary in medieval Christianity. Both Kabbalah and the monastic culture of the Middle Ages were essentially contemplative movements, a return of the wisdom tradition into religious culture: in neither case does the feminine principle represent woman as such but rather the *eros* of the soul's relationship with God.[5]

---

4 Shekhinah – 'divine presence' (fem.) – is said specifically to marry Tiferet (or Rahamin) – 'divine beauty' (masc.).

5 See Kingsmill (2009: 20–21) and Turner (1995: 26). That this feminine personification of Wisdom goes back much earlier, to the time of Solomon and before, see the work of Margaret Barker (e.g. Barker 2003: ch. 10).

Books like the Zohar (written by Moses de Leon from about 1275 to 1286) went beyond Christian use of erotic language in two important ways: first, in projecting the marital relationship into the divine or heavenly realm itself; and second, in establishing a necessary bond between marital union in this world and the *mysterium coniunctionis*. This also involves a significant gender switch from traditional typecasting in the Song (or rather a non-switch, as we have seen the feminine figure in fact *leads* the narrative), in that the human lover retains his male character while the divine beloved, the Shekhinah, is female (pointed out by McGinn 1992: 218). Every husband, the Book of Zohar says, stands between two females, his wife and the Shekhinah. Sexual union on the Sabbath eve between the kabbalist and his wife was felt to partake in the conjunction of Shekhinah and the masculine principle of divine beauty.[6]

Thomas Aquinas (d.1274) wrote that, after the love that unites us to God, conjugal love is the 'greatest form of friendship' (Aquinas 2015: III, 123; cf. Aristotle 1984: 174). But elsewhere he reduces this simply to body: 'We are told that woman was made to be a help to man … Yet she was not fitted to help except in generation, for another man would have provided a more effective help in everything else' (Aquinas 1981: 1, question 98, part 2)! Aquinas may have benefitted from his younger contemporary Dante's own comments on this passage! If anyone was to prove a beneficent influence on Dante's soul in his life (and the seminal help to his spirit in the afterlife) it was Beatrice. Not only did her prayers bring him to repentance but Virgil's help came through her until she herself became his guide through paradise. The figure of Beatrice exemplifies how a human person comes to more than signify but actually *make present* divine wisdom and grace. The human Beatrice of the *Vita Nuova* and the spiritual guide of *Paradiso* are one and the same girl: in heaven Dante recognises 'those eyes that I had known long before … the lures

---

6 Moses alone was called to abandon his earthly wife to be united directly and only to the Shekhinah (Moses de Leon 1983: 130).

which Love had used to capture me' (*Paradiso* 28:12).[7] And yet the earthly and the heavenly Beatrice are in 'two modes of being' (ibid.): the virtues he saw in a young girl in Florence he now finds among all the saints. Beatrice is the symbol and icon of the divine salutation of love.

Dante's *Vita Nuova* is, at one level, the record of 'boy meets girl'; at another, it is the account of the maturing of an infatuation for Beatrice into a love of her, *for what she made present to him.* At the age of nine, at a party, he met another child, almost nine, by whose appearance he was thrilled; he met her again and again, and at the age of eighteen he realised he was deeply in love. So, somewhere around the year 1283, when he was greeted by her in the streets in Florence, he felt a 'shock' of a love so strong that he was beside himself. For days, he could not speak. There is no evidence that Beatrice felt the same, or that she even felt any particular romantic love for him. If she had they may have got married, as there was no worldly reason in the Florence of their time why they could not. Except, in the end, for that most absolute of reasons – death. For Beatrice died at the age of twenty-four. Dante went on to lead an active political as well as literary life, he married, had children, was exiled, but he never forgot that he had once seen another person (in his case, of the opposite sex) in a blaze of beauty and goodness that made them almost divine. To him this young woman was 'the destroyer of all evil and the queen of all good', the equivalent of heaven to him.

Now, one could say this is a pure projection and has very little to do with the actual person whom Dante met, and can hardly have got to know very well in his passing meetings. However, Dante felt he did 'know her'; the qualities he perceived in her were expressed outwardly, in her appearance. Moreover, he is at pains to show that the *effect* she had on him was what was really significant. He says

---

7 All quotations from *The Divine Comedy* in this section are from Mark Musa's translation (Dante 1986). Translations from *Vita Nuova* are from William Anderson's translation (Dante 1964).

that when she met him in the street and said good morning, he was so highly moved that he was, for the moment, in a state of complete good will and complete charity towards everyone. If anyone had at that moment done him an injury, he would necessarily have forgiven him. In other words, he has not only 'fallen in love', he is quite literally 'in love'. *Enamour* – the Italian is *innamora*, literally 'in love'. Dante writes: 'If anyone had asked me a question, I should have been able to answer only "Love"' (Dante 1964: 50). It is this spiritual *fruit* of his relation to Beatrice which makes her so significant to him, and the reason why he calls her salutation 'blessed'. In *Paradiso* she indeed guides him into beatitude.

In the *Vita Nuova* no one had known what this young woman had intended with Dante, or even if she had noticed the effect she had on him, but in *Paradiso* it is clear – she wills to be for Dante what Dante needs, as she herself tells Virgil, 'no one in the world ever moved so quickly' as she to help him (*Inferno* 2:109). Beatrice's first appearance in *The Divine Comedy* is hailed with a line from the Song: 'Come, O bride, from Lebanon' (*Purgatorio* 30:11). Before they ascend heaven Dante and Beatrice stand together in the earthly paradise, Eden; with his eyes fixed on her, purified as he is by his journey, he attains the state of Adam before the Fall, where the smile of his beloved opens onto the divine smile. Many lovers have known this. Is it a passing infatuation or a momentary re-entrance into paradise?

> In that place first created for mankind
> much more is granted to the human senses
> than ever was allowed them here on earth.
> (*Paradiso* 1:54–7)

Later, as they approach 'the heaven of the wise and learned', Dante and Beatrice see Solomon there – 'the brightest of the lights [and yet] modest' (*Paradiso* 14:34–5). In placing Solomon in heaven Dante defends him against a scholastic opinion that he was damned due to 'sensuality and pride'. The scandal of the Song fired the imagination of medieval minds:

> In what he wrote, the most beautiful of all,
> he breathes with a love so passionate
> that men hunger on earth to know his fate.
>
> (*Paradiso* 10:109–11)

Solomon explains to them the mystery of the risen flesh, when the human body will participate in the soul's beatific vision, and gives a teaching on spiritual sensuality: burning coal, though material, is hotter than fire alone.

> The effulgence that contains us now [in heaven]
> will be surpassed in brilliance by the flesh …
> the organs of our body will be strengthened
> and ready for whatever gives us joy.
>
> (*Paradiso* 14:55–60)

All things human will be transparent to the divine. And yet, higher in heaven, when Dante had seen so much love 'within her sacred eyes', Beatrice turns his attention elsewhere – 'Why does this face of mine so enamour you,' she asks, 'that you do not turn to the lovely garden of paradise itself?' (*Paradiso* 23:70–71). But still further, when Dante is questioned by St John (the greatest of contemplatives and the apostle of love) as to the nature of love, he speaks of his own eyes that had seen a young girl in Florence, which 'were the gates where she entered with the fire in which I burn forever' (*Paradiso* 26:14–15). St John accepts this is a love that is worthy of God. There, from the heights of heaven, Dante looks back at Beatrice's influence in his life: 'From the first day when I beheld her face in this life until the present moment, my song never ceased to study her' (*Paradiso* 30:28–30).

In representing Wisdom the Shulamite of the Song, like Dante's

Beatrice, is depicted as fully human, no merely ethereal form. The Song has the advantage over Dante here, in that the lovers show a real degree of physical and sexual intimacy, a joining of flesh and spirit much more than in Dante. Dante expresses his relationship with Beatrice in terms of vision – indeed, there wasn't much else! The Song, however, has a full *sensorium*: sight, hearing, touch, smell, and taste. All are equally represented and less obviously 'spiritualised' than Dante's relationship with Beatrice. The eighteenth-century German Romantic poet Novalis von Hardenberg expresses a full communion in his novel *Heinrich von Ofterdingen*, where Heinrich says of Matilde:

> My whole being should mingle with yours. Only the most boundless abandonment can satisfy my love. Therein consists my love. It is a mysterious fusion of our most secret and personal beings.
>
> (Quoted in Reynolds 1995: 21)

One of his most famous aphorisms shows this was, for him, an *embodied* experience:

> There is but one Temple in the world and that is the body of man or woman. Nothing is holier than this high form. Bending before man and woman is a reverence done to this revelation of the flesh. We touch heaven when we lay hand on a human body.
>
> (Quoted in Reynolds 1995: 21)

And yet Novalis recognises that even in the mystical marriage, 'Death is invited to the wedding.'

In the Song there is no actual death (as with Beatrice, or Sophie, the young fiancée of Novalis), and yet, because of circumstances, the human *mode* of the lovers' relationship has to come to an end. The ending of relationships that have been joyful is a death, and the extent of grief corresponds to the joy. In the Song there is great joy, and therefore great grief at its ending. Though commentators have seen the end of the Song as 'ambiguous' (Carr 2003: 137), or 'lacking in closure' (Block and Block 2006: 18–19), we have seen that, at a human level, the ending is clear and final. There is a possibility that the relationship continues in some interrupted way beyond what is recorded in the Song, in the mode of friendship, but given the circumstances this is unlikely. In either case, the Song may unwittingly speak to the modern condition of relationships that, for one reason or other, do not last. It may help in giving meaning to what proves to be temporary. What meaning? Firstly, that love survives the ending of a relationship. Couples can continue to care for each other even though they may not be able to be with each other. The loss of *eros* may indeed mean the mode of relationship changes but it need not mean the love changes, for 'Love is as strong as death.' Friendship may not be just a transition 'out of love', but a real mode of love in itself. Secondly, even where a relationship of *eros* continues, or there is still the capacity to live with each other in a committed way, a transformation of that *eros* takes place which can feel like a death, yet is an opening to deeper and more other-centred love. Vatican II speaks of 'the friendship proper to marriage' (Flannery 1992: 952). In the words of Pope Benedict XVII:

> Even if *eros* is at first mainly covetous and ascending, a fascination for the great promise of happiness, in drawing near to the other, it is less and less concerned with itself, increasingly seeks the happiness of the other, is concerned more and more with the beloved, bestows itself and wants to 'be there for' the other. The element of *agape* thus enters into this love, for otherwise *eros* is impoverished and even loses its own nature.
>
> (Benedict 2006: 16)

The Song of Solomon in its entirety expresses *both* sexual passion *and* personal friendship. It is the combination of both which, in recent Church teaching, is seen as the key to marriage: Pope Francis asserts that 'Sexuality is inseparably at the service of this conjugal friendship, for it is meant to aid the fulfilment of the other person' and 'Marriage is likewise a friendship marked by passion, but a passion always directed to an ever more stable and intense union' (Francis 2016: 89, 74).

The end of the Song should not, therefore, be taken necessarily as its *conclusion* but as a *counter-balance* to what went before, introducing an element of realism to the flights of romance, of the necessity to live in this world. The 'great day' depicted in the Song may be more about 'falling in love' than the demands of 'staying in love' (while contending with the pressures of work, children and extended family). As such the ending of the Song may be a bit of a 'wake-up call'. Personal love is usually tried by the difficult situations lovers find themselves in. No couple is an island, independent or sufficient unto themselves. Learning to love within the demands of day-to-day life is the real practice. On the other hand, the end of the Song also points to a meaning of love *beyond this world*. Human love is never limited to this life. Just as we can love those who have passed through the transfiguration of death, so the Song points to a passion 'stronger than death, more relentless than the grave.' Maybe a balance is what keeps love healthy. Prioritising of one over the other may fit different 'seasons of love' for (as Solomon was supposed to have said), 'there is a time to embrace, and a time to refrain from embracing' (Ecclesiastes 3:5).

Ancient readings reviewed

If the Song is to be read for what it is – inspired literature – it must have a literal meaning, that is, the meaning of the poem is *in the words*, not just in suppositions, theories or hypotheses drawn from them. But in the Song the literal is not obvious. In fact, it seems the author intends mystery, partly concealing and masking the narrative root of the poem, as if he/she had created 'a closed garden, a fountain sealed.' However, the sense of impenetrability is because most interpreters have chosen to approach the poem didactically rather than as poetry. This may be because readers of the Bible often expect to be *instructed* rather than *moved* in response to its poetic language. In no way does the Song offer instruction on how to achieve romantic love, let alone some form of moral precept. It is a love story. The 'moral of the story' (which all good stories have) has to come *from the story*. Kingsmill here is right: '[Metaphorical] suggestions can only be sustained if they correspond to something within [the text], otherwise, their being imposed from without leads, sooner or later, to disbelief and rejection' (Kingsmill 2009: 26). If passion for union between two human beings is the *prima materia* of the Song, how does this relate to the spiritual, and specifically the monastic readings through the centuries? Psychologically, unless *eros* is engaged with it remains an untapped aspect of self-knowledge and of relationship. 'Moral qualities are only proved in situations that are morally dangerous,' as Carl Jung said (Jung 1945: 222). But the morally dangerous aspect of the Song has been consistently evaded. Even today Orthodox Jews follow ancient Rabbinic proscriptions that guard the Song's holiness: it should not be read by those under the age of thirty, nor should it be a subject of public discourse (even in Synagogue). And Christian exegesis must ask these questions: Could the Shulamite be a prophetic symbol of the Virgin Mary? Or is the relationship of Jesus with his disciples symbolically reflected by the 'fulfilment' of the lovers' relation in the Song? Certainly many of the ancient and medieval allegories seem far-fetched, though one can but wonder at the capacity for theological imagination in former times.

The earliest entire commentary we have of the Song comes from the Targum, a Chaldean paraphrase of the Hebrew Scriptures written around 550 CE. The Targum reads the Song as an elaborate allegory, describing prophetically the history of the Jewish nation, beginning with their Exodus from Egypt, detailing their doings and sufferings down to the coming of the Messiah, and the building of the Third Temple. The lover is the Lord; the beloved maiden the congregation of Israel; the 'companions of the beloved' (described in 1:7) are the Edomites and the Ishmaelites; the 'daughters of Jerusalem' (at 1:5) are the gentile nations, (at 2:7, 3:5 and 8:4) the congregation of Israel and (at 5:8) the prophets; the 'brothers of the maiden' are the false prophets; the angels are the ones who (at 8:8) speak of 'the little sister' (who is also a personification of Israel); and 'the companions' (at 8:13) are the Sanhedrim of Jewish elders. So, for example (and thousands could be taken), 'I am dark but shapely' (1:4) refers to the congregation of Israel at Sinai who became dark in making the golden calf but were brought into shape by the Ten Commandments. The 'beams' and 'rafters' of Solomon's house in 2:16 prophesy the building of a new temple by a King-Messiah, replacing that destroyed in 70 CE.

In the Middle Ages Jewish commentaries often took a more psychological approach, influenced by the recovery of Aristotle's understanding of the faculties of the soul, seeing the lover of the Song as the 'active intellect' (*mens*) and the beloved as the receptive, material intellect (*spiritus*); their love was what kept body and soul together.[8]

If we turn to Christian expositors of the Song, fragments remain of an extensive commentary by Origen (185–254 CE). Origen cites a historical literal sense of the Song as an epithalamium on the marriage of Solomon with the daughter of Pharaoh, but for him the real meaning is the marriage of Christ and the Church; the 'companions of the bridegroom' are the angels and saints in heaven, 'the daughters of Jerusalem' the believers on earth. 'Let him kiss me with the kisses

---

8 See commentary by Christian Ginsburg (1957: 46–57). Such an approach predates psychoanalytical understanding of the relation of the ego and the unconscious by 700 years.

of his mouth' (1:1) invokes the incarnation: the bride speaks to the Father, 'How long will your son, and my bridegroom, send kisses by Moses and kisses by the Prophets? I want to touch his lips. Let him come.'

The Alexandrian school of exegesis took Origen's disinterest in the literal story of the Song further under St Athanasius (296–373 CE): 'The whole book,' Athanasius contended, 'is an allegory, and it is to be understood enigmatically from the beginning to the end; its doctrines are secrets, and only those who are well versed in allegory ought to study it.' For example, 5:1 ('I have come into my garden, my sister, my spouse; I have gathered my myrrh with my spices') for Athanasius expresses the Incarnation: 'the world is Christ's garden, because it is made through him; and his whole body breathes forth fragrance, because it is joined to the Divine Word'. The parallel school of exegesis at Antioch accepted the literal sense of the Song but in doing so considered the Song inappropriate enough to bar it from the Antiochine Canon of Scripture. After the condemnations of Theodore of Mopsuestia literal interpretations were dropped.

Augustine added a certain realism in the Western Christian approach to the Song, but realism within the allegory rather than the literal sense. The maiden's query as to where her lover lies at midday (1:6) points to Christ's concern for the Church in Africa 'which lies in the meridian of the world' (a climate Augustine knew as bishop of Hippo in Carthage; Ginsburg 1957: 61–7). In the Middle Ages, the shift in Christian commentaries was towards a more personal appropriation of the meaning of the Song (though never in the strictly psychological terms of some of the Rabbinic commentators of that time). For St Bernard it was, primarily, about the relation of Christ and the soul. He divides the Song into three parts describing stages of mystical union of the soul with God as 'she' is led progressively into 'the garden', 'the cellar or storeroom', and thence into 'the bedroom.' For Bernard these images apply to the way Scripture is read: 'the garden represents the plain, unadorned historical sense of Scripture, the storeroom its moral sense, and the bedroom the mystery of Divine contemplation' (Bernard of Clairvaux 1976: 28). In the garden the wine and the spices of virtues grow, in the cellars they are made aromatic and palatable for others, in the bedroom the virtues of the soul are united to their divine source in peace and enjoyment.

Ancient Jewish and Christian commentators were prompted to find anagogical meanings (a foretaste of God's relation to the soul in the afterlife) through recognising that the Song's literal sense expresses *yearning* much more than *finding*. What made the Song so ripe for the Messianic hopes of the Jewish people and the heavenly-mindedness of the Christian mystics was the feeling of *anticipation* in the poem. The prophecies they read into the Song may have been to the detriment of the real human love story but they were based on a realisation that the poem is not about earthly marriage, let alone (as with interpreters today) simply about sex. There is a pro-lepsis in the poem, something desired, half glimpsed but not truly realisable until a future time, until a further dispensation of grace.

That the poem has been a springboard for various imaginative allegories that seem idiosyncratic to the text does not, however, discredit imaginative reading *per se*. The Song also provided a spring-board for what psychologists later called 'free-association': a word or phrase evoked further symbols and meanings relating to the commentator's own interests; theological, pastoral, mystical. Some medieval allegoric interpretations of the Song certainly went off on tangents. Reading of the Song is as much about who the reader is as about the text itself. The Song in its pauses and gaps leaves room for the reader, it asks for a type of contemplative reading where the reader learns to read their own responses. The poem is allusive and its meaning will always be an interplay between the hints and prompts of the words and those who read them. 'The spirit of the Song' cannot be tied down to fixed theological references or deconstructed into fragments that together have nothing to say. 'Free association' is something of the gift of the Song; it speaks poetically, avoids the domination of logic, and asks for a personal subjective response. Even among the Church Fathers there are a plethora of different readings of details of the Song. And the mystics bring in their own soul. John of the Cross, for example, in his Spiritual Canticle (in many ways the greatest commentary on the Song ever written, being itself a poem) weaves in his own love of solitude and of nature. He offers his own personal associations as to what the beloved means to him:

> My beloved, the mountains
> And lonely wooded valleys,
> Strange islands,
> And resounding rivers,
> The whistling of love-stirring breezes,
> The tranquil night
> At the time of the rising dawn,
> Silent music,
> Sounding solitude,
> The supper that refreshes, and deepens love.
>
> (John of the Cross 1987: 223)[9]

Body and soul/relationship and solitude

The Song often reads like a dream sequence, even an erotic dream, and yet it is the mystics rather than the psychoanalysts who have been fascinated with it. Mysticism is infused with much of the psychic elements that come up in dream-life and yet its main focus is spirit. In the light of Jungian analysis, however, much of the

---

9 One of John's disciples said that, at the point of death, John 'interrupted the prior of the Carmelites who had started to read the prayers of recommendation for his departing soul. "Tell me about the Song of Songs; this other thing is of no use to me", John gently implored. And when the verses of the Song were read to him, he commented as if in a dream: "Oh, what precious pearls!"' (Crisogono de Jesus 1982: 383).

symbolism and metaphor of the Song (while having associations with its epoch) holds resonances with 'a collective unconscious', a soul-memory. As such the Song is a reservoir of archetypes that are independent and prior to conscious (religious) interests or motivations. Moreover, modern branches of psychotherapy point out the relationship between memory and the body's sensory system. The bliss and trauma that can be experienced in infancy through affection or neglect leave a somatic residue, which can be relived and treated through the body. Body awareness can also be used for meditative purposes – as in 'mindfulness' – focusing on sensations so as to calm the body and bring the mind to stillness, but also simply enjoying sense experiences through 'life appreciation exercises'.

In this context meditation on the Song could find an important place in the search for an embodied therapy or spirituality. At a natural level the Song speaks to us through the senses and can awaken memories of union and separation, helping us to work through them. In leading to integration and personal wholeness the Song points to the ground of our being. The Song acts in drawing the senses, engaging them, and gently deploying them to the centre of who we are. It is here, at the centre of the soul (that is also the ground of our sensuality) that the mystics find God. The Song doesn't speak of God (and this, like mindfulness, makes it attractive today). And yet God is, in a sense, 'incarnated' in the words, so that the reader rises to God through the body (as in contemporary meditation practices). This is not something new to the Christian tradition: 'What we have seen with our eyes, what we have looked at and touched with our hands concerning the word of life' (1 John 1:1). For St Bernard the corporeal and 'spiritual senses' are the same senses only directed earthward or heavenward. The Song's imagery awakens the senses and directs them slowly towards love. What starts in the body ends in the soul. Bernard felt that the imagery of taste and touch invited an immediate and experiential contact with God. This contact was also reciprocal; for touch or taste always affects the object sensed, in a way sight and hearing need not (cf. Rudy 2002: 5–6, 45–8, 55–61). Christ wept with every part of his body not just his eyes (Bernard of Clairvaux 1968: 55).

For St Teresa of Ávila (who was both Jewish and Christian) it is the *scent* of the divine, which has this immediate effect:

> A person may be seized with a delightful fervour as if suddenly encompassed with a fragrance powerful enough to diffuse itself through all the senses. I do not assert that there really is any perfume but use this comparison because it somewhat resembles the manner by which the Spouse makes His presence understood, moving the soul to a delicious desire of enjoying Him.
>
> (Teresa of Ávila 1921: 170)

In the fourth mansion of *The Interior Castle* Teresa distinguishes between *feelings* of devotion, which come and go, and *consolations* that well up from within as from a fountain opened up in the soul. The characteristic of God's touch in the centre of the soul is that these consolations overflow into the body:

> After gradually filling the heart to the brim, the delight overflows throughout all the mansions and faculties, until at last it reaches the body. Therefore, I say Divine consolations arises from God and ends in ourselves, for whoever experiences it will find that the whole physical part of our nature shares in this delight and sweetness.
>
> (Teresa of Ávila 1921: 145)

When Bernard writes that what starts in the body ends in the soul, Teresa brings it full circle – what starts in the soul ends in the body. As above so below, and *vice versa*. The Song expresses the two-way dynamic: bodily experience can be a way to meet God; spiritual experience can be brought down into the body.

Why, in Christian history, did monks and nuns particularly love the Song? The greatest commentaries – from Origen to Bernard to Teresa and John – where written by celibates. *Monos* means 'alone', but monks do not live outside of relationships. Their primary relationship, however, is with God. The Song allowed them to explore and express their affectivity; particularly the sense of longing for God, who they felt was tremendously attractive. The Song enabled them to see God as a lover and sense themselves as beloved in a passionate, even erotic, way. 'Christ awakens our bodies,' writes Symeon the New Theologian (948–1022), 'Let yourselves receive the one who is opening to you so deeply … In His light we awaken as the beloved, lovely and radiant, in every last part of our body' (Symeon the New Theologian 1976: 80).

Solitary life can also be a form of romantic love. In fourteenth-century England Richard Rolle championed the solitary life as a response to the love expressed in the Song. For Rolle the *lover* was the ideal religious type and he drew in his writings from both the Song and courtly love literature. In *Ego Dormio* (the earliest of Rolle's English epistles) he writes to a young woman who is about to 'fall asleep to the world' by embarking on the solitary life. The letter is a comment on the verse from the Song, 'I sleep but my heart wakes'. Rolle woos this maiden that he loves not for himself, but for Christ: 'For thee that I love, I woo thee, that I might have thee exactly as I would, not for myself, but for my Lord! I would become that go-between to bring thee to His bed' (Rolle 1989: 133). The notion of being in bed with the divine bridegroom is expressed (depending on one's taste) with a charming or embarrassing realism by the Englishwoman Margery Kempe one century after Rolle. Margery – manager of a brewery business, wife and mother of fifteen children – came across the Song of Songs and started to aspire to be a 'bride of Christ'. She prayed in the words of the Song, 'In the clefts of the rock, in the secrecy of the high places, let me see your face, let me hear your voice, for your voice is sweet and your appearance comely' (2:14). She got a bit of a surprise in that she was answered:

> The Lord answered me in my mind and said: 'As it is appropriate for the wife to be on homely terms with her husband, be he ever so great a Lord and she ever so poor a woman when he weds her, yet they must lie together and rest together in joy and peace, just so it must be between you and me, for I take no heed for what you have been but what you would be, and I have often told you that I have clean forgiven you all your sins. Therefore I must be intimate with you. I must lie on your bed with you. Daughter, you greatly desire to see me, and you may boldly, when you are in bed, take me to you as your wedded husband, as your dear darling, and as your sweet son, for I want to be loved as a son should be loved by the mother, and I want you to love me, daughter, as a good wife ought to love her husband. Therefore you may boldly take me in the arms of your soul and kiss my mouth, my head, and my feet as sweetly as you want.
>
> (Kempe 1994: 126–7)

The *monos*, or single person, is also in relationship with others and the biblical, Classical and later Christian tradition of *spiritual friendship* can be one genuine way of reading the relationship depicted in the Song. The sexualised language of the Song should not make us forget that friendship in the Classical and the biblical world was not on a lower key to romance (as it is today) but was regarded as the highest ideal of love. The Bible does speak of the love of Isaac and Rebecca, and Jacob and Sarah, but the deepest expression of soul-kinship is between Jonathon (son of Saul) and David (son of Jesse):

The soul of Jonathan was knit to the soul of David, and Jonathan loved him as his own soul … He made a covenant with David, because he loved him as his own soul. And Jonathan stripped himself of the robe that was on him and gave it to David.

(1 Samuel 18:1-4)

Gender may not be particularly important in the highest love: 'Greater love hath no one than this, that they lay down their life for their *friends*' (John 15:13). 'There is nothing so precious as a faithful friend' (Sirach 6:15). Such expressions of brotherly/sisterly love (*philia*) with allusions to *agape* seem a far cry from the sentiments of passion expressed in the Song. But, as we have seen in the Song, the first and from then on the most favoured term of address the male figure gives the female is 'my friend'. And the maiden overwhelmingly uses 'my beloved'; in the Vulgate, *diligatus* – which means literally 'one singled out from among others'. In the Septuagint it is *adelophidos* – which means literally 'nephew, kinsman, or little brother' – in form a diminutive, which in Greek is used as a term of affection, to someone 'sweet or lovable'. In the Masoretic the Hebrew is *dôd*, which appears a total of 33 times in the Song (and only 21 times in the rest of the Hebrew Bible) – the root meaning is literally from the verb 'to boil', but (as a masculine noun) was used to refer to loved ones, but especially uncles! So terms of address in the Song are more expressive of *affection* than sexuality.

Indeed, in the Classical era friendship was viewed as the highest mode of love. 'Nature has no love for solitude, and always leans, as it were, on some support; and the sweetest support is found in the most intimate friendship', writes Cicero, 'a friend is, as it were, a second self' (Cicero 2016: 28, 12). Cicero (106–43 BCE) sees friendship as going deeper than attraction to another person (for sensuality is a limited mode): 'Friends, though absent, are still present', and 'Friendship is the only thing in the world concerning the usefulness of which all mankind are agreed' (ibid.: 28), and yet, 'it is not so much the benefits received as the affection from which they flow which gives friendship its best and most valuable recommendation' (ibid.: 20).

The English monk Aelred of Rievaux (1110–67), writing a thousand years after Cicero, takes a similar view applying it to monastic life. Friendship, for Aelred, has three parts: attraction, intention and fruition. *Attraction* involved the natural impression made on the mind by a person perceived as desirable.[10] *Intention* involved choosing that person and deciding on the mode of relation (and degree of closeness) most suited to encouraging unselfish affection. *Fruition* was to enjoy the benefits, pleasure and delights of friendship as an end in itself and its own reward. The usefulness of friendship, for Aelred, is primarily as a path beyond egocentricity and, therefore, into the spiritual life.

For Aelred fruition is when we find Christ in and through the friend: 'In this way, divine love follows on from human love, spiritual delight from emotional delight, affection for God from affection for a human being' (Aelred of Rievaulx 1977: 74). He uses the opening line of the Song to express the fruition of friendship:

> Thus does a friend, cleaving to his friend in the spirit of Christ, become one heart and one mind with him, and so, rising by steps of love to Christ's friendship, he becomes one spirit with him in one kiss. To this kiss the holy soul aspires in the words: 'Let him kiss me with the kiss of his mouth.'
>
> (Aelred of Rievaulx 1977: 74)

He goes on to write that, 'In a kiss two breaths meet, mingle and become one; and as a result there arises in the mind a wonderful feeling of delight that awakens and kindles the love of them that kiss'

---

10 Here Aelred drew from his friend St Bernard's view that carnal love is the first step of love. 'Carnal love' involves loving what God gives us in creation, reaching fulfilment when God himself became flesh 'to recapture the affections of carnal men' (Bernard of Clairvaux 1971: 152).

(ibid.). Aelred distinguishes the kiss of the body, the kiss of the heart and the kiss of the mind. The bodily kiss within the rule of St Benedict that Aelred followed is given and received as a formal expression of friendship: at the sign of peace at Mass and in receiving guests. The kiss of the heart, for Aelred, is 'the kiss of Christ which he gives not by his own mouth but by the mouth of another, breathing into two friends a most sacred affection so that it seems to them they are one soul in two bodies' (ibid.). Finally, the kiss of the mind is 'when we have become accustomed to the kiss of the heart and recognise that all the sweetness comes from Christ' (ibid.). At this point we enter into the spiritual meaning of the Song when in longing we cry out, 'Let him kiss me with the kiss of *his* mouth,' and where we rest in *his* embrace. For Aelred, however, the human stage of friendship is never a means to an end, but those who are united with a kiss of the heart remain in the bond of love.

When deployed as allegory the Song points to *relationship* as central to our encounter with God. God, as Trinity, *is* relationship, and all God does – creation, redemption, etc. – is relational. The Song can free up our view of God: desire, longing, attraction are part of divine love. Aelred's use of the Song to illustrate the path of spiritual friendship shows that for him the human dimension of the Song is not *just* allegory. It is only by affirming human love that we are able to discover the revelation of God in it. This love can take the form of love of nature, romance, marriage or friendship. All of these through the Song can be transmuted into spiritual love without losing their human aspect. As such the single life need be no bar to appreciating the relational aspect of the Song. The Song does not end with the possibility of the two lovers sharing their lives: there are many longings in life that are not fulfilled. And yet, as Rumi wrote, 'There is a passion in me that does not long for anything from any human person' (Rumi 2009: 206). Self-knowledge, through quiet contemplation, may provide the key to understanding the Song.

Gender in the Song

The Song shows that gender need not be 'essentialised' in any stereotypical or culturally constructed way. It depicts a woman who is strong-minded and in charge of her own destiny, as well as being loving and self-giving. The man, caring and undomineering, makes no attempt to mould her according to his wishes; twice he insists that she be not 'roused' until *she wishes*. Alongside delicate images she is described as incredibly *strong*: 'terrible as the camps of an army ordained to battle', 'all excelling as the sun'. Her neck is singled out by her lover ('As the tower of David, built with ramparts, on which hang a thousand shields, all the armour of valiant men'): the Jewish people who used oxen for ploughing knew that you could control the direction of the animal by hitting it on the neck, here the maiden is shown as fiercely independent, one not to be led. She herself says, 'I am a wall and my breasts are like towers.' He is described by her in far from 'macho' imagery: an apple tree among the wood of the forests, three times as a herbivore who 'feeds in the gardens', 'a roe and a young hart'; no predatory animal, but one who 'gathers lilies'. The Song is a challenge to binary concepts of what it is to be a man or a woman.

The subversive interplay of masculine and feminine in the Song culminates in the last line of the Song: the maiden says, 'O my beloved, *make thyself even as* a roe and a young hart upon the mountains of spices' (8:14). She had earlier described her lover as 'a roe and young hart' (2:9, 17), and he had described her as 'a mountain of myrrh and hill of frankincense' (4:6). She is now saying, *be like* what our relationship *is*. *Make thyself even as* the masculine and feminine together. She urges this psychological integration in him. And yet the image of gentleness (roe and young hart) is *him*, and that of strength (mountains) is *her*.

In English (as in Hebrew) gender only appears in the third person singular; and objectifies others as 'he' or 'she' – in the relational 'you' and 'we' no gender is specified, as also in the personal 'I'. In inter-personal dialogue we usually address each other without referring to gender. Relationship normally speaks as 'I', 'you' (where there is no reduction of the person to gender). However, the Song – though a dialogue – is noticeably full of third-person pronouns. In places where one would expect an *I–thou* there is a *he–she*, an interweaving throughout the Song of direct speech with narrated speech. Mystical commentators have seen in this the sense of the alternating absence and the presence of the beloved. To our sensibilities, at times, the loved one appears directly present (and can be expressed in the second person) and at times he/she is, as it were, at one step removed (and is spoken of as he/she). The important thing to note, however, is that direct presence does not need the expression of gender. Gender in language only comes in with the sense of distance.

Biological differences between men and women need not imply psychological differences any more than they prescribe social roles. And yet the Song presents the lovers clearly as *body-persons*, as a union of body and soul. Their descriptions of each other always combine *character* and *appearance*. Twice he speaks of 'that which lies hidden within' her appearance (4:1, 3). Both his and her eyes are 'as doves' because of the white in them, but also because of the gentle regard they have for each other. Nowhere in the Song, however, is gender itself used as a definition of character. Solomon's praises of his 'friend' are never simply of 'feminine charms' (as if he was to say, 'you are so womanly'), and when she is asked 'what makes your beloved more than any other beloved' her description of her lover's appearance expresses his character and in no way stereotypically, that he is 'more manly than others'.

Following from this: the 'complementarity' of the sexes – that we need our 'other half', different to us, who will complete us – poses the question of whether we can be complete in ourselves. If the Song does see the relationship between the man and the woman as complementary this is not as a *conclusion* – as if the end of the story was an outward marriage, as in the happy ending of a fairy tale.

Rather the integration of outer difference (gender as well as social class is a key duality in the Song) is a *stage* on the way to individuation. The lovers in this particular story do not *stay together*, but they do get to know much about themselves. The Song, therefore, points ultimately to the integration of opposites (including male and female) as *intra-personal*, within the soul. The maiden may be 'leaning on her beloved' but the question ultimately is who she is in herself. The inter-personal relation (between two people) may be the catalyst but the key question at the end of the Song is 'Who are you?' This is particularly the case for the woman: 'Who is she,' her lover asks, 'that advances as the dawn arising, beautiful as the moon, all excelling as the sun, terrible as the camps of an army ordained to battle?' (6:9) In contrast to the cultural conditioning that a woman's place in the world would be found in relation to a man, the Song points to a time when, in the words of Rainer Maria Rilke, 'there will be girls and women whose name will no longer signify merely the opposite of the masculine, but something in itself, something that makes one think not of any compliment and limit, but only of life and existence' (Rilke 1962: 59).

The Song shows that insofar as gender signals potential relation, it will be of two wholes, not two halves. The relationship depicted in the Song is ultimately not one of *need* but of *desire*. To *want* someone doesn't mean you *need* them. As Cicero wrote, what we *get* from friendship can never be the primary motive. Love, not lack, is the deepest root of longing. This doesn't mean in order to love we have to be 'sufficient unto ourselves'. 'Responding to the needs of another is an opportunity to show love', Cicero writes, and yet insists that 'genuine friendship is solely the offspring of pure goodwill, that is, sharing the strength we get from our common love of virtue' (Cicero 2016: 20, 12). The love between the lovers in the Song is ultimately based on their *choosing* of each other, and their sharing of strengths, rather than any co-dependence. The maiden, indeed, longs to be with her lover, 'Show me … where thou liest in the mid-day' (mid-day symbolising ordinary life) and even more 'In my bed at night I sought him' (Song 1:7, 3:1). Love is a direction, an orientation of the whole self: 'My beloved to me, and I to him', 'I to my beloved, and his turning is (ever) towards me' (2:16, 7:12).

If the Song is an antidote to binary gender characteristics, many later commentaries do not follow the lead. Reading the male figure as God or Christ, and the female figure as dependant, passive – at best receptive, at worst slothful – is simply a patriarchal reading of masculine and feminine 'traits'. Unsatisfactory stereotypes into which society has fitted women have led to equally unsatisfactory stereotypes for men. The figure of Solomon, in history or the Song, is no infallible, all-guiding divine figure. Many old commentaries impose a 'complementarity' that does not fit with the narrative of the Song. Latin Christian commentaries (favouring the tropological or moral reading under the conditions of this fallen life) often *contrast* the 'bride' with the 'groom'.[11] A key model and authority for Latin commentaries was that of Apponius, a fifth-century monk writing in Italy. In trying to emphasise the 'guiding role' of the Bridegroom, Apponius depicts the Bride as slothful and unresolved. When the male lover leaves the maiden at the end of chapter 2, and again at 8:6, it is because he is 'repelled by her sad lack of interest'. When she says, 'I sleep' at 5:2, it is her confession that she is 'occupied with the pleasures of the flesh.' The bridegroom has to rouse her through 'knocking' at her conscience; 'even though he has been rejected he returns in the darkness of the night by way of a hidden remorse'. Her excuses in opening the door at 5:3 are attempts to defer repentance. She must 'pray her Helper to come to her' but this can only happen when 'he has summoned her from her sleep of inertia by charming her' (Apponius quotations in this paragraph are taken from Norris 2003: 198).

William of St Thierry, a close friend of Bernard, interprets the

---

11 The Greek Fathers were less prone to this, reading the Song (and the relations in it) anagogically, as 'heaven already realised'.

maiden's description of herself as 'dark' (1:4) because, 'with the departure of the Bridegroom, the Bride begins to lose her former beauty and to be blackened within herself ... Hence it is that she blushes for herself because of the darkness of her troubled conscience, awareness of past sins and from the assaults of the vices' (William of St Thierry 1970: 38–9). Both Apponius and William can give high praise to the maiden as well, but she is prone to passivity, sensuality and is someone who needs guidance and help. Not far from general medieval attitudes to women (cf. Lomperis and Stanbury 1993: 146–7). Commentaries are culturally conditioned. In the Jewish and Christian traditions, readings of the male figure in the Song as God and the female as the 'Jewish people' or 'Christian Church' must, at least in terms of gender, be taken lightly. Sexual distinctiveness can only be applied to God as metaphor: nothing is outside of God and so in no way can God be defined as specifically 'male' nor 'female'. Nor – and this is more challenging – is Christ in his Resurrection body specifically *male*, for his body is the Church (Galatians 3:28), which is made up of many parts (1 Corinthians 12:27).

The Song does evoke gender, but *as a mode of relation* rather than any set of 'essential' traits. Relation between the sexes has specific qualities: it is open to the biological possibility of having children, and it has meaning at the level of the soul. As body-soul (psychophysical) persons sexual attraction provides a model for loving others as *different* and *distinct* from ourselves. But bodily difference does not determine who we are essentially, or what gender we may find sexually attractive – that would be a *reductio ad corpus* of the human person – gender difference finds its meaning within the broader diversity of people (as anthropological studies of gender and culture have shown). Does the Song speak for human sexuality as a whole? Can lesbian, gay, bisexual or transsexual people find anything for them in the literal story of the Song if it speaks only of heterosexual love? Is the Song merely alienating for those who do not subscribe to traditional 'bride and bridegroom' models of romance?

Firstly, human love stories can never speak to the whole spectrum of human experience. At a literal level the characterisation of the song is heterosexual – as Plato's models for love in the *Symposium* happen to be homosexual. And yet the unexpected characterisation of the lovers in the Song may make it meaningful for those with same-sex orientation, breaking conventional roles. Also, *if* the story and characters are read symbolically (as they have been traditionally), then the Song can carry meanings that bypass literal-physical gender completely. For example, if the female figure is read as the human soul generally then male readers can access and experience the maiden's side of the relationship. Male mystics and monastics, not just Christian but Sufi, have taken this approach through the centuries. Though the Song itself is not mentioned in Rumi's 'Reed's Song' of longing and separation, the motif of Solomon as guide of the soul, the sense that 'lovers are in each other all along', and Rumi's own passionate soul-love for Shams al-Tabriz, speak of a shared sensibility between the Song and the Masnavi.[12]

Secondly, the image of 'bridegroom' does not come into the Song at all, and there is evidence that 'bride' is used only figuratively with respect to the maiden. The maiden is called 'spouse', but this is more in terms of 'espoused' rather than wife. The Song does not speak of a settled married relation but of the state of romantic-sexual awakening that *may* (but in the case of the Song does not) lead on to marriage. More often the maiden is called 'friend' (eight times – in Hebrew *ra'yatî*), four times 'sister-bride', and only once as 'my bride' (4:8), which is balanced by the maiden's taking of his address to her as simply 'my sister' (5:2). The maiden overwhelmingly refers and speaks to Solomon as 'my beloved' (24 times), twice as 'my friend', never as

12 Though Rumi did not see marriage as such in a particularly mystical way – his expressions of love for his male teacher Shams are much more erotic than those that mention his wife – still this did not mean any lesser view of women as channels of God's grace: 'Woman is a ray of God, she is not the earthly beloved: she is creative, you might say she is not created … How did man become adversary of her who is the life of his soul?' (1 Masnavi: verses 2437-9).

'husband'. From this it seems the nuptial relation of the Song is of a betrothed rather than consummated state. The role-play of bride and bridegroom is the work of later commentators – particularly the Jewish exegetical tradition for which marriage and family was the highest social ideal. The basic relational terms (given in the Vulgate and the Masoretic text) are those of *lover* and *beloved*. These terms are much more flexible in relation to gender and do not necessarily have the association of marriage. The Septuagint (which as we have noted is the oldest extant version of the Song) actually uses the term 'kinsman' rather than beloved. The emphasis throughout is on equality and, although equality is not outside the ideal of marriage, at least in late Classical and medieval times when the commentaries on the Song were mostly written 'bride and groom' carried social and hierarchical connotations quite extraneous to the Song. If the Song does speak of a culmination of love it is more in the mode of 'spiritual friendship' – even of brother–sister relations – rather than marriage.

Thirdly, there is no evidence within the narrative of the Song that the couple *are* married, that they *get* married during the drama, or *will get* married at the end or after. The Song is no conventional fairy-tale, nor does it have any obvious happy ending. Vis-à-vis the usual end of marriage there is no mention in the Song of any motivation towards 'having children'. There is no definite evidence within the text that the relationship is consummated physically. The Song is a story about *falling in love*. As such it is an experience open to all, whatever sexual orientation. Even at a literal, narrative level, the Song shows a relation where marriage, family and physical sex are not put to the fore. This is all the more surprising as the Song comes from a Jewish context which (following God's command to 'increase and multiply') views sexual relations as having their purpose in procreation.

Many readers of the Song will be surprised to find such an ancient poem is so liberating. The Song gives a language for sexuality that is not prescriptive. The lovers are simply enjoying each other. The Song could help 'free up' conventional responses; whether they be influenced by the lingering dualism in religion – the demonisation of sexuality as evil – or reductionism in secular views – regarding sex as exclusively physical. One could go so far as to see the Song as exorcising these narrow responses to sexuality (from which women have suffered most because of their association – cultural and historical – with the physical). Instead the Song is a model of a *personal* discovery of what is attractive *to us*. Attraction can have both an inner and outer aspect, of the soul and body: the maiden in the Song loves Solomon because he is 'as the apple tree among the wood of the forests' (2:3) and yet she says 'his appearance is as a cedar of Lebanon' (5:15). His soul is humble and sweet, his outer appearance stately and grand. Love has its own reasons. Solomon, in turn, has a *plethora* of idiosyncratic images for the maiden's beauty (likening her hair to a flock of goats, etc.). They give free rein to expressing what they mean to each other and in doing so they both discover more about who they are, their affectivity, how they experience beauty and *eros*. The language of love, even of gender, is always personal.

Primary and secondary ends of love

The Song, as we have surmised, was probably written during the Jewish diaspora within the Greek-speaking world, maybe Alexandria. It is possible to read within it the influence of Classical culture and its cult of beauty, which is not generally part of the Hebrew tradition. For the Greeks, aesthetic appreciation was based much more on the male physique and homosexual attraction. Plato (*c*.428–348 BCE) was the leading philosopher in the Classical world at the time the Song was written. Plato saw 'carnal' love as a first step – necessary, but leading on to a more general love of beauty, and ultimately to love of ideal, non-material beauty. For Plato, in his *Phaedrus*, beauty is the visible aspect of the intelligible world, it guides the senses towards wisdom:

> Beauty shines most clearly through the clearest of our senses; for sight is the sharpest of the physical senses, though wisdom is not seen by it, for wisdom itself would arouse an incredible love, if such a clear image of it were granted as would come through sight … But those who are newly initiated [in the search for wisdom] when he sees a god-like face or form which is a good image of beauty, shudders at first, and something of the old awe comes over him, then, as he gazes, he reveres the beautiful one as a god, and if he did not fear to be thought stark mad, he would offer sacrifice to his beloved as to an idol or to a god … The soul is greatly troubled by its strange condition; it is perplexed and maddened, and in its madness it cannot sleep at night or stay in any one place by day, but it is filled with longing and hastens wherever it hopes to see the beautiful one. And when it sees him and is bathed in the waters of yearning the passages [to the ideal world] that were sealed are opened … Now this condition, fair boy, about which I am speaking, is called Love by men … but the immortals call him The Winged One, because he who yearns must needs grow wings.
>
> (Plato 1952: 485–91)

The mode of relationship in the Song could have influences from 'platonic love'. In the *Symposium* Plato depicts his teacher Socrates as having learnt 'the wisdom of love' from a woman, Diotima, who taught:

> This is the right way of approaching or being initiated into the mysteries of love, to begin with examples of beauty in this world, and using them as steps to ascend continually with

absolute beauty as one's aim … Gazing upon the vast ocean of beauty to which attention is now turned, we may bring forth in the abundance of love of wisdom many beautiful and magnificent sentiments and ideas.

(Plato 1951: 94, 93)

Solomon's love of the maiden in the Song also led him to wisdom. However, Plato's critic Aristotle said that the best activities are also the most useless. The best is done entirely for its own sake, not as a means to an end. Unlike ideas about marriage normative in the time the Song was written, and unlike the model of platonic love, there is no exterior motive in the lover's relation – be it childbearing, or the bringing forth of 'beautiful and magnificent sentiments and ideas.' Their relationship is of value in itself.

The emphasis in the Song is on the personal rather than the physical or social dimensions of sexual love. It homes in on what we might call the *romantic aspect* (*eros*), which brings people together rather than the *caring aspect* (*agape*) that keeps them together. The Song presents something of an *idealised love*, rather than its day-to-day living out. And yet *eros* need not be a romantic fantasy or illusion. 'Eros need not for ever be on its knees to agape; he has a right to his delights; they are part of the Way' (Williams 1930: 40). When we fall in love we do see in each other unusual beauty and glory. This may or may not be accompanied, or followed, by a direct sexual emotion; generally it is. Marriage, or a committed relationship, may follow, as the fuller living out of the way of love, but 'romantic experiences' can also break marriages if they do not fit with the physical, personal and social commitments we have already made. A passing emotion or infatuation may tell us a lot about ourselves, but is a very unsure guide as to who the other person is, or what choice we should make. The full *way of love* involves a balance of physical, personal and social relation. To quote again from Vladimir Solovyov:

The natural relation between man and woman involves three elements: (1) the *material*, namely the physical attraction, due to the nature of the organism; (2) the *ideal*, that exaltation of feeling which is called 'being in love'; and, finally, (3) the *purpose* of the natural sexual relation or its final result, namely, reproduction. In true marriage the natural bond between the sexes does not disappear but it transmuted into personal love. The chief significance [for this] belongs to the intermediate element – the exaltation or ecstasy of love. In virtue of it man sees his natural complement, his material other – the woman – not as she appears to external observation, not as others see her, but gains insight into her true essence or idea. He sees her as she was from the first destined to be, as God saw her from all eternity and as she shall be in the end. Material nature in its highest individual expression – the woman – is here recognised as possessed of absolute worth; she is affirmed as an end in herself, an entity capable of spiritualisation and 'deification'. From such recognition follows the moral duty – so to act as to reveal and realise in this actual woman and in her life that which she is and, with ever greater possibilities, will be in God's eyes.

(Solovyov 1940: 416)

It was not until the Code of Canon Law in 1917 that any conception of the *mutual support of spouses* (within the official teaching of the Catholic church) came to be appreciated as 'a secondary end of marriage'. Vatican II does not use language of two ends or purposes to marriage but throughout most of the history of Christianity the social unit of the family was perceived as the *primary* purpose of marriage. And yet, marriage, because it has its root in personal love, is still valid when there are no children. The union of spouses is the focal point from which marriage is lived out. Children manifest personal love in physical and social form, but the Song reminds us that the primary *meaning* of marriage is *between the spouses*.

If marriage is understood as a Sacrament – an expressive and, therefore, an externalised sign or oath (*sacramentum* means 'oath' in Latin) – then what is personal becomes *covenantal* love. In the Hebrew vision a covenant is made by oath (the biblical basis of sacraments): a commitment that is enacted publically, verbally or through outward gesture. This is the difference between a promise – 'I give *my* word', and an oath – 'I swear *on* something external to me'. The expansion of personal into social expression/enactment is the purpose of the vow – said and enacted before others. The expansion of personal into physical expression/enactment is the consummation of marriage. To overemphasise the demands of family and society – as in arranged marriages, compulsive sterilisation or selective childbirth (often based on prejudice about gender or 'ability') – leads to a loss of the physical and personal aspects of love. The aim is a balanced, holistic view of marriage: all intentions or objectives working together; the romantic/personal, children/physical, and society/familial.

The Second Vatican Council provides the foundations for a theology of marriage when it speaks of marriage as 'friendship', as something which must be 'nourished and developed', as 'far exceeding erotic inclination', rooted in 'free and mutual self-giving' and based on 'the equal personal dignity which must be accorded to man and wife' (Flannery 1992: 952). Marriage should be, therefore, the antidote to patriarchy, which has been implicit in our language and culture for centuries (our English word 'virtue', connoting goodness, comes from the Latin *vir* meaning male!). On the one hand, marriage *as between equals* is also the antidote to an unrealistic spiritualisation of women – a danger in courtly-love literature. Medieval courtly-love literature was based on a model of a highborn lady who elicited love and passion but remained unapproachable. If the feminine figure in the Song of Solomon was read simply as Wisdom without the human dimension revealed in the story, then this would lead to just such an over-spiritualisation. Human sexuality may be more than physical relations and yet to overemphasise the romantic/personal can lead to a separation of love from marriage, as happened with the Troubadour poets. Unlike courtly love literature the human figure of the maiden is neither unattainable nor is the love unrequited: she opens herself to her beloved, gives herself (5:5, 7:13) and she has all the earthiness of her rural origins. If anyone finds themselves placed on a pedestal in the Song it is the male figure who, as king, cannot reciprocate the completeness of her love.

The aspiration and longing for *personal union* expressed in the Song finds its primordial prototype in the male–female relationship in Genesis. In Genesis 1:27 God did not create a first man, but a first couple. Even in Genesis 2, when sequence is implied, the relational mode of male and female *from the beginning* is emphasised: they are 'companions', 'helpers'. 'It is not good for the human (*'adam*) to be by himself,' God says, 'I will make him a help (*'ezer*) corresponding (*kenegdov*) to him' (2:18). In biblical Hebrew *'ezer* does not imply subordination, in fact the one most often called 'a help' is God (e.g. Exodus 18:4; Deuteronomy 33:7; Psalm 70:6). *Kenegdov* means, literally, 'in front of, in sight of, opposite to' – as in a mirror image. They were both a help to each other, corresponding to each other's need. All they needed, or rather desired, for completion – personal, physical, social – was to be found in the one who stood by their side. Adam sees Eve as 'bone of my bone, flesh of my flesh' – Adam and Eve are together as *one reality*, an archetypal image of wholeness, an I–Thou unity. For Adam there was no question of 'knowing' Eve – that is holding her before him as an object or a problem, as something apart from, or standing over against, himself. It was a matter of *being-with* Eve, of being-with her *in the image of God*, in non-duality, in a communion of love. Religious people are prone to think of communion with God as distinct, at least formally, from communion with our neighbour, but for Adam and Eve there were not *two* communions: there was one single communion with *God-and-each other*.

The primary relation is *being together*: sexual relations being a declension or development of 'being together for each other'. In the

Genesis account, the reproductive aspect comes later (not until Genesis 4). In fact, when Scripture says, 'Adam knew his wife, and she conceived …' it places this act of knowing after the Fall, that is, *outside paradise*. Whether reproduction has anything to do with this original *being together* of the sexes is a question opened up, but not answered, by the Song. The Song is noticeably *not* orientated to the normal physical-social end of marriage – childbearing. It is set in springtime rather than harvest-time. It celebrates fertility in its 'bud and possibility' rather than in its fruit. Quite unlike biblical imperatives about marriage or many of the fertility rites to which it has been compared the Song at no point *encourages* childbearing or even a natural harvest.[13]

It has been argued that it was only outside of paradise – when the male and female became divided against each other – that being 'bone of my bone and flesh of my flesh' needed to be substantiated through sexual intercourse (Genesis 2:23).[14] The general position of Jewish and Christian commentary on Genesis is that reproduction fulfils a command written into humanity at its creation. In Genesis 1:28 to 'be fruitful and multiply' is presented as a blessing given before the Fall, and yet still *after*, or at least independently of, the creation of man and woman in the image of God (at 1:27). If the Song express-es the *regaining of paradise* and the recovery of *man and woman together*, as I contend, it could be said there is no *need* for sexual intercourse in the Song. The Song is about the original state of unity that comes from the moment of creation. It seems, from the ending of the narra-tive, that children *as a further blessing* are not given to the lovers. And yet the *primary relation* of these two lovers – on which the magnetism of sexual attraction is based – is as a *communion of persons*.

---

13 The command to 'increase and multiply' is reiterated in Genesis 1:28 and 9:1, 7. Marvin Pope, in his weighty study of the Song, tends to favour a cultic funeral and fertility role (Pope 1977: 210–29).
14 See also William Blake, 'The Book of Urizen': 'Eternity shudder'd when they saw / Man begetting his likeness / On his own divided image' (Blake 2008: 79).

Theology of the body revisited

The question of what was 'in the beginning' in Eden was explored by St John Paul II in his talks on *The Theology of the Body* (a series of 129 catechesis given on human love in the divine plan, from 1979 to 1984). John Paul proposes Genesis 2:23, in which the first man on seeing the newly created woman exclaims, 'This is now bone of my bone, and flesh of my flesh', as the biblical prototype of the Song of Songs (John Paul II 2006: 162). The biblical account describes the first couple as naked and not ashamed or embarrassed. Nowhere else in the Bible is such a reciprocal nakedness, free from shame, developed and enacted as it is in the Song. The Song depicts what was 'in the beginning'. After the fall from paradise, in Genesis 3, man and woman cover their nakedness from each other and hide from their creator's gaze.

The human body is relational from the womb; and then in the family, until there is a new self-giving in marriage: when 'a man/ woman shall leave father and mother, and cleave to their wife/ husband, and they shall be *one flesh*' (Genesis 2:24). Speaking of Genesis 2:23-25 John Paul writes of what could equally be applied to the Song:

> It seems that the second creation account has assigned to the man 'from the beginning' the function of the one who above all receives the gift. The woman has 'from the beginning' been entrusted to his eyes, to his consciousness, to his sensibility, to his 'heart.' … The man, on his part, in receiving her as a gift in the full truth of her person and femininity, enriches her by this very reception, and, at the same time, he too is enriched by the relationship. The man is enriched not only through her, who gives her own person and femininity to him, but also by his gift of self.
>
> (John Paul II 2006: 196–7)

This 'spousal aspect' of the body, John Paul argues, does not mean the other becomes 'an object for me'. It is the giving of self in answer to another, rather than 'gaining an other', which makes relationship an enrichment. The one we love is experienced as part of who we are and yet appreciated as uniquely themselves. That the body is *personal* does not mean 'sealed off' and private from others, for when we feel accepted body and soul, we give ourselves body and soul.

In a few catechesis not delivered publicly but presented in written form, John Paul presents the Song as an expression of human love rather than religious allegory: 'The words, movements, and gestures of the spouses, their whole behaviour, correspond to the inner movement of their hearts, the *fascination* they have with each other' (John Paul II 2006: 552). The wonder and admiration Adam expresses so briefly in Genesis 2:23 is amplified in the Song 'into a full dialogue, or rather a duet, in which the bridegroom's words are interwoven with the bride's, and they complete each other' (ibid.).

John Paul imposes bride and bridegroom roles onto the couple and tries, against the text, to develop the Song into a symbol of 'happy marriage'. And yet he recognises that the Song itself is much more about *betrothal*. In authentically following the sense of the poem John Paul goes beyond his own argument of using Genesis and the Song as proof texts for marriage. Really the Song is about the *romantic aspect of love*. It gives us the language of 'falling in love'. Betrothal in Jewish and traditional Catholic practice is a time when a couple get to know each other as *persons* before sexual relations. The closest the Song can be to a marriage poem is in describing a state *prior to* marriage. 'In the Song of Songs we find ourselves,' John Paul writes, 'at any rate in the vestibule of that "sexual union", and precisely for this very reason, the *poetic expressions* which allow us to grasp its profound personal dimension and meaning take on great value' (John Paul II 2006: 572).

The Song is the poetry of romance, rather than the prose of daily married life. It is deeply sensual, yet also full of yearning for and anticipation of something not yet realised. John Paul writes, correctly:

> In the Song of Songs, human *eros* reveals the face of *love* ever *in search* and, as it were, *never satisfied*. The echo of this restlessness runs through the verses of the poem … *Love* shows itself *as greater than what the 'body' is able to express.*
>
> (John Paul II 2006: 582–6, emphasis original)

John Paul notices that the term *sister-bride* 'in a simple and firm way seems to overcome any *determination* of [the Song's] "language of the body" by "libido" alone … The bride and bridegroom reciprocally feel as close as brother and sister' (ibid.: 564–6). The poem reproduces 'the human face of *eros*, its subjective dynamism as well as its *limits* and its *end*' (ibid.). The *eros* of the poem does not express the social or physical ends of marriage – family and children – but only the personal dimension. Yet the aspect of sexual love that the Song does highlight is 'as strong as death' and 'relentless as the grave'. The physical body does not survive death, nor does the social dimension of marriage exist beyond the grave – 'In the resurrection man and woman neither marry, nor are given in marriage, but are as the angels of God in heaven' (Matthew 22:30).

There is a point at which the choice for the other forms who we are. Such is marriage – impossible in the context of the Song. To read the Song as leading inevitably to marriage takes it out of its narrative context, makes little sense of the 'letting go' evident at the end of the poem, and ignores the fact that it is *only* personal love that survives death. The narrative context shows that the love of Solomon and the Shulamite was secret, illegitimate (in the view of the world), an 'antisocial' love. Even read at a symbolic level as expressing mystical experience, the Song is 'non-conjugal' in that it implies the abandonment of, or rupture with, all social and conventional moral values, which, throughout history, was the experience of the mystics. An example from the Hindu mystical tradition that has parallels with the Song is the *Gita Govinda,* composed by Jayadeva in the mid-twelfth century CE. The *Gita Govinda* depicts Krishna among the *gopīs,* or milk-maidens, many of whom he married and yet only one of them, Radha, who is the daughter of Krishna's foster father, is his real sister-bride. Like the Song, the *Gita* is set in springtime. The mystical interpretation of this Sanskrit idyll or pastoral drama has been that Krishna represents the human soul drawn alternately between earthly and celestial beauty. Krishna, at once human and divine, is attracted by the sensual pleasures represented by the *gopīs* and wastes his affections on the delights of their illusory world. Radha represents spiritual beauty and eternal delight that cannot die; she wishes to free him from his divided nature by enkindling in him a desire for her own surpassing loveliness. Krishna is enticed to focus his affections, enthrone Radha in his heart, and through her come to know his own essence as infinite love.

The love-play of Krishna with the *gopīs* and Radha is depicted in a markedly sensuous way, as in the Song. And yet, like in the Song, the lovers are not married, they have to meet in secret, as in the view of society they are of the same father. Krishna strays towards others. Jayadeva sings rather of Radha's sense of desertion, their separation due to Krishna's lack of commitment, their mutual loneliness and longing for each other as they discover what they have lost, her jealousy over his delays, and their final blissful reunion which flouts the patriarchal conventions of their time, so that 'the hearts of beautiful adulteresses rush to meet their lovers' (Jayadeva 1984: 117). Wanton waywardness and constricting conventions are both transcended in the enjoyment of love's playfulness. At the end of the *Gita* Krishna is 'playing to delight her heart' and she in turn 'tells the joyful hero to adorn her!' Jayadeva caps it all by saying that all the play of his song is for 'saffron robed monks to chant in prayer'!

Krishna: Revel in a bright retreat heaped with flowers!
           Your tender body is flowering.
           Revel in the fragrant chill of gusting sandal-forest winds!
           Your sensual singing captures the mood.
           Revel where swarms of bees drunk on honey buzz!
           Your emotion is rich in the mood of love.
           Revel where cries of flocking cuckoos sweetly sound!
           Your teeth glow like seeds of ripe pomegranate.
           Revel in tangles of new shoots growing on creeping vines!
           Your voluptuous hips have languished too long.

Radha: My ears reflect the restless gleam of doe's eyes,
           Hang earrings on them to form snares for love!
           Pin back the teasing lock of hair on my lotus face,
           It fell before me to mime a gleaming line of black bees!
           Make a mark with liquid deer musk on my moonlit brow,
           Make a moon shadow, Oh Krishna!
           Fix flowers in shining hair loosened in love-play,
           Make a peacock plumage to be the banner of Love!
           Paint a leaf upon my breasts! Put colour on my cheeks!
           Lay a girdle on my hips! Oh delight my heart!

Jayadeva: Her yellow robed lover did what Radha said.
           So let blissful men of wisdom purify the world
           By singing the adornments of this *Gita Govinda*.
                          (Jayadeva 1984: 118, 124–5, with some editing)

'Falling in love' may be of many kinds and degrees, but involves 'a vision', a joy in seeing the other as 'perfection itself,' an image of heaven. A projection, maybe, of our own wholeness: love invites us to *become* what we have seen, to maintain always the joy and completeness we temporarily fall into outside ourselves. Often the vehicle of love, the awakener, disappears. Despite its exuberant end most of the *Gita Govinda* describes the experience of loss and separation. Grief for the beloved can, however, become a transforming compassion. Even in marriage (or friendship) *eros* deepens into *agape*. Spring turns into autumn. The ego is stripped away with age. Sometimes *eros* breaks up marriages – we shall not understand why, unless we know the strength of an infatuation that breaks through all social convention. The 'romance' associated with adultery (which began with courtly-love literature and continues today), and the taboo of brother–sister love (a legal prohibition in primitive societies which continues as a psychological prohibition today), may both reflect a 'dangerous' and half-conscious longing within us for something *more* than marriage while the depersonalisation of bodies into objects to view, use or abuse reflects the reduction of human relations to something much *less* than marriage. Sometimes 'falling in love' neither leads to marriage, nor breaks it up, *but is no less all-powerful*, as with Beatrice's effect on Dante, and then falling in love points beyond this world, and is neither social nor anti-social. In view of the variety of love, maybe the wisest comment is from Rumi's teacher Shams:

> Don't ask yourself what kind of love you should seek, spiritual or material, divine or mundane, eastern or western … divisions only lead to more divisions. Love has no labels, no definitions. It is what it is, pure and simple. Love is the water of life. And a lover is a soul of fire! The universe turns differently when fire loves water.
>
> (Rumi 2009: 122)

The love of Love itself. Those we love may pass away but the love we have for them remains the same. For the lovers in the Song there is the painful letting-go that motivates her great request: 'Set me as a seal over thy heart.' The word for 'seal' in the Masoretic text is *hôtām*, which occurs only once elsewhere in the Hebrew Bible, where God says to King Zerubbabel: 'I will make you as a seal for I have chosen you' (Haggai 2:23).[15] In the Song the maiden is the *hôtām*, chosen by God. Her unique character and the indelible choice she makes to give her heart to Solomon is what binds the relationship. Normally a piece of wax or lead with an individual design stamped into it, a seal is attached to something sent, as a guarantee of authenticity. So Solomon is loosed back to his role in the world. The passion of union must be lived out in an inner way. But once a seal is set the imprint it leaves cannot be altered. A 'seal' is also a device or substance used to join two things together to prevent them coming apart, or prevent anything passing between them (not even death).

In the Middle Ages a legend developed among Jewish and Muslim Arab writers of the 'Seal of Solomon', a ring that was supposed to have been engraved by God and given to Solomon directly from heaven. Said to have been made of brass and iron, in two parts, the signet was used by Solomon to seal written commands to various spirits. The Testament of Solomon (a Greek text showing Christian influences, datable to around the third century CE) depicts the Archangel Michael offering the ring to Solomon where the two parts symbolise the male and female: 'With this ring thou shalt lock up all the spirits of the earth, male and female; and with *their* help thou shalt build Jerusalem' (Conybeare 1898: §5). The symbol on the ring was supposed to have been the two interlocking triangles of the hexagram, which, according to Kabbalist commentaries, represent the integration of dualities, fire and water, earth and heaven, but particularly of male and female.

---

15 In the New Testament it occurs seven times, always implying 'being chosen' in relation to the end times. See John 6:27; 2 Timothy 2:19; Ephesians 1:13, 4:30; Revelation 6:9, 7:2, 9:4.

A psychological approach

Emphasis on the personalities of the couple in the Song opens the possibility of a psychological approach. Jungian psychology in particular has emphasised that masculine and feminine are not just physical or social gender identities but are aspects of the *psyche*. Sexual relationship is *intra-personal* as well as inter-personal. We all have male and female within us. In fact, by bringing to consciousness the sexual aspect that is hidden from physical and social identity, we bring the *self* – that is the whole person, into focus. The love expressed in the Song may open our eyes to the oneness that pre-exists the formation of our ego identities. As such it may be a psychological expression of a personal 'Garden of Eden', an integration of opposites in original innocence. Erotic love points to a deep unity within each person, and this may be why it is normally experienced as a longing. We are broken people and are looking, quite literally, for our other halves.

But if it is the other half *of ourselves* we are looking for, we can only ultimately find it *within ourselves*. This may help to explain the ending of the Song, where the lovers have to go their separate ways, *and yet carry the other with them like a seal upon their heart*. They are, in fact, much more united than an actual marriage might make them, they are *psychically* inseparable, as a seal imprints its image (one remembers Catherine Earnshaw in *Wuthering Heights*: 'I *am* Heathcliff!'). It is no coincidence that when the maiden is given a name it is a feminine version of Solomon's own name.

Psychologically, the 'falling in love' so vividly expressed in the Song is the moment when the *anima* or *animus* comes into play. In Jungian terms, this is a threshold moment but also precarious: it puts us in touch with the unconscious but also clouds any real awareness of the other person. The real woman is lost in the projection of the unconscious *anima* by the male; the real man is swamped by the unrealised (and therefore impersonal) male archetype within the female. Romantic love is the most prone to this projection for it is most tied up with the longing for wholeness. The real person comes to wear the mask of what we feel we most need. What *starts out* as 'falling in love' often *turns out* to be a private illusion – a self-deceiving infatuation, which we wake up from with a bump when we are faced with the real *difference* of the other person. It is easy to fall in love at a distance – with film stars, pop singers, Facebook images – proximity makes things real, and we soon fall out of love. Psychologically, the advice given is to 'withdraw the projection' – and we do this only through self-knowledge, by knowing that what we have 'fallen in love with' is something we are seeking for *in ourselves.*

To see male and female as two halves needing each other is at the root of the Kabbalah. However, the Book of Zohar argues that integration must be found *within* the soul. The living out of wholeness is not dependent on finding an 'external' companion. Longing for union with another is really about personal integration. Fulfilment cannot be based on anything external to the soul. Medieval Zoharic commentators point to Genesis 3:24 as a key text: 'God drove out the man and his wife; and God placed at the entrance of the garden of Eden angels, and a flaming sword which turned every way, to keep the way of the tree of life.' 'Know that the angels are two powers: male and female,' writes Rabbi Meshulam, a thirteenth-century German Zoharist, 'The flaming sword that revolved implies that sometimes they are transformed into a male and sometimes into a female' (quoted in Elior 2007: 49). Contemporary scholar Rachel Elior sees the Zohar as concerned with combining within the mystic the two redemptive mystical aspects of the deity: the king-lover, symbolising the holy male powers, and the gazelle-queen symbolising the Shekhinah (ibid.: 92–3, 99). Re-entering the Garden of Eden the new Adam and new Eve 'turn' and 'revolve' the divine male and female within their souls.

Carl Jung found the fascination with the non-literal significance of language most evident in Gnostic and alchemical texts which used imaginative fictions to express the inner quality of experience. As the third-century CE Gospel of Philip says, 'Truth did not come into the world naked, but it came in types and images. One will not receive truth in any other way' (Robinson 1977:140). And yet to spend one's time chasing after types and images is – in the blunt words of the Gospel of Thomas – 'to make friends with a corpse' (Bauman 2002: 120). Most psychotherapy, following Freud, does not attribute independent existence to 'types and images' – as in dreams, which are seen as a product of the personal subconscious. Jung does raise them to the level of collective archetypes, which can *seem* to carry an autonomous force, acting on the psyche from outside. And yet in the end this is only a projection. Though part of a common human inheritance, the archetypes need to be brought into awareness as 'types and images' of the self. In practice they need to be distinguished from other people (or events) who may evoke them.

Yet relationship can be the lens through which we *both* better see ourselves *and* the other as distinct from ourselves. The Song affirms that relationship as the crucible for self-discovery (even if individuation may be *an* end). The alchemy of love depicted in the Song is not just within the soul but is between two people. The subjective world of the lovers is expressed, but does not swamp what is going on *between* them. The problem with applying an intra-personal or archetypal model to the Song is that it tends to make the lovers types and symbols rather than real (literary) characters. The psychologists here run up with the same problem as the spiritual allegorists. And yet the human aspect is what reveals the Song as a *story*, not a dream or private fantasy. The accolades of the lover and the beloved avoid the fixed imagery associated with psychological projection, objectifying certain aspects of a person in an obsessive way.[16] The

16 Sigmund Freud's famous discussion of the 'adhesiveness of the libido' to particular objects, when the other person is not brought into full focus as *other*. The example he gives is of the man who, due to early childhood experience, develops an exclusive fixation with feet, 'quite indifferent to the other attractions of women [he

lovers praise the many-faceted wholeness of the one whom their heart loves.

In reading the Song 'types and images' need not contrast with the 'naked truth' of the narrative. Philo of Alexandria, the great first-century CE allegorical interpreter of the Jewish Scriptures, in his treatise *On the Change of Names* says that within every person there is an external *persona* and an eternal prototype. The example he gives is Sarah, wife of Abraham, who, in Genesis 17:15, is given a new name as a *seal* stamped upon her humanity, making it stronger than death:

> Sarah had her name changed to Sarrah by the addition of one element, the letter *rho* ... Sarah means 'my personal authority', Sarrah signifies 'princess'; the former name, therefore, is a symbol of specific human virtue, but the latter is a title of complete virtue. Now the wisdom which exists in the virtuous person is the authority of themselves alone, and those who have it would not err if they were to say, my authority is the wisdom which is in me; but that which has stretched out this authority is generic wisdom, not any longer the possession of this or that person, but absolute intrinsic authority; therefore that which exists only in the specific will perish at the same time with its possessor, but that which, like a seal, has stamped the human and personal with an impression, is free from all mortality, and will remain always imperishable.
>
> (Philo 1993: 347)

The maiden in the Song carries wisdom which seals together all division; between the specific and the complete, personal and the generic, the human and divine. 'What will you see in your Shulamite,' she says to Solomon, 'except one dancing between two camps' (7:1), healing the duality.

---

could] only be plunged into irresistible sexual excitement by a foot of a particular form wearing a shoe' (Freud 1991: 392–3).

If Philo is the great Platonist of Judaism, St Maximus the Confessor (c.580–662 CE) is the one who most successfully integrated Platonism into Orthodox Christianity. 'This similarity or likeness, which, thanks to the energy that holds them in their turning, becomes *identity*, a oneness of the sharers with him in whom they share' (Maximus the Confessor 1857–66: 202). 'The deified person, while remaining completely human in nature, both in body and soul, becomes wholly God in both body and soul, through grace and the divine brightness of the beatifying glory that *permeates the whole person*' (ibid.: 1088). A garden sealed and integral, from which flows wisdom. 'The one who shares in wisdom,' Maximus writes, 'becomes God by participation and, immersed in the ever-flowing, secret outpouring of God's mysteries, they impart, to those who long for it, a knowledge of divine blessedness' (ibid.: 218–19). The maiden in the Song, immersed in the secret fountain of her identity, overflows just such knowledge and divine blessedness to her beloved.

The Spirit of God 'moved over the face of the waters' at the beginning of creation (Genesis 1:2). Coming forth, 'like a breath from the mouth of the Most High … she passes into holy souls, making them friends of God, and prophets' (Book of Wisdom 7:25-7). 'Wisdom has prepared a dwelling place for herself' (Proverbs 9:1). An incarnate wisdom, both human and divine, like Jesus who, St Paul says, 'has become for us the wisdom of God' (1 Corinthians 1:30). Jesus' humanity formed through the waters of Mary's womb and the breath of the Spirit. Water and fire, earth and heaven, female and male – the seal. According to Bernard, the seal is the kiss; the maiden asks for the seal of the Spirit when she prays to God the Father for the kisses of his Son: 'Let him kiss me with the kisses of his mouth.'

Paradise regained: wisdom and love

If Genesis shows that the first condition of human existence is characterised by a 'companionable relationship', the Song gives a detailed description of that *way of life*, before the Fall. Here a real love story expands the *personal* dimension hinted at in Genesis. What Genesis expresses in mythical form becomes poetry in the Song. In the Song two human beings are shown a way back to that primeval companionship in Eden. All real relationships take place within a physical and social context, and the Song shows a particular point in history – the reign of Solomon. The man and woman of the Song, unlike the account of Genesis, *begin* their love *outside* paradise. It is a story set within the socio-political conditions of their time. They are (in the language of Christian theology) children of the Fall: they live and love, and temporarily regain the paradisal relation, *in the context of exile*. The measure of their love is 'as strong as death … relentless as the grave' (8:6). The conditions of Eden are only fully regained with the nativity of the second Eve and the second Adam; a new dispensation which made St Paul cry out: 'O death, where is thy sting? O grave, where is thy victory?' (1 Corinthians 15:55).[17] It is as a story set *within history* that the drama and tragic pathos of the Song lies. But also the possibilities of the Song are opened up – it points to and prophesies a new dispensation of time and space. In expressing an 'ideal love' as a story set *within history* the Song instils a longing for a time and place where such a love *will* be at home. It gives the marriage relation in the 'new earth' prophesied in Isaiah 65:17-25, where 'weeping shall no more be heard, nor the voice of crying'.

The Song sings of love that has to pass through death, and yet will not die. True love is always love of what is mortal and of what is imperishable in each person. The two lovers in the Song are

---

17 Mary, like her son, always lived and loved in complete freedom, immaculately.

permitted, for some brief moments, to experience what it might be like to breathe that air of the primal paradise – the lost world of Eden. They taste of 'the tree of life', the original companionship from which children may, or may not be, the fruit. In the context of the Fall only the *personal love* of man and woman can re-enter the Holy of Holies. 'In heaven [people] neither marry, nor are given in marriage' (Matthew 22:30). The physical and social – bound to time – must wait at the door of eternity. Marriage *as a social institution* will always be influenced (and contaminated) by the conventions of history. But the angels, more than anyone, love personally – attached as they are to those whom they guard and minister to.

The relationship the Song depicts is 'a garden closed' from the world. The lovers do everything they can to forget the world, and yet ultimately they cannot. The conclusion of the Song is one of parting. The course of sacred history is the honest record of the consequences of the loss of that original unity. In the Song, however – the central point of all the Scriptures – are to be seen the figures, moving as if reflected in the still waters of a deep well (of a 'fountain sealed'), of a man and a woman who find (it would almost be more true to say *fight*) their way back to the primal condition of that first relationship, realise and hold it between them for a few brief moments, and then must part forever. Even if Solomon and the Shulamite were to go on to marriage, what would this have meant among Solomon's 700 wives! The Song presents, rather, a dream of ideal romance. In contemporary terms it speaks more to betrothal or engagement than the demands, expectations, plans and responsibilities of marriage. In the Song the lovers are evidently *getting to know each other*, discovering how they share a 'common ground', how they are *soulmates*, how they are *friends* (in the rich meaning of that word).

In the Bible the archetypal human relationship moves from myth in Genesis to literary history in the Song, however, it awaits fulfilment as historical *fact*. Marriage, as a sacrament, makes present outwardly what was 'in the beginning'. In a special way, however, the 'household' of Nazareth (depicted in Luke 1:26-38) fulfils the hope of the Song – the relationship of Joseph and his *betrothed* (to whom he is not married, yet). This very unusual household may be the historical theatre of the Song of Songs. What Solomon and the Shulamite touched, and yet in the dispensation of their time couldn't realise permanently, was fulfilled by Solomon's descendants, heirs of the house of David. The betrothal of Mary and Joseph is the immediate background to the Annunciation, that is, of *the breakthrough of eternity into time*. The Song – which was limited to the discovery of love in its personal dimension – here finds expression (albeit in a very unique way) in family and society. Isaiah's prophesy that 'the maiden is with child' (Isaiah 7:14) was not fulfilled in the Song, but in the birth of Jesus both the prophesies of Isaiah and of the Song *are* fulfilled. The God-centred relationship, and the God-child.

In this nearly 'hidden life' St Luke gives us a fleeting glimpse of the definitive recovery – the full and permanent possession – of that relationship between a man and a woman that *was* completely personal *yet now* realisable at a familial and social level. The marriage of Joseph and Mary, despite and also because of its uniqueness, constitutes in itself the archetypal form of Christian marriage. The particular aspect of this marriage is seen to be its celibate nature – this is not raised up as a model for Christian marriage! – and yet, in some cases even this has been imitated in history.[18] Yet what Mary and Joseph do model is a marital harmony that is not 'a closed garden', celebrating its own beatitude, as in the Song, but open to others – to a child, and to all who enter the ambit of its hospitality. It is no surprise that the house of Nazareth at Loretto, and modelled

---

18 The records in hagiography tend to come from aristocratic milieu (with some others whose sanctity alone made them notable). For example, in the eleventh century the Emperor Henry II and the Empress St Cunegunda of Rome; in the thirteenth century St Cunegund Queen and Boleslaw King of Poland; in the fourteenth century St Elzéar Count of Sabran and Blessed Delphine of Glandèvres, and St Catherine Princess of Sweden with Eggard Lyderssen de Kyren; and in the fifteenth century Blessed Angela of Corbara and the Count of Civitella.

at Walsingham, has the same dimensions as the Holy of Holies in Solomon's Temple (see 1 Kings 6:20).

Mary, at the wedding at Cana, is the one who notices that marriage (as an institution and convention) 'has no more wine' (John 2:3). Jesus answers her, 'Woman, what concern is that to you and to me?' Indeed – they were mother and son – what has marriage to do with them? The 'marriage of the lamb' to the New Jerusalem, that is the Church, 'has not yet come.' And yet, the steward at this ordinary human marriage at Cana is amazed 'the very best wine has been kept for *now*!' (2:10). The marriage, indeed, begins with the new Adam and the new Eve – but doesn't end with them: the wine is shared with everyone. 'The Spirit and the Bride say, "Come"' (Revelation 22:17).

The Song gives a haunting echo of the forgotten garden that was our original home, a garden guarded by cherubim with 'a sword flaming and turning to guard the way to the tree of life' (Genesis 3:24). This is the sword of love – 'I to my beloved, and his turning is (ever) towards me' (Song 7:11) – through which man and woman must pass. And the sword of peace – 'his hands as of lathe-turned gold, filled with hyacinths' (Song 5:14) – past which none but the peaceable may go. Finally, it is 'the one who is faithful and true ... who has no name except to himself ... Out of whose mouth comes a sharp sword' (Revelation 19:11-15). The expression of God's Wisdom – 'living and active, and sharper than any two-edged sword, piercing even to the dividing of soul and spirit, of both joints and marrow, and able to judge the thoughts and intentions of the heart' (Hebrews 4:12) – the root of physical, spiritual and psychological life.

Wisdom in its fierce aspect is personified in all religions. Mañjuśrī – the oldest and most significant *bodhisattva* in Mahayana Buddhism and embodiment of *prajñā*, transcendent wisdom – wields the flaming sword in his right hand, representing the realisation of absolute wisdom which cuts down ignorance and duality. The *Lotus Sutra* assigns him a 'pure land' called Vimala, which, according to *Avatamsaka Sutra*, is located in the East (as with Eden). In the *Lotus*

Sutra he guides Nagaraja's beautiful daughter to enlightenment. His wrathful manifestation is as Yamãntaka (meaning 'terminator of *Yama*, death'). On every Zen altar Mañjuśrī stands with a sword cutting through illusion. 'If you would walk the highest way,' writes the third Zen Patriarch Seng-ts'an (d.606), 'do not reject the sense domain for, as it is, whole and complete, this sense world is enlightenment' (Seng-ts'an 2001: 5). In Christianity Jesus integrates body and Spirit: his own flesh is the sword of peace that 'breaks down the dividing wall' (Ephesians 2:14). Solomon, likewise, 'learned both what is secret and what is manifest, for wisdom, the fashioner of all things, taught me' (Book of Wisdom 7:21-2).

In the end Wisdom may be personified as male or female, or neither. In Wisdom dualities do not belong. Blessed Henry Suso (1300–66) in his autobiography exclaims:

> O God, if I could but once see Love, if I could but once exchange a word with her! Ah what does the beloved look like (that has so many lovely aspects concealed within herself)? Is it God or man, woman or man, art or wisdom, or what can it be? … Now when he thought he had a fair maiden before him, he suddenly found a noble youth. At times she appeared as a wise teacher, at times she looked at him as a fair lady-love.
>
> (Suso 1982: 23)

In the Song, however, there is a very specific allegory and symbolism for the encounter with Wisdom. Henry Suso was one of the mystics who recognised this, writing of himself:

> From his youth up the Servant had a heart full of love. Now Eternal Wisdom offers itself in the Holy Scriptures very affectionately, as a fair beloved, who adorns herself beautifully in order to be well pleasing to all, speaking gently in the guise of a woman, in order to incline all hearts to herself. At

times she shows how false other lovers are, by showing how full of love and faithfulness she is. The Servant's young heart was drawn to her thereby ... She often attracted him and charmed him lovingly to her spiritual love, especially by means of the books which are among *The Books of Wisdom*. When they were read at meals, and he heard the endearments described in them, he felt joy in his heart. Hence, he was seized by longing, thinking in his loving heart: 'You should just for once try your fortune and see whether this noble friend, of whom I hear such great wonders related, could be thy beloved.'

(Suso 1982: 20–21)

Allegory, symbol and wisdom in the Bible

We have proposed that any spiritual reading of the Song needs to be built on the foundation of its literal meaning. The idea that this alone of all the books in the Bible has no 'literal meaning' comes from the fact that religious readers would not see it, and secular readers could not. The Song does have spiritual meaning, but the spiritual is in the human. The woman in the Song personifies divine wisdom because she is humanly wise. The male figure expresses the love of God because he shows tender affection for another. Any heavenly significance does not make the protagonists of the Song other than who they are.

Likewise, in the Song (as in all poetry) the meaning is *in* the words. Poetry is different from allegory. In allegory an idea, feeling, or sense of value is clothed and made perceptible in a physical image. A flag is an allegory: a geographical, cultural, historical 'space' – which cannot be visualised – becomes a concrete emblem of colours and shapes. Or an olive branch – symbolising peace because of biblical associations. Images in poetry, however, are not just pictorial tokens representing something other than what they are. In poetry, there is an intrinsic relationship between the sense impressions evoked in imagery and emotions or ideas which correspond to them. For example, within the expressions 'the height of happiness' or 'depth of despair', there is an equivalence between the 'spatial image' and the 'feeling' that is more than mere convention. (Try changing them around and it doesn't *feel* right – 'the depth of happiness'... er, perhaps not!) The same is true with thoughts: for example, the association of the visual sense of light or sight with understanding – 'much light has been thrown on the subject', 'now I *see* what you mean.' To say, 'much darkness has been thrown on the subject' gives the opposite meaning. In poetic metaphor, the sense image does not just *represent*, because of an innate correspondence it *expresses*.

One step beyond poetry is symbolism: a symbol not only represents and expresses, it carries what it signifies. There is even more intrinsic a link; one can begin to say it *is* what it signifies, as a *part* that makes present a wider *whole*. For example: the body in relation to the whole person. Our bodies represent who we are (allegory), express who we are (poetry), but it is quite possible to say our bodies *are* who we are – in a way we cannot say a flag *is* a nation, or physical light *is* understanding.

The transfiguration of the symbol into its truth takes the process a further step. It is only here (not at the level of allegory) that poetry can be infused with spiritual significance. An example is the relation of God and light. The first letter of St John says, 'God is light' (1:5); here God is not only represented by light (an allegory, as if God needed something else to stand in for him in his absence), or expressed by light (in poetry, as if he *needed* to present himself outside of his nature through created matter), but here God *is* light. 'Enlightenment' or 'seeing the light' is not just a metaphor for spiritual experience: in Eastern orthodox theology eyes see the *energia* of uncreated light, natural light carries divine luminescence. Here symbol becomes sacrament. In an emblem (like a flag or olive branch) the image serves the abstract idea, in the sacrament the intangible pours itself out completely into what can be seen, tasted, smelt and touched.

We are given two real lovers, presented in body, soul and spirit. Written as it is within the strongly non-dualistic Semitic view of the human person – the body of the lovers not only expresses their souls but is transfigured into spirit. The human person becomes a model of how the Song should be appreciated as 'a whole' – body, soul and spirit corresponding to the literal, allegorical, and mystical meanings of the text. It is no surprise, therefore, that a story about a man and woman comes to symbolise God and the soul, or Christ and the Church. It is part of the nature of poetic symbolism to give a concrete image an increasingly wider horizon of meaning. Great poetry, however, makes the final turn back to the concrete, giving universal significance to the particular image. If that image is a human person – as Beatrice is for Dante, or the Shulamite for Solomon – then the human is not just a 'guide into heaven' but is heaven itself. The Song is the greatest of all poems, the lovers – while being images of wisdom and love – become completely real characters. The great philosopher of love, Vladimir Solovyov, shows how the ideal and concrete can be held together:

> The object of true love is not simple, but twofold: We love, in the first place, the ideal creature – ideal not in the abstract sense, but as kindred to our soul – the creature whom we ought to install within our soul. And, in the second place, we love the natural human creature, who furnishes the living personal material for the realization of the former, and who is idealised by means of such a soul connection.
>
> (Solovyov 1945: 62)

Elsewhere the same philosopher shows how this 'togetherness' is, at one and the same time, a relational, psychological and theological process. As a process of integration it is *not* simply a rarefaction but involves an affirmation of the physical and particular:

> The way of higher love, perfectly uniting male and female, the spiritual and the physical, is necessarily by its very principle a union or interaction of the divine and human, or a divinely human process. Love, in the sense of an erotic emotion, always has corporality as its proper object. Corporality, however, worthy of love, that is, beautiful and immortal, does not grow up of itself from the ground, nor does it fall ready made from heaven. It is acquired by an effort of a spiritually-physical and divinely-human kind.
>
> (Solovyov 1935: 74)

If the woman in the song is a figure of wisdom, this is not to say that she is so merely figuratively, as a metaphor or motif for wisdom. In her newfound capacity to love she finds peace, and is confirmed in her own strength of character: 'I am a wall: and my breasts as a tower, since I am become in the face of him (whom I love) as one finding peace' (Song 8:10). If Job represents endurance because he endured (not only his sufferings but the criticisms of his 'comforters') – so Shulamite represents 'the wisdom of love' because she came to wisdom 'for she loved much' (Luke 7:47). A refrain of the Gospels is 'that the Scriptures might be fulfilled.' If the Book of Job prophesies Christ in his sufferings, so the Shulamite anticipates some of the female figures of the Gospel. The possibilities of human love opened up in the Song were unrealisable in the spiritual and temporal conditions of the time in which the Song was set. It awaited a future fulfilment. Jesus' meeting with Mary Magdalene at the tomb echoes the sorrowful parting of the lovers and their finding of a union that is 'as strong than death.' At the tomb Mary Magdalene 'turned' and 'turned' (John 20:14, 16). 'Now there was a garden in that place, where he was crucified' (John 19:41). A new garden. A love more powerful than the grave.

Proverbs 1-22 and 25-29, Ecclesiastes, and the much later Wisdom and Odes of Solomon all carry an attribution to Solomon. He is the historical-literary figure under which the wisdom tradition is placed. As such, if an allegory was intended in the poem then one would expect it to be about the human search for wisdom. As wisdom is the dominant trait, or at least association, of the biblical figure of Solomon, it is not without significance that the song named after him was considered as one of the Wisdom Books by the collators of the Septuagint, in fact the very central wisdom book: with Job, Proverbs and Ecclesiastes before it, and the Book of Wisdom, Sirach and the Psalms after.[19] The New Testament writers would have known the Song in the Septuagint form, and it is no surprise that they see Jesus as the fulfilment of the *embodied wisdom* of Mary. The Song prophesied the birth of wisdom in human form. In the case of the Song a feminine expression of she who, in Proverbs 8:30-31, plays before God 'delighting in the children of humanity.' The Song expresses this relationship *as a human possibility.*

The clearest parallels in the Bible with the Song's imagery are in Sirach (Ecclesiasticus): though not attributed to Solomon this late biblical text (which can be dated to just after 200 BCE) carries strong allusions to the Song. It could be said Sirach brings out more explicitly the sapiential nature of the Song. Kingsmill – favouring a Second Temple dating of the Song – argues they could be contemporary texts; the Song being a poetic concentration of the varied ethical teachings of Sirach. Yet the fact that Sirach 47:17 speaks of Solomon as 'astounding the nations with song and proverbs' hints that Ben Sirach knew of the Song, prompting a fifth- to third-century BCE dating of the Song. Ben Sirach's criticism of Solomon's relations

---

19   In the Vulgate it is the middle book of the Bible when it includes the two Testaments – a symbolically central place. In the Tanakh, the Rabbinic collation the Song was not placed among the Wisdom Books, but (as with the Psalms and Job) among the 'writings'. In Christian Bibles, even after translation from later Hebrew versions, it has ever remained among the Wisdom Books.

with women (47:19-20) and his advice on women generally shows, maybe, why he felt it necessary to give an ethical corrective to any wisdom reading of the Song:

> When you see a good looking woman, look the other way; don't let your mind dwell on the beauty of any woman who is not your wife. Many men have been led astray by a woman's beauty. It kindles passion as if it were a fire.
>
> (Sirach 9:8-9)

And yet even the last line here shows an allusion to Song 8:6: 'the lights of love are lights of fire and of flames.'

Such allusions continue in a more positive vein as Ben Sirach plays with the sapiential personification of the maiden in the Song. Where the Song says, 'Behold him, standing behind our wall, gazing through the windows, peering through the lattice' (2:9), Sirach says: 'Blessed is he who meditates on wisdom and gazes on her with understanding … who searches after her and carefully observes all her comings in; who peers through her window, and listens at her door' (14:20, 23). Where the Song says, 'Behold King Solomon with the crown with which his mother crowned him on the day of his espousals, and in the day of the gladness of his heart' (3:11), Sirach says: '[Wisdom] will meet him like a mother, and like the wife of her youth she will welcome him … So he will find gladness and a crown of rejoicing' (15:2, 6). And who cannot discern the Shulamite in Sirach 24:13-34:

> I grew tall like a cedar in Lebanon,
> and like a cypress in the heights of Hermon.
> I grew tall like a palm tree in En-gedi,
> and like the rose-bushes in Sharon,
> like a fair olive tree in the field,
> and like a plane tree beside water I grew tall.

Like cinnamon I gave forth perfume,
and like choice myrrh I spread my fragrance …
Like an oak I spread out my branches,
and my branches are glorious and graceful.
Like a vine I bud forth delights,
my blossoms become glorious, abundant fruit.
I am the mother of beautiful love,
of fear, of knowledge, and of holy hope;
being eternal I am given to all my children,
to those who are named by the Creator of all.
Come to me, you who desire me,
and eat your fill of my fruits.
For the memory of me is sweeter than honey,
possession of me sweeter than the honeycomb.
Those who eat of me will hunger for more,
and those who drink of me will thirst for more …
The first man did not know wisdom fully,
nor will the last one fathom her.
For her thoughts are more abundant than the sea,
and her council deeper than the great abyss.
As for me I was like a canal from a river,
like a water channel into a garden.
I said, 'I will water my garden
and drench my flower-beds.'
And lo, my canal became a river,
and my river a sea.
I will again make instruction shine forth like the dawn,
and I will make it clear from far away.
I will again pour out teaching like prophesy,
and leave it to all future generations.
Observe that I have not laboured for myself alone,
but for all who seek wisdom.

If grace builds on nature, then the spiritual meaning of the text is related to the personalities of the lovers depicted, including their gender. The metaphorical/allegorical readings given in Rabbinic and Christian readings (and in that of Kingsmill) contradict the personification of wisdom as feminine in the sapiential books. The allegory they read into the poem regards the male figure as the leading, guiding force, and the female as the personality in formation. However, Wisdom for the Jewish people up to the time of Jesus was considered as a feminine figure. Later tradition has ignored that the obvious allegory in the poem is that the Shulamite guides Solomon.

On showing the poem's basic narrative sense, there are few cases in the entire history of scriptural commentary and exegesis, which demonstrate so clearly the precariousness and limitations of the analogical method. Nearly all 'religious' commentaries require, in the feminine figure, either the personification of the frailty, incertitude and timorous dependence of the human soul in relation to its saviour, or the hopeful and fearful anxiety (with a kindred sense of dependence) of the Christian Church in relation to *her* Lord. At times she comes to represent simply the incorrigible waywardness and inconstancy of the Israelite people, tied to sensual pleasures, whom God has to drag, passive and moaning, into the promised land. The fact remains that in the actual poem the feminine figure is found to be a personification of qualities and characteristics entirely the opposite of these. Where the pious commentator requires a weak, yielding, fearful and inconstant figure, playing everywhere the secondary role, what the poem actually shows us is a figure with the strength and supple malleability of steel: a moral character of remarkable depth and purity, fearless, resolute and absolutely faithful in her love.[20] Moreover, one who everywhere dominates the *action*.

---

20 The *Navarre Bible* says, 'the lover's character is defined by his faithfulness and by the way he wins over the love of his beloved in the end' is *exactly* the reverse of the case: the maiden, from the beginning, shows no wavering or fickleness in her love, Solomon's *exclusive* fidelity is far from sure' (*Navarre Bible* 2003: 482).

The love between Solomon and the Shulamite is indeed mutual. Solomon is quickly responsive, but it is she who guides in love. Solomon the wise was to learn that there is no wisdom without love. As St John says, 'The one who does not love does not know God, for God is love' (1 John 4:8). Throughout the Song the Shulamite is sensitive to what is appropriate for the expression and flourishing of love in each moment. Solomon is also a great lover – because he is a lover of wisdom – but as the Book of Wisdom recognises:

> All good things come to me along with her, and in her hands uncounted wealth. I rejoiced in them all, because wisdom leads them; but I did not know that she was their mother … I loved her and sought her from my youth, and I desired to take her for my bride, and I became enamoured of her beauty … For she is an initiate in the knowledge of God, and an associate in his works.
>
> (Book of Wisdom 7:11-12; 8:2, 4)

A clear reading of the narrative of the poem similarly shows that the morally and spiritually paramount male figure evoked by religious commentators in both the Jewish and Christian traditions – often symbolising no less than God – has no counterpart in that of the very human lover of the poem itself. That great and entirely sovereign figure of the 'Bridegroom' is the creation of devout and mystical souls and simply not in the poem. Solomon, in the Book of Wisdom, recognises, 'I also am a mortal, like everyone else' (7:1). In terms of *plot* the Song has no 'hero': it has only a heroine. Certainly, the male figure is praised for who he *is* – but, in terms of narrative action, the woman is the one who draws attention for what she *does*. And this is no surprise if we situate the Song as a wisdom text, celebrating the feminine spirit of Wisdom with attributes not difficult to associate with the Shulamite in the Song: 'For in her there is a spirit that is intelligent, holy, unique, manifold, subtle, mobile, clear, unpolluted, distinct, invulnerable, loving the good, keen, irresistible, beneficent, humane, steadfast, sure, free from anxiety' (Book of Wisdom 7:23).

Conclusion

The religious associations with the imagery in the Song have prompted its reading as a series of metaphors for spirituality. However, it is just as likely that the author of the Song used such imagery to enrich and deepen an expression of human love. As I have argued, the key to interpreting the Song is in understanding that it represents the human embodiment of divine love whereby human love expresses God. This is clearly expressed in 1 John 4:20: 'Anyone who says, "I love God", and hates his brother or sister, he is a liar; for the one who does not love the brother or sister whom he has seen cannot love God whom he has not seen.' It is this *correspondence* which makes the poem symbolic. Human love doesn't only represent, it expresses and carries divine love. They are intrinsically linked, so that one can say human love *is* divine. This assumes, however, that human love is functioning properly: according to the Church Fathers the *communicatio idiomatum* (the transfer of properties between the human and divine) only completely works in the person of Jesus. And yet the Word of God also sounds in the inspired words of Scripture, of which the Song is a paramount example. As with Jesus the human is not subsumed into the divine, the literal 'nature' of the Song should not be abstracted into religious ideas. Rather the Song gives a foretaste that God has poured himself out into flesh. The love of God can be seen, tasted, smelt and touched in the human beloved. The Song offers an embodied *experience* of wisdom because it teaches the wisdom of love.

When we read the Song we imagine we are outside, like Solomon at the door of the Shulamite's house, peering in through the fragmentary words of the poem. As we pray the Song may open its meaning, lying as much in the gaps between the words. The Song is latticework. At times we feel blessed and anointed by the dew of its refreshment, at times we feel left out in the night. We return to it, often, gently knocking. No one can push their way into the Song with scholarship alone. The door only opens from the inside. We ponder and wait, patiently, until one day we hear a sound of the bolt opening. Then with the door slightly ajar and we catch a glimpse of the one inside the house – the Shulamite. We reach out (from the ingrained habit of trying to understand) but what we catch is not something we can hold, it is a perfume. It is the perfume of Wisdom that we must follow.

The greatest commentary ever made on the Song was just one line. If we had listened to it we would never have tried to read divine characteristics into Solomon. Two millennia ago someone who indeed lived the non-duality of the human and the divine expressed in the Song said, simply, 'Something greater than Solomon is here!' (Matthew 12:42; Luke 11:31).

Wisdom, as we have seen, lives both with God and with humanity: 'She glorifies her noble birth by living with God' and yet 'God loves nothing so much as the person who lives with her' (Book of Wisdom 8:3, 7:28). In the Song, we have seen, she is a child of Wisdom and a child of her own earthly mother. Ironically, in view of complaints that there are no female images of God in the Bible, here one is found, literally (and in the Vulgate) exactly, in the middle of the Bible. And among the many feminine heroines of the Hebrew Bible – Judith, Esther, Susanna, Ruth, Sarah – we can add the Shulamite. And like the woman 'with an alabaster jar of very costly ointment' in the Gospels – who 'filled the whole house with the fragrance of the perfume' (John 12:3) – wherever the Song is read, 'what she has done will also be told in memory of her' (Matthew 26:13; Mark 14:9). And yet like that woman she has no name except that which comes from her relation to the one she loves.

PLATE 1: *The Shulamite*, John B. Trinick (1969) (with Latin verse 7:13 from the Song: 'Let us go up early to the vineyards, let us see if the vineyards flourish, if the flowers be about to bring forth fruit, if the pomegranates blossom: there will I give thee my breasts.')

PLATE 2: *Icon of Holy Wisdom*, Annie Shaw (2017)

Painted especially for this book, following a traditional (though not too common) image of Holy Wisdom from medieval Russian iconography.
The Orthodox view Divine Wisdom as an uncreated energy of God. She is presented as a crowned and winged female figure, wearing the royal red, seated in the Holy of Holies in the Jerusalem Temple, on the Mercy Seat. She has the moon and the stars beneath her feet, the seven days of creation depicted by the rainbow, and the seven pillars of wisdom holding up the Temple veil, with two cherubim to her left and right, and the dove (Spirit) descending upon her.

PLATE 3: *My love is for me, and I am for him*, Icon of the Spouses (2010), Atelier Iconografico del Monastero di Bose, Italy.

PLATE 4: *Song of Songs* 4 (detail), Marc Chagall (c.1965)

PLATE 5:
My Only Desire,
'Lady and the
Unicorn' (detail).
Tapestry, early
1500 Flanders

PLATE 6: *The Madonna of the Rose Garden* (detail), Stefano da Verona (1435)

PLATE 7: *The Shulamite* (detail), Juliet Asher (2015)

PLATE 8: *'Until Love be Ready' Solomon and the Shulamite*, Juliet Asher (2013)

PLATE 9: *His Right Arm under My Head and His Left Arm Embraces Me,* or *The Seal of Solomon,* Juliet Asher (2015)

PLATE 10: *Radha and Krishna in the Grove,* Pahari, Kangra, ca. 1780 © Victoria and Albert Museum, London

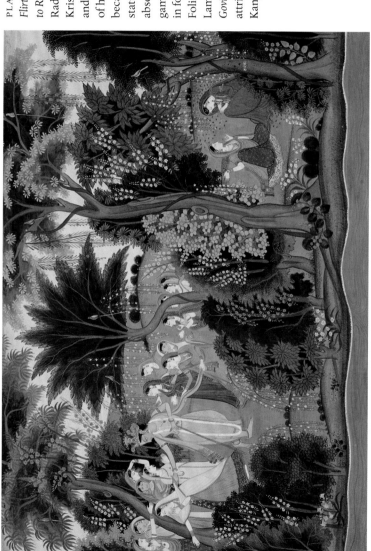

PLATE 11: *Krishna Flirting with the Gopis, to Radha's Sorrow.* Radha challenges Krishna to a unique and exclusive love of her; while Krishna, because of his royal status, has been absorbed in amorous games with the Gopis in forgetfulness of her. Folio from the Lambagraon *Gita Govinda*, ca. 1810, attributed to Purkhu, Kangra, India

PLATE 12: *Jayadeva worshipping Radha and Krishna*
The twelfth-century author and poet Jayadeva has a vision of Krishna and
Radha, which inspires him to write of their love in the *Gita Govinda* (*Song
of God*), an erotic poem which has always been read by Hindus as expressing
the mutual longing of the soul and God. Manak, Bahsoli Pahari (ca.1730),
painting on paper.

PLATE 13: *Radha and Krishna
on a Bed at Night* (ca. 1830),
Punjab, India, ink and
watercolor on paper.

Glossary

Anima
According to Jungian psychology it is the feminine component of the unconscious male psyche which functions as a filter, bridge, guide, and mediator between the ego and the deeper layers of the unconscious. Often personifies *eros*; the personal, relatedness element which, for Carl Jung, characterises a woman's psychology and a man's *anima*. The *anima*, according to Carl Jung, passes through four stages in the male psyche corresponding with a man's maturity: Eve, Helen of Troy, Mary, and Sophia (Wisdom).

Animus
According to Jungian psychology it is the male component of the unconscious female psyche. Often personifies 'spirit' and 'intellect'. For Jung the *animus* evolves through four stages: the physical man, the romantic man or man of action, the bearer of the word, and the wise spiritual guide.

Apostles
Those chosen by Jesus during his life or soon after to carry on his ministry.

Authorised Version
The King James Bible of 1611 translated into English from the Hebrew Masoretic (Cambridge MS).

Biblical criticism
A form of literary criticism developed in nineteenth-century Europe, and continuing today, seeking a more scientific analysis of the Bible. Independent texts are scrutinised in terms of their possible authorship, date, readership, intention, historical context, unification, transmission over time, literary genre and how they came to be included in the Bible.

Church Fathers
Christian theologians post the death of the Apostles whose voices are reflected in the Church councils up to the eighth century (see also 'Patristic era').

Coincidentia oppositorum

Meaning 'coincidence of opposites', a term used by Christian mystics (especially Nicholas of Cusa 1401–1464) to describe God who, in his transcendence, integrates all contradictions.

Communicatio idiomatum

Meaning 'transfer of properties', an approach developed at the Church councils of the fifth century seeking an understanding of how the human and the divine natures of Christ relate. In order to protect the unity of the person of Jesus it was argued that in him the human and the divine natures were always in interaction. Recently, the philosopher Johann Hamann (2007: 99) argued that the communicatio idiomatum applies not just to Christ, but should be generalised to cover all human action.

Dead Sea Scrolls

Ancient Jewish religious, mostly Hebrew, manuscripts found in the Qumran Caves near the Dead Sea. The scrolls are from various dates from 300 BCE to 70 CE. The fragments of the Song found in the Dead Sea Scrolls date from 30 BCE to 70 CE.

Deuterocanonical writings (or Apocrypha)

Texts that are part of the Septuagint collation of the Hebrew Bible but not in the later Masoretic. Though they are considered important in both Jewish and Protestant communities they are not included in the Bible except as Apocrypha. They are accepted as fully canonical by the Catholic and Orthodox Christian communities.

Deuteronomic editors

Sixth-century BCE Levitical editors of the Hebrew Scriptures who, during the exile of the Jews to Babylon, emphasised the Law and the Covenant with Moses rather than the Kingship and Temple Priesthood (which, during that period of exile, were anyway not practicable).

Ecclesia

Literally, 'those called out' – used to describe the Christians as 'church'. Also used in Medieval Kabbalah as a feminine noun to describe the embodiment of the Shekhinah in the Sabbath gathering of the community of Israel.

Energia or Divine Energies (in Orthodox theology)

St Gregory Palamas (1296–1359), Archbishop of Thessaloniki, upheld the doctrine that the human body played an important part in prayer. God can be experienced through the radiation of *energies*, through the purification of the senses and the practice of stillness (*hesychia*), even while the *essence* of God remains completely invisible and ineffable.

Fall, the

Christian term, although not named in the Bible, expresses an interpretation of Genesis, chapter 3: At first, Adam and Eve lived with God in the Garden of Eden, but they succumbed to the temptation to eat the fruit from the tree of knowledge of good and evil, which God had forbidden, and they 'fell' from the paradisal state, and (by the end of chapter 3) were expelled from Eden. An interpretation that is shared (with some differences) in Judaism and Islam.

Hermeneutics

The theory and methodology of interpreting texts concerned with meaning and values, especially of biblical texts, wisdom literature, and philosophical texts.

Hieros gamos

From the Ancient Greek, meaning a sacred marriage between a God and a human, often, in ancient Greece, enacted in a symbolic ritual where human participants represent the deities.

Hypostasis (as used in Christian theology)

A Greek philosophical word, literally meaning 'standing out', which, in the Patristic era, was used to explain how the *persons* of the Trinity express one underlying divine nature. Also used to express how the human *person* of Jesus is a manifestation of the Divine Word (which is also personal) – *hypostatic union*. At times, though less commonly, *hypostasis* was used by the Church Fathers to describe how every human person is a *hypostasis* (an expression) of human nature.

Kabbalah

The mystical tradition of Judaism, which draws on both the Hebrew Bible and Rabbinic literature, yet offers more esoteric meanings both to the texts and Jewish practice. Historically, Kabbalah emerged, after earlier forms of Jewish mysticism, in twelfth- to thirteenth-century southern France and Spain.

Kethubim
Hebrew 'writings' – third section of the Rabbinic collation of the Hebrew
Scriptures that includes the Song of Solomon, the Psalms, Ecclesiastes, Job,
Esther and other texts.

Masoretic text/Masorite editing
Tenth-century CE Rabbinic versions of the Hebrew Scriptures (in three
main versions – Leningrad, Aleppo and Cambridge MS). Culmination of
Masorite editing that started in the eighth century CE. The Masorite editors
fixed the pointing (see 'Pointing of Hebrew Texts') of earlier and Hebrew
texts so as to give a more definite meaning, an edit which necessitated
interpretative choices. The Masoretic Text is the source of Protestant and
Catholic Bibles today.

Mishnah
c.200 CE. A written compendium of Rabbinic Judaism's Oral
commentaries on the Hebrew Bible during the first two centuries of the
Common Era.

Mixta composita
Mixed entities. Latin term derived from Aristotle's understanding of how
form and matter are combined in the human person. Used by Carl Jung in
a letter to John Trinick: 'We are not liberated by leaving something behind
but only by fulfilling our tasks as *mixta composita* i.e. human beings between
the opposites of spirit and matter' (Jung 1976: 396).

Mysterium coniunctionis
Mysterious conjunction. Title of Carl Jung's last major work on the
synthesis of opposites in alchemy and psychology. Describes the final
alchemical synthesis of ego and unconscious, matter and spirit, male and
female that brings forth true self (symbolised by the philosopher's stone).

Orthodox theology/Orthodox Church
The Eastern and Oriental Christian Churches (not in communion with
Rome) which base their theology on the early Church councils and
the writings of the Church Fathers. There are, however, disagreements
between the Eastern (e.g. Greek and Russian) and the Oriental (e.g. Coptic,
Armenian and Ethiopian) as to which of the early Church councils are
valid. Eastern Orthodox theology developed with some assistance from
Platonic philosophy and tends to be more Platonic than that of the Catholic
Church since the scholasticism of the Middle Ages. Based on the teaching

of the early Church fathers, it is more open to the understanding of *theosis* or divinisation as the end and aim of the Christian life.

Patristic era
Period after the death of the Apostles (*c*.100 CE) when Christian theology was worked out at general Church councils. Ending after the last council in the eighth century.

Pointing of Hebrew texts
Early written Hebrew has only consonants (evolving from an Oral language where vowels were supplied). Both Deuteronomic and later Rabbinic interpreters gave vowel 'pointers' in written texts, stresses, that indicated how they believed Oral tradition understood or spoke the words.

Prima materia
In alchemy, *prima materia* (first matter) is the ubiquitous starting material required for the creation of the philosopher's stone. The alchemical work involves raising this formless and chaotic base of all matter into the stability and luminescence of the stone.

Projection
In Jungian psychology unless *anima* and *animus* are assimilated as autonomous personality-fragments of the Self, they are usually projected onto an outer woman or man, confusing the psychic image with an external person.

Rabbinic Judaism
Rabbinic Judaism grew out of Pharisaic Judaism. After the destruction of the Second Temple in 70 CE Jewish religion realigned itself on the covenant with Moses, the Law and the Oral tradition of teachings (which were first codified in the Mishnah and further and more extensively in the Talmud). The Rabbis replaced the Priests as the leaders of the Jewish community, synagogues replaced the Temple, personal practice of the law and traditions replaced external sacrifice and offering (of fruits, grain and animals).

Rosh Hashana
Jewish religious New Year festival. According to Judaism, Rosh Hashanah marks the beginning of the year because it is held on the traditional anniversary of the creation of Adam and Eve.

Sapiential
Adjective meaning 'relating to wisdom' (from the Latin *sapientia*, wisdom).

Scholastic theology
Style of Christian theology based on questions and responses that developed from the twelfth century in the West, especially in the new universities, involving a new use of the philosophy of Aristotle as a background to reflecting on Christian faith. A parallel assimilation of Aristotle's ideas into Jewish thought occurred.

Second Temple/First Temple
Jewish Holy Temple which stood on the Temple Mount in Jerusalem during the Second Temple period between 516 BCE and 70 CE. According to Jewish tradition, it replaced Solomon's Temple (the First Temple), which was destroyed by the Babylonians in 586 BCE, when Jerusalem was conquered and part of the population of the Kingdom of Judah was taken into exile to Babylon.

Septuagint
Third- to late-second-century BCE Greek version of the Hebrew Scriptures translated by 70 Jewish scholars in Egypt. Remains the definitive text (in translation into modern languages) for the Orthodox Church today.

Shekhinah
English transliteration of a Hebrew word meaning 'dwelling' or 'settling', denotes the gift of the divine presence of God. The Shekhinah is a feminine aspect of Divinity. In the Kabbalah she is invoked as the Sabbath Bride, when the divine presence is embodied in the devotions of the Jewish community.

Sophia
'Wisdom' in ancient Greek (σοφία).

Sufism
The mystical aspect of Islam. The term is a creation of nineteenth-century British oriental studies and refers to the Arabic word *taṣawwuf* – the ascetic and spiritual practice of Sufis.

Syncretism
Blending or amalgamating of two or more religious belief systems into a new system, or the incorporation into a religious tradition of beliefs from unrelated traditions.

Talmud
Translates literally as 'instruction' in Hebrew – a central text of Rabbinic Judaism, which contains the Mishnah and extensive later reflections on the Hebrew Bible. The Munich Talmud, the oldest full manuscript, dates from 1342.

Tanakh
Jewish name for the Hebrew scriptures approved at the Council of Jamnia in 90 CE. *Ta-Na-Kh* is an acronym of the first Hebrew letter of each of the Masoretic Text's three traditional subdivisions: Torah ('Teaching'), Nevi'im ('Prophets') and Kethubim ('Writings').

Tantra
Sankrit word meaning 'weaving together' – in Vedic Hindu and early Buddhist teaching it refers generally to religious learning and meditative practice. Later, around middle of the first millennium CE, more esoteric traditions of tantra co-developed in Hinduism and Buddhism, including some practices where sexual practice was used to raise spiritual energy. In popular culture today this small aspect of tantra has tended to overshadow the broader meaning and tradition behind it.

Targum
Chaldean Aramaic commentaries and paraphrases of the Hebrew Scriptures written around 550 CE, but representing earlier oral material.

Torah
The early historical and legal books of the Hebrew Scriptures (also known as the Five Books of Moses): Genesis, Exodus, Leviticus, Numbers and Deuteronomy.

Vulgate
Fourth-century CE translation of the Bible from Hebrew and Greek into Latin by St Jerome, replaces older Latin versions of the Bible, becomes definitive text for Western Europe during the Middle Ages.

Wisdom Books
The collation of texts in the Bible in the Septuagint into a section dealing with Wisdom – includes a selection of the Kethubim ('Writings') that refer directly to Wisdom. However, also includes Sirach ('Ecclesiasticus') and the Book of Wisdom, which were not considered biblical by the Rabbis at Jamnia in 70 CE and not in the later Masoretic text. Christian Bibles keep

the Septuagint subdivision (though Protestant Bibles do not include Sirach or the Book of Wisdom).

Yom Kippur
Also known as the Day of Atonement – the holiest day of the year in Judaism. Yom Kippur completes the annual period known in Judaism as the High Holy Days or Days of Awe that commences with Rosh Hashanah.

Zen
A school of Mahayana Buddhism starting in China after the middle of the first millennium CE which places emphasis on the practice of meditation, initiation and interaction with an experienced teacher over external ritual and religious learning.

Bibliography

Aelred of Rievaulx. (1977) *Spiritual Friendship*, trans. M. Laker. Collegeville, MN: Cistercian Publications.

Alexander, Philip (ed.). (2003) *The Targum of Canticles*. Collegeville, MN: Liturgical Press.

Aquinas, Thomas. (1956) *Corpus Thomisticum*. Pamplona: University of Navarra. Retrieved on 5 March 2018 from www.corpusthomisticum.org.

Aquinas, Thomas. (1981) *Summa Theologiae*, trans. English Dominicans. New York: Christian Classics.

Aquinas, Thomas. (2015) *Summa Contra Gentiles*, trans. English Dominicans. London: Aeterna Press.

Augustine of Hippo. (1964) *Sermons*, Patrologiae Latina, vol. 38, ed. Jean Pierre Migne. Paris: Migne.

Aristotle. (1984) *Nicomachean Ethics*, ed. J. Bywater. Oxford: Oxford University Press.

Arnold, Gottfried. (1963) *Die Geheimnis der Göttlichen Sophia*. Stuttgart: F. Frommann.

Baile, David. (1981) The God with Breasts: *El Shaddai* in the Bible. *History of Religions* 21(3): 240–256.

Balthasar, Hans Urs von. (1982) *The Glory of the Lord: A Theological Aesthetics, Vol. 1: Seeing the Form*, trans. E. Leiva Merikakis. Edinburgh: T. & T. Clark

Barker, Margaret. (2003) *The Great High Priest: The Temple Roots of Christian Liturgy*. London: Continuum.

Baudelaire, Charles. (1995) *Selected Poems*, trans. Carol Clark. London: Penguin.

Bauman, Lynn (trans.). (2002) *The Gospel of Thomas: The Wisdom of the Twin*. Ashland, OR: White Cloud.

Benedict XVI, Pope. (2016) *Deus Caritas Est (God is Love): Encyclical Letter on Christian Love*. Dublin: Veritas.

Berlyn, Patricia. (1996) The Great Ladies. *Jewish Bible Quarterly* 24(1): 26–35.

Bernard of Clairvaux. (1968) *Opera Omnia*, vol. 5, ed. J. LeClercq. Rome: Editiones Cistercienses.

Bernard of Clairvaux. (1971) *On the Song of Songs*, vol. 1, trans. Kilian Walsh. Collegeville, MN: Cistercian Publications.

Bernard of Clairvaux. (1976) *On the Song of Songs*, vol. 2, trans. Kilian Walsh & Irene Edmonds. Collegeville, MN: Cistercian Publications.

Bernard of Clairvaux. (1980) *On the Song of Songs*, vol. 4, trans. Irene Edmonds. Collegeville, MN: Cistercian Publications.

Bernard of Clairvaux. (1987) *Selected Works*, trans. G. Evans. New York: Paulist Press.

Bernard of Clairvaux. (1995) *On Loving God: An Analytical Commentary by Emero Stiegman*, trans. Robert Walton. Collegeville, MN: Cistercian Publications.

Blake, William. (2008) *The Complete Poetry and Prose of William Blake*, ed. David V. Erdman. Berkeley, CA: University of California Press.

Block, Chana and Block, Ariel. (2006) *The Song of Songs: The World's First Great Love Poem*. New York: Modern Library.

Bloy, Leon. (2015) *The Woman Who Was Poor*, trans. I. Collins. South Bend, IN: St Augustine's Press.

Boyarin, Daneil. (1990) *Intertextuality and the Reading of the Midrash*. Bloomington, IN: Indiana University Press.

Brugg, John. (1995) *Commentary on Song of Songs*. Milwaukee, WI: Northwestern Publishing.

Budde, Karl. (1894) The Song of Solomon. *The New World* 3: 56–77.

Budge, Wallis (trans.). (2000) *The Queen of Sheba and her only Son Menyelek: Kebra Nagast*. Ontario: In Parenthesis Press.

Bulgakov, Sergei. (1993) *Sophia the Wisdom of God: An Outline in Sophiology*, trans. P. Thompson. New York: Lindisfarne Press.

Bulgakov, Sergei. (2002) *The Bride of the Lamb: On the Divine Humanity, Part 3*, trans. Boris Jakim. Edinburgh: T. & T. Clark.

Carr, David. (2003) *The Erotic Word: Sexuality, Spirituality and the Bible*. Oxford: Oxford University Press.

Cassian, John. (1985) *Conferences*, trans. C. Luibheid. Mahwah, NJ: Paulist Press.

Catholic Church (1994) *Catechism of the Catholic Church*, 2nd edition. New York: Doubleday.

Cicero, Marcus Tullius. (2016) *Treatises on Friendship and Old Age*. trans. Evelyn Shuckburgh. London: Pantinos Classics.

Conybeare, F. C. (trans.). (1898) The Testament of Solomon. *Jewish Quarterly Review* (October). Facsimile retrieved on 10 February 2018 from www.jstor.org/stable/10.2307/1450398.

Crenshaw, James. (2010) *Old Testament Wisdom: An Introduction*, 3rd edition. Louisville, KY: John Knox Press.

Crisogono de Jesus. (1982) *Jean de la Croix: Sa Vie*. Paris: Cerf.

Danielou, Jean. (1951) *Platonisme et Théologie Mystique: Essai sur la Doctrine Spirituelle de St Grégoire de Nysse*. Brussels: Desclée de Brouwer.

Dante [Dante Alighieri]. (1964) *Vita Nuova*, trans. William Anderson. London: Penguin.

Dante [Dante Alighieri]. (1986) *The Divine Comedy*, trans. Mark Musa. London: Penguin.

Davis, Ellen. (1989) *Proverbs, Ecclesiastes and the Song of Songs*. Louisville, KY: John Knox Press.

Davis, Ellen. (2001) *Getting Involved with God: Rediscovering the Old Testament*. Cambridge, MA: Cowley.

Delitzsch, Franz. (1975) *Proverbs, Ecclesiastes, Song of Solomon, Vol. 6: Commentary on the Old Testament*. Grand Rapids, MI: Eerdmans.

Dirksen, Piet. (2004) *Canticles*, 4th edition, Biblia Hebraica. Stuttgart: Deutsche Bibelgesellschaft.

Dostoevsky, Fyodor. (1986) *The Idiot*, trans. David Magarschack. London: Penguin.

Douay-Rheims. (2009) *The Holy Bible: Douay-Rheims Version*. Charlotte, NC: TAN Books.

Elior, Rachel. (2007) *Jewish Mysticism: The Infinite Expression of Freedom*. Oxford: Littman Library.

Eliot, T. S. (2015) *The Poems of T. S. Eliot, volume I: Collected and Uncollected Poems*, ed. Christopher Ricks and Jim McCue. London: Faber & Faber.

Ellis, Havelock. (1933) *Psychology of Sex*. London: Medical Books.

Enoch. (1921) *The Books of Enoch*, trans. R. Charles. London: SPCK.

Epstein, I. (ed.). (Undated) *Sanhedrin*, trans. Jacob Shachter and H. Freedman. Retrieved on 5 March 2018 from www.judentum.org/talmud/traktate/sanhedrin/sanhedrin_101.html.

Flannery, Austin (ed.). (1992) *Vatican Council II: The Conciliar and Post Conciliar Documents*. Dublin: Dominican Publications.

Ford, Julia Ellsworth. (1908) *King Solomon and the Fair Shulamite*. New York: Sherman.

Francis, Pope. (2016) *Amoris Laetitia (The Joy of Love): Apostolic Exhortation on Love in the Family*. Dublin: Veritas.

Freud, Sigmund. (1991) *Introductory Lectures on Psychoanalysis*, Penguin Freud Library vol. 1. London: Penguin.

Ginsburg, Christian. (1957) *The Song of Songs*. London: Longman.

Goldin, Hyman (ed.). (1918) *The Babylonian Talmud: Mishna Bava Kamma*. New York: Hebrew Publishing Co.

Gregory of Nyssa. (1955) *Vita Moysis*, ed. Jean Daniélou. Paris: Éd du Cerf, Sources Chretiénnes.

Gregory the Great, Pope. (1971) *Exposition on the Song of Songs, Corpus Christianum: Continuatio Mediavalis*. Turnhout: Brepols.

Hahn, Scott (ed.). (2009) *Catholic Bible Dictionary*. New York: Doubleday.

Hamann, Johann. (2007) *Writings on Philosophy and Language*. Cambridge: Cambridge University Press.

Hardy, Thomas. (1902) 'The Darkling Thrush'. In his *Poems of the Past and the Present*. London: Harper & Brothers.

Hess, Richard. (2003) *Song of Songs*. Grand Rapids, MI: Baker Commentary.

Hill, Andrew and Walton, John. (2010) *A Survey of the Old Testament*. London: HarperCollins.

Hillesum, Etty. (1999) *An Interrupted Life: the Diaries and Letters of Etty Hillesum 1941–43*. London: Persephone.

Hillman, James. (1989) *A Blue Fire: Selected Writings*. London: HarperCollins.

Hocking, David and Hocking, Carole. (1986) *Romantic Lovers: The Intimate Marriage*. Eugene, OR: Harvest House Publishers.

Ibn Al Arabi. (1911) *Tarjuman al-Ashwaq*, trans. R. Nicholson. London: Royal Asiatic Society.

Jámi, Nur ad-Din Rahman. (1904) *Salámán and Absál: An Allegory Translated from the Persian of Jámi*, trans. Edward FitzGerald. London: De La More Press.

Jastrow, Morris. (1921) *The Song of Songs, Being a Collection of Love Lyrics of Ancient Palestine*. London: Lippincott.

Jayadeva. (1984) *The Gitagovinda of Jayadeva: Love Song of the Lord*, trans. B. Stoler Miller. Delhi: Motilal Banarsidass.

John of the Cross. (1960) *Poems*, trans. Roy Campbell. London: Penguin.

John of the Cross. (1987) *Selected Writings*, trans. K. Kavanaugh. Mahwah, NJ: Paulist Press.

John Paul II, Pope. (2006) *Man and Woman He Created Them: A Theology of the Body*, trans. M. Waldstein. Boston, MA: Pauline Books.

Jung, C. J. (1945) *Contributions to Analytic Psychology*. London: Kegan Paul.

Jung, C. J. (1965) *Answer to Job*, trans. R. Hull. London: Hodder & Stoughton.

Jung, C. J. (1976) *Letters of C. J. Jung*, vol. 2. London: Routledge.

Jung, Emma. (1957) *Animus and Anima*. New York: Psychology Club of New York.

Keel, Othmar. (1994) *The Song of Songs: A Continental Commentary*. Minneapolis, MN: Fortress Press.

Kempe, Margery. (1994) *The Book of Margery Kempe*, trans. B. Windeatt. London: Penguin.

Kierkegaard, Søren. (1946) *The Concept of Dread*. trans. Walter Lowrie. London: Oxford University Press.

King, Nicholas. (2008) *The Old Testament: A Translation of the Septuagint*, volume 3. Stowmarket: Kevin Mayhew.

Kingsmill, Edmée. (2009) *The Song of Songs and the Eros of God: A Study in Biblical Intertextuality*. Oxford: Oxford University Press.

Lancel, Serge. (1995) *Carthage: A History*. Hoboken, NJ: Wiley-Blackwell.

Lawrence, D. H. (2007) *Women in Love*. London: Penguin.

Lewis, C. S. (1936) *The Allegory of Love: A Study in Medieval Tradition*. Oxford: Oxford University Press.

Lewis, C. T. and Short, C. (1996) *A Latin Dictionary*. Oxford: Oxford University Press.

Lichtheim, Miriam (ed.). (1976) *Ancient Egyptian Literature*. Berkeley, CA: University of California Press.

Lomperis, Linda and Stanbury, Sarah (eds). (1993) *Feminist Approaches to the Body in Medieval Literature*. Philadelphia, PA: University of Philadelphia Press.

Maccoby, Hyam. (1980) The Queen of Sheba and the Song of Songs. *Society for Interdisciplinary Studies Review* 4(4) (Spring): 98–100.

Manjhan, Mir Sayyid. (2000) *Madhumālatī: An Indian Sufi Romance*, trans. A. Behl and S. C. R. Weightman. Oxford: Oxford University Press.

Maximus the Confessor. (1857–66) *Questions to Thalassius*, Ambigua, vols 90–91, ed. J. P. Migne. Paris: Imprimerie Catolique.

Maximus the Confessor. (1990) Centuries of St Maximus. In *Philokalia*, vol. 2, trans. G. E. H. Palmer, P. Sherrard and K. Ware. London: Faber & Faber.

McGinn, Bernard. (1992) The Language of Love in Christian and Jewish Mysticism. In S. Katz (ed.), *Mysticism and Language*. Oxford: Oxford University Press.

McGinn, Bernard. (1994) *The Growth of Mysticism: From Gregory the Great to the Twelfth Century*. Norwich: SCM.

Meek, Theophile. (1924) The Song of Songs and the Fertility Cult. In Wilfred Schoff (ed.), *The Song of Songs: A Symposium*. Philadelphia, PA: Commercial Museum.

Mitch, Curtis & Hahn, Scott. (2013) *Proverbs, Ecclesiastes and the Song of Solomon*. San Francisco, CA: Ignatius Press.

Moses de Leon. (1983) *Zohar: The Book of Enlightenment*, trans. D. Matt. New York: Paulist Press.

Murphy, Roland. (1990) *The Song of Songs. Hermeneia*. Minneapolis, MN: Fortress Press.

Navarre Bible. (2003) *Navarre Bible*. Dublin: Four Courts.

Neusner, Jacob (trans.). (1988) *The Mishnah*. New Haven, CT: Yale University Press.

Neusner, Jacob. (1989) *Song of Songs Rabbah*. Atlanta, GA: Scholars Press.

Nizami of Ganja. (1924) *The Haft Paykar* [*The Seven Beauties*], trans. C. E. Wilson. London: Probsthain & Co.

Norris, Richard (ed.). (2003) *The Church's Bible: The Song of Songs*. Grand Rapids, MI: Eerdmans.

Novalis [Friedrich von Hardenberg]. (1987) *Novalis Gedichte*. Berlin: Insel Taschenbuch.

Origen. (1956) *Commentary on the Song of Songs*, trans. R. Lawson. New York: Newman Press.

Origen. (1966) *Homilies on the Song of Songs*. Paris: Cerf.

Origen. (1979) *On First Principles*, trans. R. Greer. London: SPCK.

Origen. (2017) *Against Celsus*. Philadelphia, PA: Dalcassian Publishing Co.

Patmore, Coventry. (1913) *Principle in Art Religio Poetae and Other Essays*. London: Duckworth.

Philo. (1993) *The Works of Philo*, trans. C. Yonge. Peabody, MA: Hendrickson.

Plato. (1925) *Plato in Twelve Volumes*, vol. 9, trans. W. Lamb. London: Heinemann.

Plato. (1951) *The Symposium*, trans. W. Hamilton. London: Penguin.

Plato. (1952) *Phaedrus*, trans. H. Fowler. London: Heinemann.

Pope, Marvin. (1977) *Song of Songs: A New Translation with Introduction and Commentary*. New York: Doubleday.

Pritchard, James (ed.). (1974) *Solomon and Sheba*. London: Phaidon.

Reynolds, Simon. (1984) *The Vision of Simeon Solomon*. Stroud: Catalpa Press.

Reynolds, Simon. (1995) *Novalis and the Poets of Pessimism*. Norwich: Michael Russell.

Rilke, Rainer Maria. (1962) *Letters to a Young Poet*, trans. M. D. Herter Norton. New York: W. Norton.

Robinson, James (ed.). (1977) *The Nag Hammadi Library*. New York: Harper & Row.

Rolle, Richard. (1989) *The English Writings*. London: SPCK.

Rosenroth, Christian Knorr von. (1912) *The Kabbalah Unveiled*, trans. S. MacGregor Mathers. New York: Theosophical Pub. Co.

Rudy, Gordon. (2002) *Mystical Language of Sensation in the Later Middle Ages*. London: Routledge.

Rumi, Jalāl ad-Dīn. (1957–67) *Divan: Shams i' Tabriz*, ed. B. Furuzanfar. Tehran: University of Tehran Press.

Rumi, Jalāl ad-Dīn. (2000) *Feeling the Shoulders of the Lion: Poetry and Teaching Stories of Rumi*, ed. C. Barkes. Boston, MA: Shambhala.

Rumi, Jalāl ad-Dīn. (2009) *Diwan Al' Shams*, trans. A. Arberry, *Mystical Poems of Rumi*. Chicago, IL: University of Chicago Press.

Rumi, Jalāl ad-Dīn. (2011) *The Essential Rumi*. London: HarperCollins.

Rupert of Deutz. (1974) *In Cantica Canticorum De Incarnatione Domini Commentaria*, ed. Hrabanus Haake, Corpus Christianorum Continuatio Mediaevalis, vol. 26. Turnhout: Brepols.

Scholem, Gershom. (1995a) *Major Trends in Jewish Mysticism*. New York: Schocken Books.

Scholem, Gershom. (1995b) *On the Kabbalah and its Symbolism*, trans. R. Manheim. New York: Schocken Books.

Seng-ts'an. (2001) *Hsin-hsin Ming: Verses on the Faith Mind*, trans. Richard Clarke. New York: White Pine Press.

Singer, Isidore (ed.). (1906) *The Jewish Encyclopedia*. 12 vols. New York: Funk & Wagnalls.

Solovyov, Vladimir. (1935) *The Life Drama of Plato*. London: Centenary Press.

Solovyov, Vladimir. (1940) *The Justification of the Good: An Essay on Moral Philosophy*. London: Centenary Press.

Solovyov, Vladimir. (1945) *The Meaning of Love*. London: Centenary Press.

Steindorff, George and Steele, Keith. (1942) *When Egypt Ruled the East*. Chicago, IL: University of Chicago Press.

Suso, Henry. (1982) *The Life of the Servant*, trans. J. Clark. Cambridge: James Clarke.

Symeon the New Theologian. (1976) *Hymns of Divine Love*, trans. G. Maloney. Denville, NJ: Dimension Books.

Teresa of Avila. (1913) Conceptions of the Love of God on Some Verses of the Canticle. In *Minor Works of St Teresa*, trans. Benedictines of Stanbrook. London: Thomas Baker.

Teresa of Avila. (1921) *The Interior Castle*, trans. Benedictines of Stanbrook. London: Thomas Baker.

William of St Thierry. (1970) *Exposition on the Song of Songs*, Cistercian Fathers Series, vol. 6. Dublin: Irish University Press.

Turner, Denys. (1995) *Eros and Allegory: Medieval Exegesis of the Song of Songs*. Collegeville, MN: Cistercian Publications.

Turner, W. J. (1925) *The Seven Days of the Sun*. London: Chatto & Windus.

Tyldesley, Joyce. (1994) *Daughters of Isis: Women of Ancient Egypt*. London: Penguin.

Unterman, Alan (ed.). (1976) *The Wisdom of the Jewish Mystics*. London: Sheldon Press.

Vaux, Roland De. (1997) *Ancient Israel: Its Life and Institutions*, trans. John McHugh. Grand Rapids, MI: Eerdmans.

Virey, Philippe. (1890) *The Official Life of an Egyptian Officer from the Tomb of Amen-em-heb at Thebes*, ed. A. Sayce, Records of the Past, series 2, vol. 4. Retrieved on 9 February 2018 from www.sacred-texts.com/ane/rp/rp204/rp20404.htm.

Von Franz, Marie Louise. (1966) *Aurora Consurgens*. London: Routledge.

Von Rad, Gerhard. (1972) *Wisdom in Israel*. Norwich: SCM.

Welburn, Andrew (ed.). (1994) *Gnosis: The Mysteries and Christianity; An Anthology of Essene, Gnostic and Christian Writings*. Edinburgh: Floris Books.

Williams, Charles. (1930) *Religion and Love in Dante*. London: Dacre Press.

Würthwein, Ernst. (2011) Song of Solomon. In *Encyclopedia of Christianity Online*. Retrieved on 9 February 2018 from http://dx.doi.org/10.1163/2211-2685_eco_SI.49.

Yeats, W. B. (1989) *Yeats's Poems*, ed. A. Norman Jeffares. Basingstoke: Macmillan.

Index

Note: italic page numbers indicate illustrations;
numbers in brackets preceded by *n* are footnote numbers.

DR STEFAN GILLOW REYNOLDS is Retreat Director at Mount Melleray Abbey, Co Waterford, Ireland. He has a PhD from London University in Christian Spirituality, an MA in History of Christianity and an MA in Inter-Religious Dialogue. He is the author of *Living with the Mind of Christ: Mindfulness in Christian Spirituality* (Darton, Longman & Todd, 2016). He wrote the online course *Roots of Christian Mysticism* for the World Community for Christian Meditation. He teaches Christian Meditation in a contemporary context and leads retreats internationally. He also paints icons and writes poetry.